"I have always loved Leah Koenig's books, but it should come as no surprise that this 'sweet' one holds an extremely special place in my heart. Beautifully photographed and expertly researched, this tome of Jewish desserts is the cookbook we didn't know our collections were sorely missing. From Black-and-White Shortbread Cookies to Chocolate Pull-Apart Cake to Apple Cider Sufganiyot with Salted Caramel to Flan Napolitano, I want to bake and eat everything in here, and there is no question that you will, too."

—JESSIE SHEEHAN, author of *Snackable Bakes*

"Leah Koenig's love letter to Jewish sweets gives us not just rock-solid recipes—tender apple cakes, hypnotic babkas, jam-swirled meringues—but thoughtful, deeply researched storytelling from the global Jewish diaspora. (In what other book could we learn about the origins of the egg cream, the Sachertorte, and Bazooka Bubble Gum?)"

—KRISTEN MIGLORE, author of *Genius Desserts*

THE DESSERT TABLE

100 JOYFUL JEWISH SWEETS

LEAH KOENIG

photography by Nico Schinco

W. W. NORTON & COMPANY
Independent Publishers Since 1923

To my family,
for making life so sweet

Strawberry Cloud Meringues (page 93)

CONTENTS

INTRODUCTION

When I was a child, my primary motivation for going to synagogue on Saturday mornings had very little to do with religion and nearly everything to do with the dessert table. As soon as the service ended, all the children would stream from the sanctuary into the social hall, where our prize for being patient lay: a long table lined with platters of crumbly sprinkle cookies, spongy slices of honey cake and marble cake, and, rather curiously, green fondant-covered petit fours in the shape of frogs. (Thirty years later, I still can't explain those frogs.)

The congregation would recite the blessing over tiny cups of grape juice and sweet wine. Then we kids would fill our plates with a sugar high's worth of treats and blissfully make our way through the haul as our parents chatted nearby. Looking back with a more mature palate, I know that the desserts themselves were not particularly transcendent. But for a kid, it was heaven.

My connection with Jewish tradition has naturally deepened and evolved over the years. But to this day, many of my most beloved Jewish memories and moments revolve around dessert. There's the spread of crackly-topped brownies, airy meringues, and chocolate-dipped apricots my mom served after our Passover seder. There's the raspberry jam–filled hamantaschen we baked together on Purim, and her impossibly tender Rosh Hashanah apple cake.

There's the triumph I felt after baking my first successful babka in my early twenties, and the oozy centers of the jelly doughnuts I ate at Hanukkah parties in Brooklyn. More recently, there's been the thrill of delighting friends with a decadent cheesecake or homemade strudel after a Shabbat or holiday dinner, and stamping out menorah- and dreidel-shaped sugar cookies with my kids, using the same cookie cutters my mom bought for me and my brother decades ago.

These memories are as central to my Jewish identity as any prayer or ritual. That is because, perhaps more than any part of the meal, the desserts made for us by loved ones, or that we make for others, are so often imbued with love and connection. We shower one another with sweets during happy occasions and bake to comfort those in mourning. Desserts bring joy to the holidays and warmth to all the days in between. No matter which corner of the Jewish diaspora I travel to, I am routinely greeted with a little something sweet upon arrival—either just baked or pulled from the freezer for exactly such an occasion. I now keep my own freezer stocked with a few batches of cookies to shower upon unexpected guests.

I have been writing about Jewish cuisine for the better part of two decades, always with the intent of shining a light on recipes and stories from around the world. *The Dessert Table* continues in this tradition. Throughout history, Jewish communities have lived—and baked—all across the globe, which means the Jewish dessert canon includes cookies, cakes, and confections from France, Hungary, and Poland to India, Morocco, Curaçao, and other far-flung locales. How each community expresses itself through sweets varies widely from place to place. But what ties these disparate sweets together is their ability to inject joy into times of celebration, soothe in times of sorrow, and make anyone feel instantly at home.

Some of the recipes in this book—like the Classic Walnut Baklava (page 202) and Persian Rice Pudding (page 210)—are made very much the same way as they have been for hundreds of years. Others, like the Chocolate Turtle Babka (page 174) and Orange and Almond Cake (page 132), offer my modern interpretations of classics. And still others, including the Almond Kiss Blondies (page 54) and No-Churn Coffee Hawaij Ice Cream (page 265), transform flavors from the Jewish diaspora into something entirely new. I pulled inspiration for these treats from sweets I have personally enjoyed, and reached out to some of my favorite pastry chefs and food professionals for their most beloved and innovative desserts. Together, the recipes offer an homage to the past while demonstrating the ways that the Jewish dessert table has evolved—and continues to evolve—in America and around the world.

As you read through the recipes—perhaps deciding what to bake for a birthday or a holiday—I invite you to spend a little time with the headnotes. Each one of them shares the history and stories behind the individual recipe and situates it in a larger framework of heritage and tradition. I truly believe that knowing that, for example, Israel's famous Hanukkah jelly doughnuts have roots in the Polish shtetl (see page 184) or that Jews with ancestry from Cochin, India, celebrate Rosh Hashanah with a cardamom-spiced semolina coconut cake (see page 131), makes the sweets taste even more delicious. Throughout the book, you will also find stand-alone essays on dessert-relevant subjects including the role Jews played in the sugar trade (see page 212) and chocolate trade (see page 49), and the way Jewish American bakeries once shaped their communities (see page 146).

It might be ill-advised to admit this considering the subject of this cookbook, but I have not always been a confident baker. I used to prefer the free-wheeling, taste-as-you go approach to savory cooking more than the precision and patience required for desserts. But over time, I have learned that just as onions plus oil, low heat, and a pinch of salt will always yield a pile of browned onions, butter, eggs, flour, and sugar also act in predictable ways when treated with care. I developed the recipes in this book to be accessible to any home cook, regardless of baking experience. So, whether you are an avid baker or feel a little nervous around a cake pan (if so, start with the "I Can't Bake" Dessert Recipes, page 278), I hope this collection of recipes inspires you to explore the stunning diversity—and otherworldly deliciousness—of the Jewish dessert table.

JEWISH DESSERTS ACROSS THE DIASPORA

Over the last 2,000-plus years, Jews have lived and cooked in communities all over the world. As a result, Jewish cuisine cannot be readily defined by geographical lines or a particular set of ingredients. Instead, it is made up of a kaleidoscope of dishes from the myriad countries and regions where Jewish people and families have made their homes. Any attempt at organizing Jewish food into neat categories is further complicated by the fact that throughout history, Jews have relocated time and again, and their traditional weekday, Shabbat, and holiday dishes have evolved to mirror their new homes' own flavors and customs. Yet while the global nature of Jewish cuisine can lead to some confusion and blurring of boundaries, it is also fundamental to its unique appeal.

Just like the savory side of Jewish cuisine, the scope of Jewish desserts defies easy definition. But understanding a few broad-stroke categories can help set the context while you bake, share, and enjoy the sugary diversity from across the Jewish diaspora.

ASHKENAZI DESSERTS

Ashkenazi cuisine has roots in western Germany and eastern France and eventually expanded to include large portions of Central and Eastern Europe. Many home-baked Ashkenazi desserts—like German Jewish coffee cakes, Hungarian sweet cheese strudels, Polish babkas, and crunchy Lithuanian almond cookies—provided comfort and warmth to offset the relatively cold European climate. The Ashkenazi Jewish dessert canon also reflects the skills of professional Jewish bakers—like Austria's famous Sachertorte, which was invented by a young Jewish pastry chef in the 1800s (see page 156). American Jewish desserts are widely associated with the Ashkenazi pastry case, although many of the classic sweets, like rugelach (see page 75) have evolved significantly here.

SEPHARDI DESSERTS

Sephardi cuisine originated in the Iberian Peninsula, specifically Spain and Portugal. But it spread widely throughout the Mediterranean, Middle East, North Africa, and elsewhere starting in the late fifteenth century, in the wake of the persecution under the Spanish Inquisition. Because Sephardi Jews tended to live in warmer regions, their desserts are noticeably lighter than Ashkenazi desserts. Many Sephardi desserts, like Spanish orange cakes and chewy Italian almond cookies, are made with ground almonds or other ground nuts instead of (or in addition to) wheat flour. The Sephardi dessert table also includes a variety of custards and puddings thickened with eggs and rice flour, along with airy fritters sweetened with honey.

MIDDLE EASTERN/ MIZRAHI DESSERTS

Jews hailing from the Middle East and North Africa (including Syria, Egypt, Yemen, Iran, Iraq, Morocco, Libya, Tunisia, and Algeria) prior to the arrival of Sephardi Jews are identified as Mizrahi. The desserts from these warm-weather communities include a wide variety of cookies, from buttery shortbreads (sometimes made with oil instead of butter to meet kosher requirements) to sweet biscuits flavored with anise or citrus. Cold rice puddings, sweet custards enhanced with cardamom and rose water, and candied fruits and preserves also helped combat the heat. Another signature feature of the Middle Eastern/Mizrahi dessert table is cakes and pastries that are painted with or soaked in a sweet, glistening sugar syrup after they emerge from the oven.

DESSERTS FROM ELSEWHERE IN THE DIASPORA

In Jewish communities with long-standing roots in other parts of the diaspora, the desserts tend to reflect the flavors and ingredients of their locales. Some Indian Jews, for example, end holiday and Shabbat meals with puddings or cakes made with semolina, ghee or coconut oil, and coconut milk. In South and Central America, home to Jewish communities from both Ashkenazi and Sephardi backgrounds, you might find hamantaschen filled with guava paste on Purim or flan served as a flour-free sweet after the Passover seder. And in Central Asian countries, like Uzbekistan, Jewish meals traditionally ended with fruit preserves, tea, or fried dough sprinkled with confectioners' sugar or drizzled with honey and chopped nuts.

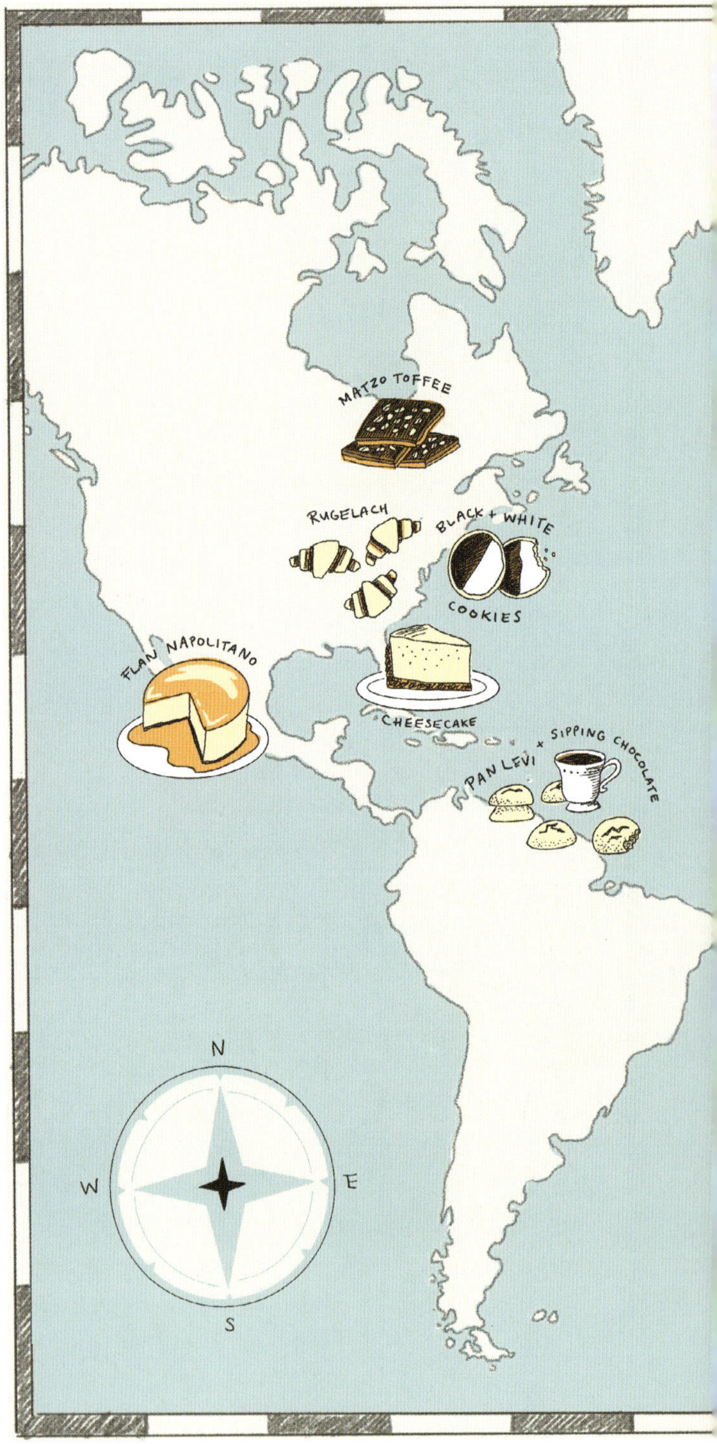

TIEGLACH
HONEY CAKE
BABKA
MANDELBREAD
FÁNK
APPLE SHARLOTKA
ROSEY MARZIPAN
HAMANTASCHEN
STRUDEL (RETES)
PALMIERS
MARUNCHINOS
BAKLAVA
PERSIAN
RICE PUDDING
ORANGE + ALMOND
CAKE
LOUKOUMADES
APAM
TRAVADOS
GRAYBEH
SUFGANIYOT
KA'AK B'SUKAR
CHAROSET BALLS
MELKTERT

THE JEWISH HOLIDAYS

The Jewish calendar is filled with holidays of reflection, spirituality, connection, and celebration. And each of these special days comes with its own important foods, including desserts. If you are baking for a holiday and are curious to try a traditional recipe from global Jewish cuisine, these sweets offer a great place to start.

SHABBAT

Every week from Friday at sunset through Saturday at sundown

Shabbat honors the seventh day of creation in the Torah and is a day of complete rest. Shabbat-observant families abstain from driving, using electricity, and active cooking, focusing instead on prayer, family, community, and food. The weekly holiday includes a festive dinner on Friday night, a midday lunch on Saturday, and *seudah shlishit* (literally "third meal") on Saturday afternoon. Many families also bake simple cakes or cookies in advance to enjoy throughout the holiday.

- Kiddush Sprinkle Cookies (page 60)
- Citrus-Glazed Pistachio Mandelbrot (page 62)
- Citrusy Cookie Twists (page 104)
- Sour Cherry Coffee Cake (page 123)
- Blueberry Streusel Cake (page 124)
- Orange and Almond Cake (page 132)
- Chocolate-Frosted Poppy Seed Cake (page 140)
- Caramelized White Chocolate–Lime Babka (page 171)
- Chocolate Turtle Babka (page 174)
- Rice-Flour Pudding (page 211)
- Chocolate-Covered Pretzels (page 255)
- Rosy Marzipan (page 256)

ROSH HASHANAH

Early fall, usually September/October

Rosh Hashanah is the Jewish New Year, and it helps to usher in the autumn festival season known as The High Holidays. It is customary to enjoy sweet foods on Rosh Hashanah, including apples dipped in honey and baked goods flavored with honey, apples, pumpkin, and/or pomegranate, as an edible symbol of one's hopes for a sweet year ahead.

- Chewy Chocolate Gingersnaps (page 52)
- Back Pocket Apple Cake (page 118)
- Apple Sharlotka (page 119)
- Jam Cake (page 126)
- Venetian Pumpkin Cake (page 130)
- Coconut-Cardamom Semolina Cake (page 131)
- Triple-Pomegranate Cake (page 137)
- Honey Cake with Apple Butter Frosting (page 144)
- Grape Spoon Sweet (page 235)
- Cheater's Teiglach (page 257)

YOM KIPPUR

Ten days after Rosh Hashanah, typically September/October

Yom Kippur, which is also called the Day of Atonement, is among the most solemn and spiritual holidays on the Jewish calendar. It is the day when Jewish people ask forgiveness for their wrongdoings from the previous year. Observant Jews fast from both food and drink for the entirety of the holiday's twenty-five-hour duration. After nightfall, they break the fast, often in community with others, with a celebratory meal.

- Sour Cherry Coffee Cake (page 123)
- Blueberry Streusel Cake (page 124)
- Venetian Pumpkin Cake (page 130)
- Honey Cake with Apple Butter Frosting (page 144)
- Sweet Cheese Bougatsa (page 204)
- Rice-Flour Pudding (page 211)
- Coffee Soda (page 272)

SUKKOT

Five days after Yom Kippur, usually in October

Sukkot commemorates the forty years the Israelites wandered in the desert after being freed from enslavement in ancient Egypt. The holiday also marks the fall harvest festival. Observant Jews build temporary outdoor huts called *sukkot*, and eat their holiday meals inside them. Autumnal foods and stuffed foods that symbolize the season's abundance are typically served.

- Triple-Pomegranate Cake (page 137)
- Spiced Chiffon Cake with Brown Sugar Frosting (page 147)
- Hungarian Apple Squares (page 194)
- Sweet Walnut and Almond Turnovers (page 199)
- Ancient-Grains Apple Crisp (page 224)

HANUKKAH

Usually December

Also called the Festival of Lights, Hanukkah commemorates the rededication of the Holy Temple in Jerusalem following the Maccabees' victory over the ancient Greek king Antiochus. The story says that the Maccabees found only enough olive oil to light the temple's menorah (candelabra) for one night, but that it miraculously lasted for eight. In honor of this miracle, Jews around the world light Hanukkah menorahs and eat foods fried in oil thoughout the eight-day holiday.

- Whole Wheat Hanukkah Sugar Cookies (page 57)
- Pumpkin Cake Doughnuts (page 182)
- Apple Cider Sufganiyot with Salted Caramel (page 185)
- Fluffy Apricot Jam Doughnuts (page 187)
- Greek Doughnuts with Honey and Walnuts (page 191)

TU BISHVAT

Usually January

Tu Bishvat, which is also called the New Year of the Trees, began in ancient times as a tax holiday, deliniating one year's tree crops from the next. Over the centuries, it was transformed into a celebration of everything that grows on trees. There are not many traditional dishes served on Tu Bishvat, but it is customary to eat tree fruits as well as the seven specific species associated with the land of Israel (wheat, barley, dates, grapes, figs, pomegranates, and olives). Some Jews also hold a Tu Bishvat "seder"—a ritual begun by the Jewish kabbalists in the sixteenth century.

- Tu Bishvat Trail Mix Cookies (page 51)
- Triple-Pomegranate Cake (page 137)
- Grape Spoon Sweet (page 235)

PURIM

February/March

Purim celebrates the biblical story of Queen Esther, the Jewish Queen of Persia who saved her people by outsmarting Haman—a royal vizier who wanted to eradicate all of Persia's Jews. Today Jews celebrate Purim by reading Esther's story, dressing up in costumes, holding festive parties, giving to charity, and sharing gifts of food. The most recognizable Purim dessert is hamantaschen, the triangular-shaped Ashkenazi cookies meant to resemble Haman's pockets, hat, or ears, depending on whom you ask.

- Oatmeal–Sour Cherry Hamantaschen (page 66)
- Triple Chocolate Hamantaschen (page 68)
- Orange Blossom Butter Cookies (page 110)
- Sweet Walnut and Almond Turnovers (page 199)
- Chocolate and Cinnamon Palmiers (page 201)
- Rice-Flour Pudding (page 211)
- White Wine–Poached Pears with Chocolate Sauce (page 233)

PASSOVER

March/April

Passover is one of the most widely observed Jewish holidays. It commemorates the Israelites' exodus from enslavement in ancient Egypt. Many Jewish families hold Passover seders—festive meals that include a retelling of the Passover story and feature symbolic foods. Observant Jews refrain from eating chametz (foods made from wheat, barley, spelt, oats, or rye) throughout the week-long holiday, substituting unleavened matzo. Some Ashkenazi Jews also avoid kitniyot—corn, legumes, rice, and other foods said to closely resemble chametz. One of the dessert recipes below contains kitniyot and is marked as such.

- Cherry–Coconut Flake Macaroons (page 86)
- Lemon Curd Macaroon Thumbprints (page 89)
- Pistachio Macaroons (page 91)
- Strawberry Cloud Meringues (page 93)
- Flourless Chocolate Walnut Cookies (page 96)
- Passover Jam Thumbprints (page 99)
- Best Passover Banana Bread (page 128)
- Best Passover Chocolate Zucchini Muffins (page 129)
- Flourless Fudge Cake with Apricot Sauce (page 156)
- Flourless Chocolate Espresso Cake (page 159)
- Persian Rice Pudding (kitniyot) (page 210)
- Baked Pumpkin Pie Custard (page 213)
- Flan Napolitano (page 219)
- Charoset Truffle Balls (page 254)
- German Chocolate–Matzo Toffee (page 258)
- Egg Cream Float (page 267)

SHAVUOT

Forty days after Passover, May or June

Shavuot celebrates God's revelation of the Torah to the Israelites at Mount Sinai after forty years of desert wandering. It also marks the end of the ancient barley harvest and the beginning of the wheat harvest. Many Jewish communities observe the customs of studying Jewish texts on Shavuot and eating foods made with dairy products to symbolize "the land of milk and honey."

- Sour Cherry Coffee Cake (page 123)
- Chai-Spiced Cheesecake (page 151)
- Sweet Cheese Bougatsa (page 204)
- Persian Rice Pudding (page 210)
- Milk Tart (page 220)
- Tea Biscuit Tiramisu (page 217)

ESSENTIAL BAKING TECHNIQUES

Set yourself up for success by learning and following these basic baking techniques.

BEATING EGG WHITES

Several of the recipes in this book call for egg whites to be beaten to firm peaks. Beating egg whites traps air inside the egg's proteins, which helps add lift and leavening to cake batters and cookie doughs. For the best results, start with room-temperature eggs and a very clean, dry bowl (oil and water both inhibit the process). A stand mixer fitted with the whisk attachment works best, but you can also use a handheld electric mixer or a large wire balloon whisk. When the eggs reach the firm peak stage, they will be glossy and voluminous and will stand straight up when the whisk is lifted.

CHILLING COOKIE DOUGH

Some cookie recipes recommend that you chill the dough (or batter) before baking—either in the bowl before scooping or on the baking sheet after the cookies are formed. Chilling dough firms up the fats, which helps keep the cookies from spreading in the oven. It also allows the dough to hydrate and the flavors to meld and concentrate. If a recipe instructs you to chill your dough, I strongly recommend abiding by it.

COOLING CAKES AND COOKIES

When she was five my daughter told me, "Mama, you are as impatient as a hiccup." That made me laugh, but she's not wrong! And one of the things I'm most impatient about is waiting for baked goods to cool. But if you can manage it, it's definitely a good idea. Many cookies firm up and develop more sweetness and flavor as they cool. And if you try to frost a cake that is still warm, you will end up with melted frosting that slides off it. So take a deep breath, or set a timer, and let those baked goods cool before digging in.

GREASING A BAKING PAN

Applying a thin layer of oil, butter, or cooking spray to the inside of a baking pan helps prevent whatever cake or baked good you are making from sticking to it. I typically grease the pan with a little more of whatever fat the recipe calls for, using a pastry brush to apply oil or rubbing the end of a stick of butter around the pan to coat the entire surface. Cooking sprays are a convenient way to apply grease, but many brands include anti-foaming agents and chemical propellants. Look for natural cooking sprays that are 100-percent oil and free from preservatives and synthetic propellants.

MEASURING FLOUR

All of my recipes include weight measurements in grams, and for the most consistent baking results, I recommend measuring everything–particularly flour–with a digital scale. If you have only measuring cups, I recommend following the "scoop and sweep" method, whereby you scoop the flour into your measuring cup with a spoon and then level off the full cup with the back of a butter knife. Measuring this way, rather than dipping your measuring cup into the flour container, helps keep the flour from getting tightly packed into the cup–which can result in more flour than you want and dry baked goods.

MISE EN PLACE

Mise en place is a French culinary term that means "everything in its place." In professional kitchens, pastry chefs make sure to have all equipment out and all ingredients measured and prepped before they begin baking. I recommend that home bakers adopt the practice in their own kitchens, taking stock of the ingredients they have on hand and measuring out everything before starting. Can you make a simple cake on the fly? Sure. But it is such a bummer to be halfway through a recipe only to realize you are missing an essential ingredient or tool.

ROTATING PANS

If there is one thing that is consistent about conventional ovens, it is that they are inconsistent when it comes to heat distribution. Most ovens have hotter spots and cooler spots, which can affect how quickly something bakes. The best way to ensure that your baked goods bake evenly–especially when you are baking two sheets of cookies at a time–is to rotate the sheets from top to bottom and back to front halfway through baking.

SIFTING INGREDIENTS

Sifting dry ingredients–either with a crank-handled sifter or through a fine-mesh sieve–incorporates air, making them easier to mix together. It also breaks up any clumps that have formed. Sifting is particularly useful for ingredients like flour, cocoa powder, and confectioners' sugar, which tend to form lumps in their containers.

SOFTENING BUTTER

Most butter-based cookie recipes instruct you to start with softened butter, meaning butter that is at or near room temperature. This is because cold butter will not break down in a mixer, which makes creaming it together with the sugar nearly impossible. You can take your butter (or vegan butter) out of the refrigerator an hour or so before you plan to bake to let it soften up. Or you can pop the stick into the microwave for 10 to 20 seconds (no longer, or you will end up with melted butter) and then proceed with your recipe.

ESSENTIAL BAKING TOOLS

You do not need super fancy equipment to turn out high-quality desserts and baked goods. But having the right basic tools to do the job makes a big difference. Here are some essentials that will help you make the most of your baking projects.

BAKING PANS

One of the most frustrating things that can happen when baking a cake is that you get halfway through a recipe only to realize you do not have the right-size pan. Fortunately, baking pans are relatively inexpensive and stack neatly in your cupboard without taking up too much space, so it is easy to keep a range of sizes on hand. From my experience, I know that a well-stocked kitchen should include:

- 8- and 9-inch (20 and 23 cm) round cake pans (ideally two of each, for layer cakes)
- 8- and 9-inch (20 and 23 cm) square cake pans
- 9 × 5-inch (23 × 12 cm) loaf pan
- 8½ × 4½-inch (22 × 11.5 cm) loaf pan
- 9 × 13-inch (22 × 23 cm) baking pan
- 12-cup muffin tin
- 9-inch (23 cm) pie pan

This collection of pans will accommodate most baking projects. From there, you can add additional pieces—like a Bundt pan or novelty-shaped pan—as needed. When it comes to cake pans, material matters. I bake exclusively in light-colored metal pans, because they conduct heat gently and evenly. Darker metal pans tend to burn the outside of baked goods. Glass and ceramic pans hold heat longer, which means the outside of whatever you are making will bake more quickly than the inside and can lead to uneven or burnt results. If you only have glass or ceramic pans, reduce the oven temperature by 25°F to compensate—and consider switching to light-colored aluminum pans.

BAKING SHEETS (HALF SHEET PANS)

Rimmed baking sheets, which measure 18 × 13 inches (46 × 33 cm), are an absolutely essential item for any home baker. From cookies and galettes to strudels and bourekas, they provide a sturdy heat-conductive surface in the oven. They are also useful for batch-toasting nuts and, when lined with paper towels, for draining doughnuts after frying. I recommend stocking your kitchen with at least two of these sheets.

COOKIE SCOOP (DISHER)

A cookie scoop, also called a disher, lets you portion out uniform amounts of cookie dough onto baking sheets. To use one, press the scoop into the dough to fill it up, and smooth off the side with a clean finger or by dragging it across the side of the bowl. Then use the spring-loaded handle to release the dough onto the baking sheet. Cookie scoops come in many sizes, from tiny to extra large. To keep things simple, all of the cookies in this book call for a 1½-tablespoon cookie scoop. Depending on the brand, this size might (rather confusingly!) also be labeled "medium," "0.75 ounce," or "size #40."

DIGITAL KITCHEN SCALE

Measuring cups vary slightly in size from brand to brand, which can lead to inconsistent results. Using a digital kitchen scale ensures that you end up with the exact amount of flour (or sugar, or sour cream, etc.) the recipe calls for every time. Kitchen scales are also useful for weighing whole ingredients like apples, carrots, and other kinds of produce, and they save time on cleanup since you can weigh everything in the same bowl and avoid washing several measuring cups.

FINE-MESH SIEVE

A fine-mesh sieve is made with woven wire mesh that allows only very fine particles to pass through it. I use my sieve all the time when baking—for sifting flour and other ingredients, straining lumps out of custard, and dusting the tops of cooled cookies and cakes with confectioners' sugar, cocoa powder, or cinnamon, among other tasks.

ICE CREAM MAKER

There are two main types of electric ice cream makers: canister-style and compressor-style. Canister-style ice cream makers include a mixing bowl that has insulated walls filled with a cooling liquid that must be prefrozen for 16 to 24 hours in order to churn your liquid base into scoopable ice cream. Compressor-style models have built-in freezers that simultaneously chill and churn the base. Canister-style models are typically smaller and less expensive, while compressor-style models are more convenient (no prefreezing time required) but typically cost more and have a larger kitchen footprint. When deciding which type of model to buy, consider your budget, your cabinet and counter space, and how important it is for you to be able to make ice cream on a whim.

MICROWAVE

You do not really need a microwave to be a successful dessert maker, but there are times when having one comes in quite handy. Forgot to soften your stick of butter for a batch of cookies? Twenty seconds in the microwave, and you are good to go. Want to melt chopped chocolate without setting up a double boiler and waiting for the water to simmer? A few twenty-second bursts in the microwave, stirring after each one, is all it takes. And reheating day-old yeasted pastries, like babka, in the microwave rather than the oven or toaster oven also helps soften them.

MIXING BOWLS

Any decent-sized bowl can be a mixing bowl, but I particularly love my stainless steel bowls. I have a set of three—small, medium, and large—that are coated on the bottoms with silicone to prevent them from sliding across the counter while I work. They are lightweight, durable, and easy to clean, unlike heavier glass bowls or plastic bowls, which stain easily and can retain odors after washing.

PARCHMENT PAPER

Parchment paper is magical stuff. Oven-safe, usually silicone-coated, and nonstick, it can be used for lining baking sheets and cake pans, keeping baked goods from sticking and making for easy cleanup. It comes in rolls or pre-cut sheets for convenience. (Do not substitute wax paper, which is not heat resistant.) I typically reuse a piece of parchment two or three times before throwing it away. If you prefer to go with a completely reusable option, substitute silicone baking mats, which function similarly to parchment but can be washed and reused for years.

PASTRY BRUSH

I never realized how useful a pastry brush was until mine broke. From cleanly and evenly painting pastries with egg wash or simple syrup to brushing melted butter onto stacked phyllo dough, they are really a baking necessity. Pastry brushes are made with natural, nylon, or silicone bristles. Buy one that is large enough (at least 1½ inches / 4 cm wide) to coat pastries quickly and effectively. Always wash and thoroughly dry the brush immediately after use.

RASP-STYLE GRATER

Nothing enlivens a batch of cookie dough or a cake batter quite like citrus zest. And nothing removes zest from a lemon, orange, or lime quite like a rasp-style grater (also referred to as a zester or a Microplane, which is one of the most popular brands). The grater's small, sharp teeth turn out fluffy zest without pulling up the bitter pith underneath. These graters can also be used for whole nutmeg, fresh ginger, garlic, and hard cheeses.

ROLLING PIN

From rolling out sugar cookies and babka dough to crushing nuts or biscuits into smaller pieces or crumbs, rolling pins come in handy for a variety of tasks. There are two basic types: pins with handles on either end and dowel-style pins, without handles. Both get the job done, but I prefer the control and heft of a wooden dowel-style rolling pin.

ROUND COOKIE CUTTERS

When I was a kid, we—like so many other Ashkenazi Jewish families—dipped the rims of juice glasses in flour and used them to stamp out circles of dough for hamantaschen. You can absolutely do that if you'd like. But for easier and more precise cutting, you could switch to round stainless steel cookie cutters. They often come in packs of three or more cutters of different sizes. Use them for stamping out biscuits, doughnuts, and other pastries as well as cookies.

RULER (OR MEASURING TAPE)

Sometimes you need to measure things when you are baking, whether it's dough thickness, the diameter of a pastry circle, or the length of a babka log. I always keep both a straight-edge ruler and a small measuring tape in my utensil drawer.

SILICONE SPATULA

I use my silicone spatula so often—for both savory and sweet recipes—that it almost never makes its way back into the kitchen drawer. The spatula's gentle, flexible head is perfect for folding delicate whipped egg whites or whipped cream into recipes and for scraping every last bit of cake batter from the mixing bowl into the pan. Make sure to buy a heatproof spatula.

STAND MIXER (OR ELECTRIC HAND MIXER)

Our great-grandmothers may have mixed everything by hand, but that does not mean we have to. Electric mixers let you cream butter and sugar together quickly and effectively and to effortlessly whip air into cake batters, egg whites, and heavy cream. If you have the budget and space for a stand mixer, these are the gold standard—nimble enough for cookie doughs and powerful enough for kneading yeast doughs. But a handheld electric mixer, which is smaller and typically less expensive, works well for many baking projects too.

THERMOMETER (DIGITAL)

Digital thermometers are a great tool for quickly checking the temperature of meat, bread, or other recipes where it is difficult to tell from visual cues when something is done. For this book, they come in most handy for the doughnut recipes (pages 182, 185, 187, and 191), where the frying oil must be held at a precise temperature.

THERMOMETER (OVEN)

I wish this weren't the case, but many of our ovens lie to us, running either hotter or colder than indicated. Fortunately, the fix is as simple as buying an inexpensive oven thermometer, which hangs from an oven rack and gives you a much more accurate picture of the actual temperature inside your oven. After preheating the oven, take a peek at the thermometer inside and adjust the temperature if necessary.

WHISK

A handheld whisk is a multifunctional tool that can be used to whip egg whites or heavy cream to soft or stiff peaks, beat lumps out of custards or cake batters, emulsify sauces, or blend dry ingredients together. I prefer stiffer stainless steel whisks to floppier silicone ones for their better control and precision.

Apple Sharlotka (page 119)

ROSE WATER
BURLAP & BARREL
SINGLE ORIGIN SPICES
ROYAL
Superior
Sadaf
Sour Pomegranate Molasses
Melasse de Grenade
NET 10 FL OZ (300 mL)
Espresso
Instantáneo
SIEMPRE PURO Y PLENO DE
COMO NINGÚN OTRO
PESO NETO
100% CAFÉ PURO
NIELSEN-MASSEY
FINEST QUALITY
PURE VANILLA
NET CONTENTS 8 FL OZ
A BROOKLYN ORIGINAL SINCE 1900
Fox's
ORGANIC
MIGHTY SESAME CO.
NIELSEN-MASSEY
PURE VANILLA BEAN PASTE
WATKINS
PURE ALMOND EXTRACT
EXTRAIT D'AMANDE PURE

THE DESSERT PANTRY

As a recipe developer, I strive to use ingredients that are readily accessible to most home cooks. But in some cases, a less common ingredient really helps turn a dessert from good to great. Investing in these specialty ingredients will help you set up your baking cupboard for success.

ALMOND EXTRACT

Almond extract is made from bitter almond oil blended with alcohol and water. It enhances the almond flavor in many cookies, cakes, and other pastries. Look for pure almond extract rather than an imitation extract; these are made from synthetic flavors and have an ersatz, notably saccharine flavor. Pure almond extract is powerful stuff, so use it sparingly—a little goes a long way.

ALMOND FLOUR

Almond flour, sometimes labeled almond meal, is blanched or raw almonds that have been ground into a powdery flour. Ground almonds and other nuts are an important part of Sephardi baking traditions and show up in many traditional cakes and cookies. The flour is mildly sweet and nutty tasting, and it helps baked goods stay moist. Since almond flour doesn't contain gluten, it cannot be used interchangeably with all-purpose flour in most recipes. To extend its shelf life, store almond flour in an airtight container in the refrigerator or freezer.

APPLE BUTTER

This thick, concentrated fruit preserve is made from apples, sugar, and spices cooked together for an extended period over low heat. Apple butter can be spread on bread, stirred into yogurt, or used to add flavor to cakes and frostings. Despite the name, apple butter contains no dairy products.

BAKING APPLES

A few of the recipes in this cookbook call for "baking apples," which refer to apples that maintain some of their texture when baked, rather than collapsing into mush in the oven. Some of my favorite baking-friendly apples include Honeycrisp, Pink Lady, Fuji, Mutsu, and Braeburn. I recommend experimenting with a few varieties to see which you prefer.

BARLEY FLOUR

Barley flour is made from barley grains that have been dried and finely ground. It is high in fiber, protein, and B vitamins, and it lends a sweet, nutty flavor to breads and other baked goods. It is not gluten free, as barley contains gluten. Look for high-quality stone-ground flour made from whole-grain barley. To extend its shelf life, store barley flour in an airtight container in the refrigerator or freezer.

BUCKWHEAT FLOUR

Buckwheat flour is made from dried buckwheat groats that have been finely ground. It has an assertively earthy, slightly bitter flavor that complements both sweet and savory dishes. The flour also adds a distinctive dark color to baked goods. Buckwheat, which is botanically a seed rather than a true grain, is gluten free and rich in fiber and protein. To extend its shelf life, store buckwheat flour in an airtight container in the refrigerator or freezer.

CARDAMOM

This aromatic spice, which is a member of the ginger family, has a peppery, floral flavor that lends warmth and spicy sweetness to many baked goods. There are three varieties of cardamom, green, black, and white (which is actually green cardamom that has been bleached), with green being the most commonly found in stores. Whole cardamom pods are often added to savory dishes to infuse them with flavor, then removed before serving. Ground cardamom is stirred in directly to whatever you are making.

CLARIFIED BUTTER

Clarified butter is butter that has been heated and strained to remove the milk proteins and water, leaving only butterfat behind. After being clarified, butter has a longer shelf life and higher smoke point that works well for sautéing and other types of cooking. If allowed to cook further, the milk solids begin to brown, giving the butter a rich brown color and nutty flavor that adds depth to baked goods.

COCOA POWDER

During the chocolate-making process, cacao beans are fermented and roasted, and then the nibs are ground to extract the cocoa butter. The remaining solids are then pulverized into a concentrated powder that is used to flavor a variety of desserts. Natural cocoa powder, which is most commonly found in grocery stores, is light brown in color and slightly acidic. Dutch-process cocoa powder is treated with an alkali solution to increase its pH level. It tends to be mellower in flavor and darker in hue. All of the recipes in *The Dessert Table* were developed using natural cocoa powder, which is often just labeled as unsweetened cocoa powder.

COCONUT CREAM

Coconut milk and coconut cream are like milk versus heavy cream in that the cream contains a higher fat content and is thicker and richer. Canned coconut cream can be used in place of heavy cream to make dairy-free versions of some frostings and ganache. These will have a subtle but noticeable coconut flavor. In the grocery store, be sure to select "coconut cream," not "cream of coconut," which is mixed with sugar and not the same as pure coconut cream.

CORNSTARCH

Cornstarch, which is sometimes called corn flour, is a powdery white starch derived from the endosperm of the corn kernel. It is commonly used as a thickening agent for stews, gravies, glazes, and custards, and it is also sometimes added to baked goods to improve their texture. (See also Potato Starch, page 35.)

CREAM OF TARTAR

Despite its name, cream of tartar is not creamy and contains no dairy. Rather, it is a powdery acidic by-product of the wine-fermenting process. Adding a small amount of cream of tartar to egg whites as you whip them helps to stabilize their airy texture.

DATE SYRUP (SILAN)

Date syrup, also commonly called *silan*, is a thick, molasses-colored syrup made from boiled dates. This natural sweetener is widely used in Middle Eastern and North African cooking, prized for its rich, jammy-sweet flavor. Some scholars write that the honey mentioned in the Torah actually refers to date syrup, not bees' honey.

DIAMOND CRYSTAL KOSHER SALT

All of the recipes in this book were developed using Diamond Crystal kosher salt, which is widely considered the gold standard in the food industry. I like its delicate flavor and relatively large and coarse crystals, which dissolve easily. If you substitute another brand of kosher salt, like Morton (which has an objectively stronger, saltier taste), or table salt (which packs more tightly into a measuring spoon), I recommend using between half and two-thirds of the amount of salt called for in the recipe.

DRIED UNSWEETENED COCONUT

Dried unsweetened coconut comes in several forms, from tiny flecks and thin shreds to larger flat flakes or chips. It is sold both toasted and untoasted. Unlike dried sweetened coconut, which is moist and spongy because of the added sugar, dried unsweetened coconut has a crisp, meaty texture. The different types of dried unsweetened coconut cannot always be used interchangeably, so make sure to read your recipe closely before buying.

DULCE DE LECHE

Popular across Latin and South America, this "milk jam" is made by slowly heating milk and sugar together until the mixture takes on a thick, spreadable, caramel-like consistenry. It is traditionally used for filling pastries or spreading on toast. In recent years, vegan versions of dulce de leche (made from almond or coconut milk) have become available.

EDIBLE FLOWERS

Edible flowers like pansies, nasturtiums, chamomiles, and elderflowers, among others, add elegance to frosted and glazed cakes and other special baked goods. They can be purchased at specialty food stores or ordered online. They are delicate and have a short shelf life, so they should be used within a day or two after purchase.

GLUTEN-FREE ALL-PURPOSE FLOUR

Gluten-free all-purpose flours combine a variety of non-wheat flours (such as rice, tapioca, millet, and sorghum) and starches (like potato starch, arrowroot, and cornstarch) to mimic the structure and texture provided by regular all-purpose flour. The specific mix of ingredients varies from brand to brand, and not all work as consistently as others, so it is worth trying out a few to see what works best in your kitchen. Look for one that contains xantham gum, which helps provide elasticity to batters and doughs.

HAZELNUT FLOUR

Also known as hazelnut meal, hazelnut flour is made from finely ground hazelnuts. Gluten-free and high in fiber and protein, it lends a delicately sweet, buttery flavor to baked goods. To extend its shelf life, store the flour in an airtight container in the refrigerator or freezer.

INSTANT COFFEE GRANULES

Instant coffee granules are made from brewed coffee that has been dehydrated and freeze-dried into small crystals that will dissolve in hot water. They are often used in baking to add flavor to cookies and cakes. Adding a little bit of instant coffee to chocolate desserts also helps intensify the chocolate's flavor. Instant coffee granules are available in regular and decaf versions.

MATZO MEAL

Matzo meal is made from sheets of matzo (the unleavened bread eaten on Passover) that have been ground. It is used for making matzo balls and as a substitute for flour in many Passover baking recipes. Matzo cake meal is simply finely ground matzo meal. I personally prefer the airy texture that matzo meal gives baked goods over cake meal, which can result in denser baked goods.

NATURAL FOOD COLORING (AND SPRINKLES)

Conventional food colors, sold as either liquids or powders, are made from chemicals formulated to add an array of colors to foods. They are beautiful, but the petroleum-derived chemicals have been linked to a variety of health risks. Natural food colors do not contain anything artificial; they are derived from vegetables, fruits, spices, algae, and other natural sources. Natural food colors tend to be slightly less vibrant than synthetic colors, but they still add beauty to dishes.

NEUTRAL VEGETABLE OIL

Many of the recipes in this cookbook call for neutral vegetable oil, which means an oil that does not impart noticeable flavor to a finished dish. Neutral oils tend to have high smoke points, which makes them useful as frying oils. Some of my favorite neutral vegetable oils include sunflower, safflower, grapeseed oil, and light olive oil.

ORANGE BLOSSOM WATER

Orange blossom water (sometimes sold as orange flower water) is used across Mediterranean, Middle Eastern, and North African cuisines. It is made from the flowers of the bitter Seville orange tree, which are boiled and then distilled to create an aromatic flavoring that lends a heady, floral fragrance to pastries, custards, and other dishes.

PETIT BEURRE BISCUITS (TEA BISCUITS)

Two of the recipes in this cookbook, Tea Biscuit Tiramisu (page 217) and Chocolate Salami (page 245), call for petit beurre–style biscuits (or cookies). These French shortbreads are crisp, barely sweetened, and—as their name, which translates to "little butter" suggests—small and buttery. They are also known as tea biscuits, and they are commonly served alongside that warming drink. Kosher nondairy brands of petit beurre biscuits are popular throughout Israel and in religiously observant communities in America.

PHYLLO (FILO)

Phyllo is a super-thin unleavened dough widely used across Middle Eastern and Balkan cuisines for making baklava and other pastries. To make these delicacies, many sheets of phyllo are stacked on top of one another, with butter or oil brushed onto each layer, yielding a crisp and airy texture after baking. (Although phyllo dough and puff pastry are often sold next to one another in the supermarket freezer section, they cannot be used interchangeably.)

POMEGRANATE MOLASSES

Pomegranate molasses is a thick, syrupy reduction made from boiled pomegranate juice. (Some commercial brands also contain sugar.) The tart syrup is commonly used in Middle Eastern cuisine, primarily in savory dishes, but it also lends a concentrated pomegranate flavor to baked goods.

POPPY SEEDS

The tiny blue-black seeds of the poppy plant are used as an ingredient in cooking and baking and are also pressed for their rich oil. Called *mohn* in Yiddish, the seeds are popular throughout Central and Eastern European Jewish cuisine. Poppy seeds spoil quickly, so be sure to buy them fresh, store them in the freezer, and only grind them right before use.

POTATO STARCH

Potato starch is a light, powdery, bright-white starch extracted from potatoes. Like cornstarch, it is often used to thicken sauces and custards. Since it is free of chametz (the five types of grain forbidden during the Passover holiday), it has also become a common addition to the Passover baking pantry. It is naturally gluten free. (See also Cornstarch on page 33.)

PUFF PASTRY

A laminated dough, which alternates layers of dough and butter, puff pastry bakes up airy and flaky. The layers of butter melt during baking, creating airspaces in the dough that puff up into crisp, separate layers by steam. Puff pastry is traditionally made with butter, but there are also dairy-free brands that substitute vegetable shortening. (While puff pastry and phyllo dough are often found next to each other in the supermarket freezer section, they usually cannot be used interchangeably.)

RICE FLOUR

Rice flour is made from white, brown, or glutinous rice that is finely milled. It is a common ingredient in gluten-free flour mixes, and it is also used as a thickening agent for sauces and puddings. To extend its shelf life, store rice flour in an airtight container in the refrigerator or freezer.

ROSE WATER

Popular in Middle Eastern and many other cuisines across the globe, rose water adds a delicate floral flavor to baked goods, puddings, and sweet drinks. It is made by boiling and steeping rose blossoms and then distilling their fragrant vapor into a concentrated liquid. Some brands of rose water pack a stronger punch than others, so try a few and see what you like.

SEMOLINA

Semolina is a coarse flour made from durum wheat (the same wheat used for making pasta). It is commonly used in Mediterranean, Middle Eastern, and South Asian cuisines, and it is the base of many cakes and puddings. It has a slightly nutty, sweet taste. At the grocery store, look for finely ground semolina, which retains some of its texture (similar to cornmeal), rather than semolina flour, which is milled into a finer powder.

SILKEN TOFU

This variety of tofu has a soft, wobbly texture and a mild, milky flavor. It is commonly used fresh in Japanese cuisine, served topped with soy sauce, ginger, sesame seeds, and scallions. But it can also be used as a creamy, dairy-free base for puddings.

SOUR CHERRIES

Also called tart cherries, sour cherries are a species of the Prunus genus that has a lower sugar content and higher level of acidity than sweet cherry varieties. The bright-red, mouth-puckering fruit is typically used in baking or transformed into a sweet-tart jam. Sour cherries have a limited season, from late spring into midsummer. If you see a display of sour cherries at your farmers' market, buy a bunch of them, pit them with a cherry pitter, and freeze until needed. Out of season, you can sometimes find frozen sour cherries in the supermarket. Avoid bottled and canned sour cherries, which typically have a flat or "tinny" flavor.

SUMAC

Sumac is a brick-red spice made from sumac berries that have been dried and ground into a powder. It has a tart, lemony flavor, thanks to a high malic acid content. It is widely used in Middle Eastern cuisines.

SWEETENED CONDENSED MILK

Sweetened condensed milk is milk that has been cooked down to remove some of the water content and sweetened with sugar. It has a thick texture and rich, caramel-sweet flavor and is used to make custards, ice cream, and drinks. In recent years, vegan sweetened condensed milk (made from coconut or oat milk) has become available. Do not confuse sweetened condensed milk with evaporated milk, which has also had some of the water content cooked out but is not sweetened.

TAHINI

Made from sesame seeds that have been crushed to release their oils and ground into a smooth, creamy paste, tahini is the sesame equivalent of peanut butter. Used throughout Middle Eastern cooking, it is prized for its rich mouthfeel and nutty, mildly bitter flavor. Often used in savory contexts, it also lends complexity to baked goods and desserts.

VANILLA BEAN PASTE

Vanilla bean paste, or vanilla paste, is made of finely ground vanilla pods and seeds that are blended with thickeners to make it viscous and scoopable. It imparts both a lovely flavor and visible flecks of vanilla bean seeds to baked goods, ice creams, and custards.

VANILLA EXTRACT

Vanilla extract is made by steeping whole vanilla beans in water and alcohol to create a concentrated, flavorful liquid that is then strained. It imparts a clean vanilla taste to baked goods and other desserts.

VEGAN BUTTER

I use the term *vegan butter* throughout this cookbook to mean any nondairy butter substitute. (See more about the evolution of margarine and vegetable shortenings to vegan butters on page 85.) There is a wide variety of vegan butters on the market today, and they do not all work equally well in baking recipes. Look for a brand that specifies that it is formulated for baking, rather than as a spread or for cooking.

Honey Cake with Apple Butter Frosting (page 144)

A NOTE ON THE KOSHER LAWS AND *THE DESSERT TABLE*'S RECIPES

All of the recipes in *The Dessert Table* follow the kosher laws. Many of the recipes are naturally pareve, meaning they contain no butter, milk, cream, or other dairy products. Other recipes are dairy but offer simple ingredient substitutions to make them pareve. Any recipe that includes a substitution was tested to make sure the substitute ingredient worked as well as the original.

A handful of recipes—including Chai-Spiced Cheesecake (page 151) and Raspberry and Sweet Cheese Strudel (page 197)—that are dairy do not include recommended substitutions because I was not able to create a dairy-free version that lived up to the original. My intention and hope is that whether you are a kosher keeper or not, you will find plenty of desserts that both meet your needs and delight your sweet tooth.

COOKIES & BARS

BLACK-AND-WHITE SHORTBREAD COOKIES

Makes about 24 cookies

As with many iconic recipes, the origin of the black-and-white cookie is disputed. One theory posits that they were first introduced at Glaser's Bake Shop (owned by Bavarian immigrants) in Manhattan during the first years of the twentieth century. Other stories insist that they originated at Hemstrought's Bakery in Utica, New York, where the two-toned cookies are called half-moons, and then later took root in New York City. Regardless of their origin, black-and-white cookies are deeply entwined in the childhood memories of a generation of New Yorkers who would find them in the pastry cases at Jewish bakeries around the city.

I have always admired how unapologetically itself the black-and-white cookie is. Where other cookies skew chewy or crisp, black-and-whites are tender and cakey. And while other cookies often go unadorned, black-and-whites are dramatically swooped with a rich fondant icing. But as much as I love and respect them, sometimes I just want a little more than the typical Jewish bakery cookie can deliver. More texture, more oomph. These shortbreads fit the bill. The frosting is every bit as familiar as that of a traditional black-and-white (though I do like to add a little instant coffee to the chocolate to deepen the flavor), but the cookie itself is snappy, firm, and buttery, providing exactly the right amount of crave-worthy contrast.

FOR THE SHORTBREAD

16 tablespoons (2 sticks / 227 g) unsalted butter or vegan butter, cut into pieces and softened

⅔ cup (80 g) confectioners' sugar, sifted

½ teaspoon kosher salt

1 teaspoon almond extract

2 cups (280 g) all-purpose flour, plus more for rolling

NOTE: If your dough is too soft to roll immediately, refrigerate it for 30 minutes before rolling.

1. Make the shortbread: Preheat the oven to 325°F (160°C). Line two baking sheets with parchment paper.
2. Combine the butter, confectioners' sugar, salt, and almond extract in the bowl of a stand mixer fitted with the paddle attachment. (Or use a handheld electric mixer and a large bowl.) Beat at medium speed until the butter and sugar are fully combined.
3. Add the flour in two additions, beating at low speed and scraping down the sides of the bowl as necessary, until just combined.
4. Gather the dough together, press it into a rough disk, and transfer it to a floured work surface. With a lightly floured rolling pin, roll the dough out to a 1/8-inch (3 mm) thickness. Using a 2½-inch (6 cm) round cookie cutter, cut out as many circles of dough as possible. Using a thin metal spatula, transfer the cookies to the prepared baking sheets, leaving about ½ inch (12 mm) between them. Gather the dough scraps together and repeat the process.

FOR THE ICING

2½ cups (300 g) confectioners' sugar, sifted, plus more if needed

2½ tablespoons milk or nondairy milk, plus more if needed

¾ teaspoon vanilla extract

1½ teaspoons fresh lemon juice

2 tablespoons unsweetened cocoa powder, sifted

½ teaspoon instant coffee granules (regular or decaf)

5. Bake, rotating the pans back to front and top to bottom halfway through baking, until the cookies are lightly golden and firm to the touch, 18 to 22 minutes. Remove from the oven and transfer the cookies to wire racks to cool.

6. Once the cookies are fully cooled, make the icing: Stir together the confectioners' sugar, milk, vanilla extract, and lemon juice in a medium bowl. The mixture should be thick but spreadable. If it is too loose or runny, stir in a little more confectioners' sugar. If it is too thick to spread, stir in a little additional milk.

7. Transfer half of the icing to a second bowl. Add the cocoa powder and instant coffee, and stir to combine. Add more milk if needed to achieve a thick but spreadable consistency.

8. Set the wire racks over sheets of parchment or newspaper. Using a butter knife or spatula, carefully frost one half of each cookie with white icing. Repeat the process with the chocolate icing, frosting the other halves of the cookies. As you work, set the frosted cookies icing side up on the racks, and allow the icing to firm up.

9. Store the cookies in an airtight container in the fridge for up to 5 days, or in the freezer for up to 6 months.

BUCKWHEAT CHOCOLATE CHIP COOKIES

Makes about 36 cookies

Anyone who has ever enjoyed a kasha knish or kasha varnishkes (the beloved Ashkenazi dish of bow-tie noodles, browned onions, and toasted buckwheat groats) likely thinks of buckwheat in a decidedly savory context. But buckwheat flour has plenty of dessert potential, as in this wholesome spin on chocolate chip cookies. The flour, which is popular throughout Eastern Europe, has an earthy, slightly bitter flavor that plays nicely with all that butter, sugar, and chocolate. Think of these as a slightly more sophisticated, grown-up chocolate chip cookie—though my kids happily devour them too.

- 1¼ cups (175 g) all-purpose flour or gluten-free all-purpose flour
- ¾ cup (120 g) buckwheat flour
- ½ teaspoon baking powder
- ½ teaspoon baking soda
- ½ teaspoon kosher salt
- 16 tablespoons (2 sticks / 227 g) unsalted butter or vegan butter, softened
- ¾ packed cup (150 g) light brown sugar
- ½ cup (100 g) granulated sugar
- 1 large egg
- 1½ teaspoons vanilla extract
- 1½ cups (270 g) bittersweet or semisweet chocolate chips
- Flaky sea salt for topping (optional)

1. Whisk together the all-purpose flour, buckwheat flour, baking powder, baking soda, and salt in a medium bowl.
2. In the bowl of a stand mixer fitted with the paddle attachment (or using a handheld electric mixer and a large bowl), beat together the butter, brown sugar, and granulated sugar until fluffy, about 2 minutes. Add the egg and vanilla and beat to combine. Add the dry mixture in two stages, beating at low speed and scraping down the sides of the bowl as needed, until just combined. Beat in the chocolate chips. Cover the bowl and refrigerate the dough for 30 minutes.
3. Preheat the oven to 375°F (190°C). Line two large baking sheets with parchment paper.
4. Using a 1½-tablespoon cookie scoop, scoop the dough onto the baking sheets, leaving about 1 inch (2.5 cm) between the cookies. Sprinkle the cookies lightly with flaky salt, if desired, and bake, rotating the pans back to front and top to bottom halfway through baking, until the tops are set and the cookies are darker around the edges, 14 to 17 minutes. Transfer the cookies to wire racks to cool.
5. Store the cookies in an airtight container in the fridge for up to a week or, well wrapped, in the freezer for up to 6 months.

JEWS AND THE CHOCOLATE TRADE

Cocoa beans, which are indigenous to Central America, were introduced into Spain in the early sixteenth century by Christopher Columbus. At first, the aristocrats found the unsweetened chocolate beverage favored by the Aztecs to be bitter and unappetizing. But a few decades later, another voyager, Hernando Cortés, shared a different beverage that mixed the roasted and pounded beans with sugar, vanilla, and cinnamon. That drink—essentially hot chocolate—became a runaway hit among Spain's upper crust. The subsequent introduction of chocolate into Europe would lead to a seismic shift in the global food trade. And from nearly the beginning, Sephardi Jews played a central role in that trade.

In her book *On the Chocolate Trail*, Rabbi Deborah Prinz makes a convincing case that Jews helped introduce chocolate to the wider world. "Jews exiled from Spain in 1492 and then from Portugal in 1496 engaged in international trade," she writes. Just as with sugar (see page 212), Sephardi Jewish and crypto-Jewish shippers and traders "played a critical . . . part in the cocoa business," exporting cacao beans to Europe.

These Jews also helped spread recipes and techniques for transforming cacao beans into chocolate throughout European cities. By the seventeenth century, chocolate making was considered a Jewish specialty in the Netherlands. Moreover, Prinz writes, Jews in Bayonne, France, "were crucial leaders in the contraband trade with Spain, including the business of exporting, re-exporting, and smuggling cacao." They also helped set up some of that French region's first chocolate factories—only to then be temporarily evicted from Bayonne's chocolatier guild in the eighteenth century by the non-Jewish locals they had taught the trade to. Despite the antisemitic persecution they faced along the way, the efforts of these Jews were successful enough to establish Bayonne's reputation as the chocolate capital of France.

Sephardi Jews with connections to the colonies also helped usher chocolate into North America in the seventeenth century. Newburgh, New York, is home to the oldest extant Jewish residence in America—a homestead founded by the Gomez family, one of the area's most prominent Sephardi families. "The Gomez family's chocolate business was built on a granular chocolate, which was . . . commonly imbibed as a beverage," writes Prinz. And in Newport, Rhode Island, a wealthy Portuguese Jew named Aaron Lopez traded in many products, among them rum, candles, and chocolate.

The chocolate business shifted dramatically over the following decades, as drinking chocolate was eventually joined by edible chocolate confections. "Until 1828, chocolate was primarily consumed as a drink or in cakes," writes Gil Marks in his *Encyclopedia of Jewish Food.* But starting in the nineteenth century, developing technology allowed manufacturers to extract cocoa butter from ground cocoa beans and create chocolate bars and candy. And the center of cocoa production shifted from Central America to Africa. But while, as Marks writes, "Jewish control of the European chocolate trade declined," Jewish entrepreneurs remained at the forefront of chocolate manufacturing. For more about Jewish chocolate and candy makers in the United States, see page 49.

TU BISHVAT TRAIL MIX COOKIES

Makes about 36 cookies

Tu Bishvat (literally the fifteenth day of the Hebrew month of Shvat) began in ancient Israel as a mundane tax holiday—a way to differentiate a tree's fruit production for one tax year from the next. Over time, and with thanks to Jewish mystics living in sixteenth-century Tzfat, the holiday became layered with symbolic significance and ritual. Today many people celebrate Tu Bishvat by holding seders and eating fruits and nuts that come from trees. This recipe combines a bevy of tree fruits—cherries, walnuts, coconut, and chocolate from cacao pods—to transform trail mix cookies (the nut-and-dried fruit–packed cookies beloved by hikers and campers) into an edible ode to those trees. These are the perfect mix of crisp and chewy and absolutely brimming with goodies.

- 2 cups (200 g) old-fashioned rolled oats
- 1 cup (140 g) all-purpose flour or gluten-free all-purpose flour
- 1 teaspoon baking powder
- ½ teaspoon kosher salt
- 12 tablespoons (1½ sticks / 170 g) unsalted butter or vegan butter, softened
- ⅔ packed cup (130 g) light brown sugar
- ⅔ cup (130 g) granulated sugar
- 2 large eggs
- 1 teaspoon vanilla extract
- ¾ cup (135 g) semisweet or bittersweet chocolate chips
- ½ cup (70 g) dark or golden raisins
- ½ cup (65 g) dried cherries, roughly chopped
- ½ cup (50 g) walnuts, roughly chopped
- ⅓ cup (25 g) unsweetened dried shredded coconut

1. Whisk together the oats, flour, baking powder, and salt in a medium bowl.
2. In the bowl of a stand mixer fitted with the paddle attachment (or using a large bowl and a handheld electric mixer), beat the butter, brown sugar, and granulated sugar together at medium speed until light and fluffy, about 2 minutes. Beat in the eggs and vanilla, scraping down the sides of the bowl as necessary, until fully combined.
3. Add the flour mixture to the butter mixture in two stages, beating at low speed to combine. Add the chocolate chips, raisins, dried cherries, walnuts, and coconut and beat until fully incorporated. Cover the bowl and refrigerate the dough for 30 minutes.
4. Preheat the oven to 350°F (180°C). Line two large baking sheets with parchment paper.
5. Using a 1½-tablespoon cookie scoop, scoop the batter onto the prepared baking sheets, leaving about 1 inch (2.5 cm) between the cookies. Bake, rotating the pans top to bottom and back to front halfway through baking, until the cookies are golden and set but still a little soft on top, 15 to 18 minutes. Transfer the cookies to wire racks to cool.
6. Store the cookies in an airtight container in the fridge for up to 1 week or in the freezer, well wrapped, for up to 6 months.

VARIATIONS: You can substitute an equal amount of chopped dried figs or apricots for the cherries and raisins, or use almonds or pecans in place of either the coconut or the walnuts.

CHEWY CHOCOLATE GINGERSNAPS

Makes about 36 cookies

When I spoke with Eli Sussman, he told me he wasn't much of a sweets person. But his personal history suggests a different story. As the chef and co-owner of Brooklyn's Jewishly-inspired restaurant, Gertrude's, he makes a mean potato latke and dill pickle–brined roast chicken. But Gertrude's is undoubtedly best known for Sussman's Black & White Seven-Layer Cake—a towering strata of vanilla and chocolate cake with fudgy ganache frosting influenced by the cakes Sussman ate after synagogue as a child. "I have really strong memories of loading up a little paper plate with all these sweets and sitting on a bench in the social hall making my way through them," he said.

Sussman also recalled his mother's gingersnap cookies, which she often baked for Rosh Hashanah and other holidays. He is so fond of the gingersnaps that he served a version of them at Samesa, the Middle Eastern restaurant he cofounded with his brother Max. "The recipe almost definitely came from *The Joy of Cooking*," he said, although his family personalized it over the years. Here I've tweaked it even further, adding cocoa powder to the batter and stirring in chopped bittersweet chocolate for a complex chocolate-ginger cookie that brings a familiar treat into new territory.

- 1¾ cups (245 g) all-purpose flour
- ⅓ cup (25 g) unsweetened cocoa powder
- 1½ teaspoons baking soda
- 2 teaspoons ground ginger
- 1 teaspoon ground cinnamon
- ¼ teaspoon ground cloves
- ½ teaspoon kosher salt
- 10 tablespoons (1¼ sticks / 142 g) unsalted butter or vegan butter, softened
- ½ cup (100 g) granulated sugar
- ½ packed cup (100 g) light brown sugar
- ¼ cup (85 g) unsulphured molasses
- 1 large egg
- 4 ounces (113 g) bittersweet chocolate, chopped into roughly ¼-inch (6 mm) pieces

1. Whisk together the flour, cocoa powder, baking soda, ginger, cinnamon, cloves, and salt in a medium bowl.
2. In the bowl of a stand mixer fitted with the paddle attachment (or using a handheld electric mixer and a large bowl), beat together the butter, granulated sugar, and brown sugar at medium speed until light and fluffy. Beat in the molasses and egg, scraping down the sides of the bowl as necessary.
3. Add the the flour mixture in two stages, beating at low speed until just combined. Fold in the chopped chocolate. Cover the bowl and refrigerate for at least 1 hour, or up to overnight. (If you chill it overnight, you may need to let the dough stand at room temperature for 10 minutes before scooping.)
4. When ready to bake, preheat the oven to 350°F (180°C). Line two large baking sheets with parchment paper.
5. Using a 1½-tablespoon cookie scoop, scoop out the dough, roll into balls, and place on the baking sheets, leaving about 1 inch (2.5 cm) between the cookies. Gently press down on the cookies with your fingertips to flatten them slightly.

6. Bake the cookies, rotating the baking sheets back to front and top to bottom halfway through baking, until the edges are set and tops are slightly cracked, 12 to 14 minutes. Transfer the cookies to wire racks to cool. The cookies will still feel soft straight from the oven but will firm up as they cool.

7. Store the cookies in an airtight container at room temperature for up to 3 days or in the fridge for up to 1 week. Or wrap them well and freeze for up to 6 months.

ALMOND KISS BLONDIES

Makes one 8-inch square pan

For decades, many American Passover dessert tables—particularly in New York City, but also beyond—featured a metal tin filled with Barton's Almond Kisses. Each bite-size treat consisted of two whole roasted almonds encased in a soft nugget of chocolate caramel. (See page 248 for more about Barton's Candy Corporation.) Unfortunately, the beloved confection was discontinued in 2009, becoming only a memory of a bygone era. Instead of wallowing, I decided to create these blondies as an homage to one of my favorite Jewish candies. They have all the plush, chewy texture and caramelized sweetness you love in a classic blondie, plus the mix of roasted almonds and dark chocolate that made Barton's Almond Kisses so irresistible.

¾ cup (105 g) all-purpose flour
¼ cup (25 g) almond flour
¼ teaspoon baking powder
½ teaspoon kosher salt
10 tablespoons (1¼ sticks / 142 g) unsalted butter or vegan butter
1 packed cup (200 g) light brown sugar
1 large egg
1 teaspoon vanilla extract
¼ teaspoon almond extract
½ cup (70 g) roasted unsalted almonds, roughly chopped
½ cup (90 g) semisweet chocolate chips

1. Preheat the oven to 350°F (180°C). Lightly grease an 8-inch (20 cm) square baking pan. Line the pan with parchment paper, letting the paper hang over two opposite sides, then lightly grease the parchment. Set aside.
2. Whisk together the all-purpose flour, almond flour, baking powder, and kosher salt in a medium bowl. Set aside.
3. Melt the butter in a medium heavy-bottomed saucepan over medium-low heat, then continue cooking, stirring and swirling the pan often, until the butter starts to brown and smell toasty, about 5 minutes (see Note if using vegan butter). Watch carefully so that it does not burn.
4. Pour the browned butter into a medium bowl (leaving any darker solids at the bottom of the pan behind) and let cool slightly. Stir in the brown sugar, followed by the egg, vanilla extract, and almond extract. Add the flour mixture and stir until just combined, then fold in the chopped almonds and chocolate chips.
5. Transfer the batter to the prepared pan, smoothing the top and gently nudging it into the corners. Bake until the top is golden and a cake tester inserted into the center comes out mostly clean with a few moist crumbs clinging to it, 22 to 25 minutes. Transfer the pan to a wire rack to cool.
6. Use the overhanging parchment to lift the blondies out of the pan and transfer them to a cutting board to slice. Store the blondies in an airtight container at room temperature for up to 3 days, in the fridge for up to 1 week, or well wrapped in the freezer for up to 6 months.

NOTE: Since vegan butters do not contain milk solids, they do not effectively brown. If you are using vegan butter, simply heat it until melted and warm.

MAPLE-TAHINI RICE KRISPIES TREATS

Makes one 8-inch square pan

In the late 1930s, Kellogg's hired a food economist named Mildred Day to develop recipes using their crisped rice cereal. Her efforts resulted in the recipe for one of the most beloved and enduring American sweets, the Rice Krispies Treat, which first appeared on cereal boxes in 1941. There have been countless variations and spins on Day's recipe in the decades since. I am particularly fond of this one, which stirs tahini and maple syrup into the buttery melted marshmallows. The tahini lends just a hint of bitter nuttiness to the mix, while the maple syrup complexifies the marshmallows' sweetness. These gooey, crunchy bars are equally at home tucked into a child's lunch box or gracing the table at a Shabbat potluck.

5 cups (125 g) Rice Krispies cereal

6 tablespoons (¾ stick / 85 g) unsalted butter or vegan butter

One 10-ounce (285 g) bag marshmallows (not mini)

⅓ cup (80 g) well-stirred tahini

2 tablespoons pure maple syrup

1½ teaspoons vanilla extract

½ teaspoon kosher salt

Toasted sesame seeds for topping (white, black, or a mix)

1. Line an 8 × 8-inch (20 cm) square baking dish with parchment paper, letting the parchment hang over two opposite sides. Set aside.
2. Pour the cereal into a large bowl and set nearby.
3. Melt the butter in a medium heavy-bottomed saucepan over medium-low heat, then continue cooking, stirring and swirling the pan often, until the butter starts to brown and smell toasty, about 5 minutes (see Note if using vegan butter). Watch carefully so that it does not burn.
4. Turn the heat down to low, add the marshmallows, and stir until fully melted and smooth. Remove from the heat and stir in the tahini, maple syrup, vanilla, and salt to combine. Pour the mixture over the rice cereal and stir to fully combine.
5. Working quickly, transfer the mixture to the baking dish and use a piece of parchment paper to press it evenly into the pan. (Do not pack it down too firmly, or it will be too compacted.) Sprinkle the top with toasted sesame seeds. Let the mixture cool for about 30 minutes, then use the overhanging parchment to carefully lift the treats out of the pan and transfer to a cutting board.
6. Cut the treats into squares and serve slightly warm or at room temperature.
7. Store the treats in an airtight container at room temperature for up to 3 days.

NOTE: Since vegan butters do not contain milk solids, they do not effectively brown. If you are using vegan butter, simply heat it until melted and warm.

WHOLE WHEAT HANUKKAH SUGAR COOKIES

Makes about 36 cookies

As for so many American Jews, baking roll out–style sugar cookies together was one of my family's favorite Hanukkah traditions. A few years ago, my mom gave me the set of vintage Jewish-themed cookie cutters we used when I was a kid (there's a menorah, a dreidel, a candle, a Star of David, a Lion of Judah, and a shofar) so I could pass the holiday baking tradition down to my two children. I updated my family's recipe with whole wheat flour to give the cookies a slightly more nutritious spin while keeping all the sweetness and fun. A touch of cinnamon in the dough complements the natural nuttiness of the whole wheat flour and adds a bit of cozy warmth to the cold-weather holiday.

FOR THE COOKIES

- 1 cup (140 g) all-purpose flour, plus more for rolling
- ¾ cup (90 g) whole wheat flour
- 1 teaspoon ground cinnamon
- ½ teaspoon baking powder
- ½ teaspoon kosher salt
- 8 tablespoons (1 stick / 113 g) unsalted butter or vegan butter, softened
- ¾ cup (150 g) granulated sugar
- 1 large egg
- 1 teaspoon vanilla extract

FOR THE ICING AND DECORATING

- 2 cups (240 g) confectioners' sugar, sifted
- 2 tablespoons milk, plus more if needed
- 1 tablespoon light corn syrup
- ¼ teaspoon vanilla or almond extract
- Natural food colorings (optional)
- Natural sprinkles (optional)

1. Make the cookies: Whisk together the all-purpose flour, whole wheat flour, cinnamon, baking powder, and salt in a medium bowl; set aside.
2. Combine the butter and sugar in the bowl of a stand mixer fitted with the paddle attachment (or use a handheld electric mixer and a large bowl) and beat at medium speed until light and fluffy, 1 to 2 minutes. Beat in the egg and vanilla until combined.
3. Add the flour mixture in two stages, beating at low speed and scraping down the sides of the bowl as necessary, until a dough forms. Turn out the dough, divide it into 2 equal pieces, form each piece into a disk, and wrap each one well in parchment paper. Refrigerate for at least 2 hours, or up to overnight.
4. Preheat the oven to 375°F (190°C). Line two large baking sheets with parchment paper.
5. On a floured work surface, roll out one piece of dough (keep the remaining piece refrigerated) to a ¼-inch (6 mm) thickness. Use cookie cutters to stamp out as many cookies as possible and then use a thin metal spatula to transfer them to one of the baking sheets. Gather up and reroll the dough scraps and stamp out additional cookies. Repeat the process with the second piece of dough.
6. Bake, rotating the baking sheets back to front and top to bottom halfway through, until the cookies are lightly golden with slightly darker edges, 8 to 10 minutes. (They will continue to darken in color as they cool.)

recipe continues

NOTE: If you are baking with young kids, you can give them small clean paintbrushes for applying the icing to the cookies.

7. Remove the baking sheets from the oven and set on wire racks to cool for 2 to 3 minutes, then transfer the cookies to the racks to fully cool.

8. Make the icing: Stir together the confectioners' sugar, milk, corn syrup, and vanilla extract in a bowl to make a thick but spreadable icing. If the icing is too thick to spread, stir in a litte more milk 1 teaspoon at a time, as necessary.

9. If you want to make colored icing, divide the icing among several smaller bowls and stir a few drops of food coloring into each to reach the desired shade. Use a small offset spatula or butter knife to spread the icing onto the cooled cookies, then set the cookies icing side up on the racks. Decorate with sprinkles, if using, and let the icing set.

10. Store the cookies in an airtight container at room temperature for up to 3 days or in the fridge for up to 1 week.

KIDDUSH SPRINKLE COOKIES

Makes about 40 cookies

When I was a child, kiddush cookies were the highlight of my Saturday mornings. On Shabbat at my family's synagogue, the congregants would spill out from the sanctuary after the service into the social hall, where we would sip tiny cups of grape juice and pile our napkins with an assortment of cookies. They were sweet, they were crumbly, and they were magnificent. Chief among them were the sprinkle cookies (sometimes called confetti cookies)—snappy circles brightly festooned with rainbow sprinkles. Equally beloved in twentieth-century Italian and Jewish bakeries (made with butter in the former, and with margarine or oil in the latter), they were the only motivation I needed to sit through the lengthy Shabbat service. Now that I am grown and my family's primary baker, we can enjoy them the rest of the week too.

2½ cups (350 g) all-purpose flour
1 teaspoon baking powder
¼ teaspoon baking soda
½ teaspoon kosher salt
16 tablespoons (2 sticks / 227 g) unsalted butter or vegan butter
1¼ cups (250 g) granulated sugar
1 large egg
1 tablespoon vanilla extract
About 2 cups (320 g) natural rainbow sprinkles

1. Preheat the oven to 375°F (190°C). Line two baking sheets with parchment paper. Whisk together the flour, baking powder, baking soda, and salt in a medium bowl.
2. In the bowl of a stand mixer fitted with the paddle attachment (or using a handheld electric mixer and a large bowl), beat together the butter and sugar at medium speed until fluffy. Add the egg and vanilla and beat to combine. Add the flour mixture in two stages, beating at low and scraping down the sides of the bowl as needed, until just combined.
3. Pour the sprinkles into a shallow bowl. Scoop out a level tablespoon of dough and roll it into a ball. (If the dough is too soft to roll, refrigerate it for 20 to 30 minutes.) Drop the ball into the sprinkles and gently roll it around to coat on all sides, then transfer to the baking sheets and press on it with your fingers to flatten it into a ½-inch- (12 mm) thick circle. Continue the process with the remaining dough and sprinkles, leaving about 2 inches (5 cm) between the cookies.
4. Bake, rotating the baking sheets back to front and top to bottom halfway through, until the cookies are very lightly golden, 10 to 12 minutes. Remove from the oven and let the cookies cool on the baking sheets for 5 minutes, then transfer to wire racks to cool fully.
5. Store the cookies in an airtight container at room temperature for up to 5 days, or in the fridge for up to 2 weeks or, well wrapped, in the freezer for up to 6 months.

CITRUS-GLAZED PISTACHIO MANDELBROT

Makes about 36 cookies

Mandelbrot (literally, "almond bread" in Yiddish) is biscotti's Ashkenazi Jewish cousin. Like the Italian cookie, mandelbrot is first baked as a slab, then cut into long, thin slices and baked again, which gives the cookies their distinctive crisp, crunchy texture. Older recipes for mandelbrot are typically quite simple, and the cookies were served as a weekday snack or dessert, or as an accompaniment to tea or coffee on Shabbat afternoon. Many more contemporary recipes, like this one, amp up the flavor by mixing different kinds of nuts, chopped chocolate, citrus zest, or other ingredients into the dough. I also like to dress them up with a beautiful sweet-tart lemon glaze.

FOR THE MANDELBROT

3 cups (420 g) all-purpose flour
1 teaspoon baking powder
1 teaspoon baking soda
½ teaspoon kosher salt
1 cup (200 g) plus 2 tablespoons granulated sugar, divided
Grated zest of 2 medium lemons
Grated zest of 2 medium oranges
16 tablespoons (2 sticks / 227 g) unsalted butter or vegan butter, softened
4 large eggs
1½ teaspoons vanilla extract
1 cup (140 g) roasted unsalted almonds, roughly chopped
½ cup (50 g) roasted unsalted pistachios, roughly chopped

1. Make the mandelbrot: Preheat the oven to 350°F (180°C). Line two large rimmed baking sheets with parchment paper.

2. Sift together the flour, baking powder, baking soda, and salt into a medium bowl.

3. Combine 1 cup (200 g) of the sugar, the lemon zest, and orange zest in the bowl of a stand mixer fitted with the paddle attachment. (Or use a handheld electric mixer and a large bowl.) Rub the sugar and zest together between your fingers until fragrant and well combined, about 2 minutes. Add the butter and beat on medium speed, scraping down the sides of the bowl as necessary, until light and fluffy, 2 to 3 minutes. Add the eggs and vanilla and beat to fully combine.

4. Add the flour mixture in two additions, beating at low speed until just combined. The dough should be soft and spreadable. Add the almonds and pistachios and beat briefly to combine.

5. Divide the dough into 4 equal portions. Place 2 portions of dough on one baking sheet, leaving ample space between them, and use a butter knife or an offset spatula to spread each one into a long rectangle about 9 × 4 inches (23 × 10 cm) and ½ inch (1.3 cm) thick, leaving about 2 inches (5 cm) of space between the rectangles. Repeat with the remaining dough on the second baking sheet. Bake the mandelbrot, rotating the sheets top to bottom and back to front halfway through, until puffed and lightly browned, about 20 minutes. Remove from the oven and let cool slightly.

FOR THE GLAZE

1½ cups (180 g) confectioners' sugar

2 tablespoons fresh lemon juice, plus more if needed

6. Slice the rectangles, still on the baking sheets, crosswise into ¾-inch (2 cm) slices, then turn the slices onto their sides and sprinkle with 1 tablespoon of the remaining sugar. Bake for 10 minutes, remove the sheets from the oven, flip the cookies over, and sprinkle with the remaining 1 tablespoon sugar. Bake until firm, 5 to 10 minutes more. Remove from the oven and transfer the cookies to wire racks to cool.

7. Make the glaze: Sift the confectioners' sugar into a bowl. Add the lemon juice and stir to form a thick, spreadable glaze. If the glaze is too thick to spread, stir in a little bit more lemon juice. Use a butter knife or offset spatula to spread a layer of glaze over the top of each cookie. Set the cookies back down on the racks to allow the glaze to set.

8. Store the cookies in an airtight container at room temperature for up to 3 days, in the fridge for up to 1 week, or in the freezer for up to 6 months.

VARIATIONS: Change up the recipe by swapping in different nuts or adding dried cranberries or finely chopped candied orange peel or crystallized ginger. Just keep the overall amount of mix-ins the same.

BAKING WITH CHILDREN

Baking with kids can be an absolute joy. What could be better than passing down treasured recipes or celebrating the Jewish holidays by pulling something sweet and comforting out of the oven together? Some of my fondest childhood memories include the days leading up to Purim, when my mom, brother, and I would use juice glasses to stamp out circles of hamantaschen dough and fill them with sticky-sweet jam.

But now that I am a parent of two school-aged kids, I know that baking together is not always a dreamy process. Sometimes you get everything all set up, only to find out your kids aren't in the mood to bake. Sometimes the cookies end up looking more like amorphous blobs than the circles you envisioned. Sometimes (usually) the counter ends up splattered with egg yolk and oil and the floor is covered in floury footprints.

Over the last decade of being a parent—and lots of trial and error—I have developed some strategies that have made baking with my kids smoother and more enjoyable for everyone involved. I hope that these inspire readers to bake more with the children in their lives and to create new traditions together.

✻ Prioritize fun (and connection) over perfection. As a professional recipe developer, my job is to make sure that the recipes I create turn out consistently well. So when I first started baking with my kids, it was difficult to let go of my typical standards. But I eventually realized that the process is more important than the product. (Perhaps that seems obvious, but, unfortunately, it took me some time to get there.) So what if the apple cake turns out uneven, or more jam ends up in the kids' mouths than in the sufganiyot? If all parties had fun, shared moments of connection, and came away with a memory and a sweet treat, that is really what matters. So when working with kids—especially younger ones—focus the baking project around having a good time rather than perfection.

✻ Start them young. Whenever you begin baking with kids is the right time, but there is no reason to wait for them to reach a certain age. Will a 2½-year-old be able to crack eight eggs for a cake—maybe! (But probably not.) What they can almost definitely do, however, is dump the ingredients you measured out into a bowl and help mix them together, line a muffin tin with paper liners, or just play with a lump of babka dough while you roll out the rest and place it in the loaf tin. As your kids grow, they can take on more responsibilities, but getting an early start will make them feel at home in the kitchen.

✻ Get their input. Solicit kids' opinions when deciding what to bake. If Hanukkah is coming up, ask if they would rather make sugar cookies (page 57) or doughnuts (page 187). Or if Purim is on the horizon, take a poll on their favorite fillings for hamantaschen. (Be sure to let them know that chocolate, page 68, is definitely an option.) The more you communicate with them in advance, and the more input they have in the process, the more likely they are to feel engaged.

✻ Prep ahead. Some baking recipes require long stretches of down time, and children might not always have the patience to wait for two hours while a batch of dough rests on the counter or chills in the fridge. Whenever possible, do some of the prep work ahead yourself—like making and refrigerating the cookie dough, kneading a yeast dough and letting it rise, or simply gathering all the ingredients together—so you and your pint-size co-chef can jump right into the active part.

✻ Clean up together. Seeing my kitchen (which is both a professional work space and where I cook meals for my family) get trashed when making cookies with the kids is admittedly still hard. But baking is often a messy endeavor, even when I am doing it solo. With practice, I have learned to calm my nerves when the sugar inevitably spills. But I also involve my kids in the cleanup process. The older one gets a broom and a dustpan. The younger one gets a spray bottle filled with water and a sponge. We turn on music, and while they work, I put away the ingredients and load the dirty dishes into the dishwasher. Usually by the time we are done, the cookies are baked and out of the oven and ready to taste.

BAKING WITH KIDS? START HERE

- ✻ Tu Bishvat Trail Mix Cookies (page 51)
- ✻ Chewy Chocolate Gingersnaps (page 52)
- ✻ Maple-Tahini Rice Krispies Treats (page 56)
- ✻ Whole Wheat Hanukkah Sugar Cookies (page 57)
- ✻ Kiddush Sprinkle Cookies (page 60)
- ✻ Triple-Chocolate Hamantaschen (page 68)
- ✻ Passover Jam Thumbprints (page 99)
- ✻ Blueberry Streusel Cake (page 124)
- ✻ Best Passover Banana Bread (page 128)
- ✻ Best Passover Chocolate Zucchini Muffins (page 129)
- ✻ Triple-Pomegranate Cake (page 137)
- ✻ Chocolate Layer Cake with Advieh Buttercream (page 161)
- ✻ Chocolate and Cinnamon Palmiers (page 201)
- ✻ Silky Vegan Chocolate Pudding (page 216)
- ✻ Tea Biscuit Tiramisu (page 217)
- ✻ Berries with Honey and Sour Cream (page 238)
- ✻ Chocolate-Covered Pretzels (page 255)
- ✻ Egg Cream Float (page 267)

OATMEAL–SOUR CHERRY HAMANTASCHEN

Makes about 24 cookies

Hamantaschen, the triangular-shaped Ashkenazi Purim cookie, got its name from its original filling. Medieval Germans enjoyed a poppy seed–filled pastry called *mohntasche*, literally poppy seed (*mohn*) pockets (*tasche*). German Jews noted the similarity to the name of the Purim story's villain, Haman and, unable to resist a good pun, started baking hamantaschen ("Haman's pockets") filled with ground sweetened poppy seeds or, later, thick apricot or prune jam. Those classic hamantaschen flavors remain popular today, but now many home cooks view these Purim cookies as an opportunity for creative expression, filling them with everything from Nutella to lemon curd. This version combines the cozy-hug vibes of an oatmeal cookie with a quick sweet-tart jam made from dried cherries and orange juice.

FOR THE SOUR CHERRY JAM

1¼ cups (190 g) dried cherries
½ cup (100 g) granulated sugar
½ cup orange juice
½ cup water
½ teaspoon ground cinnamon

1. Make the jam: Combine the dried cherries, sugar, orange juice, water, and cinnamon in a medium saucepan and cook over medium-high heat, stirring occasionally, until the mixture begins to bubble. Turn the heat down to low, cover the saucepan, and cook, stirring once or twice, until the mixture thickens and only a few tablespoons of liquid remain, 25 to 30 minutes.

2. Remove the pan from the heat and use an immersion blender or food processor to puree the cherries into a thick paste. Let cool before using as a filling; the jam will continue to thicken as it cools. (*The filling can be stored, covered, in the fridge for up to 1 week. Return to room temperature, or briefly microwave to loosen it before filling the cookies.*)

3. Make the dough: Whisk together the flour, oats, baking powder, cinnamon, and salt in a medium bowl.

4. In the bowl of a stand mixer fitted with the paddle attachment (or using a handheld electric mixer and a large bowl), beat together the butter and brown sugar at medium speed until fully combined. Add the eggs and vanilla and beat to combine, scraping down the sides of the bowl as necessary. Add the flour mixture in two additions, beating at low speed to combine.

5. Gather the dough together and gently knead it a few times in the bowl, then divide it in half and form into 2 disks. Wrap each one tightly in parchment paper and refrigerate for at least 2 hours, or up to overnight.

FOR THE DOUGH

2 cups (280 g) all-purpose flour

1 cup (100 g) old-fashioned rolled oats

½ teaspoon baking powder

1½ teaspoons ground cinnamon

¼ teaspoon kosher salt

8 tablespoons (1 stick / 113 g) unsalted butter or vegan butter, softened

1½ packed cups (300 g) light brown sugar

2 large eggs

1½ teaspoons vanilla extract

6. Preheat the oven to 350°F (180°C). Line two large baking sheets with parchment paper.

7. Remove one piece of dough from the fridge (keep the other half chilled). On a lightly floured surface, using a lightly floured rolling pin, roll the dough out to a ⅛-inch (3 mm) thickness. If the dough is too cold to roll at first, let it rest at room temperature for 5 or 10 minutes and then proceed.

8. Using a 3-inch (7.5 cm) round cookie cutter, stamp out as many rounds of dough as possible and transfer them to the prepared baking sheets. (If the dough is sticking, use a bench scraper, thin metal spatula, or butter knife to help release it.) Gather the scraps, reroll, and cut out additional rounds.

9. Spoon 1 rounded teaspoon of the jam into the center of each dough round. Fold the left side over on an angle, followed by the right side. Fold the bottom flap up, tucking one end under the side flap to make a pocket with filling still visible in the center. Repeat with the remaining dough and jam.

10. Bake the cookies, rotating the baking sheets back to front and top to bottom halfway through baking, until lightly browned at the corners, 15 to 20 minutes. Let the cookies cool on the baking sheets for 5 minutes, then transfer to wire racks to cool completely.

11. Store the cookies in an airtight container in the fridge for up to 5 days or in the freezer for up to 3 months.

TRIPLE-CHOCOLATE HAMANTASCHEN

Makes about 24 cookies

Chocolate lovers, these cookies are for you. I admit that they stretch the boundaries of traditional hamantaschen, which are made with a mildly sweet vanilla dough and filled with jam or a poppy seed filling. Other than their triangular shape, they basically break all standard hamantaschen conventions. But some traditions are worth breaking, especially when that means ending up with a tender cocoa-powder–enriched dough wrapped around an intensely chocolatey brownie-textured filling. I originally developed this recipe for readers of my newsletter, "The Jewish Table," and they were such a hit, I knew I had to share them with the world.

FOR THE DOUGH

2½ cups (350 g) all-purpose flour or gluten-free all-purpose flour, plus more for rolling

½ cup (40 g) unsweetened cocoa powder

½ teaspoon baking powder

1 teaspoon instant coffee granules (regular or decaf)

½ teaspoon kosher salt

8 tablespoons (1 stick / 113 g) unsalted butter or vegan butter, softened

1 cup (200 g) granulated sugar

2 large eggs

Milk or nondairy milk, as needed

FOR THE FILLING

2 ounces (57 g) bittersweet baking chocolate, roughly chopped

2 tablespoons unsalted butter or vegan butter, cut into pieces

2½ tablespoons granulated sugar

⅛ teaspoon kosher salt

1 large egg

1 tablespoon all-purpose flour or gluten-free all-purpose flour

½ cup (90 g) semisweet chocolate chips

1. Make the dough: Whisk together the flour, cocoa powder, baking powder, instant coffee, and salt in a medium bowl.

2. In the bowl of a stand mixer fitted with the paddle attachment (or using a handheld electric mixer and a large bowl), beat together the butter and sugar on medium speed until pale and fluffy, about 3 minutes. Add the eggs and beat to fully combine. Add the flour mixture in two additions, beating at low speed and scraping down the sides of the bowl as necessary, until a firm but pliable dough forms. If the dough is too dry, beat in a little milk, 1 teaspoon at a time, until the desired consistency is reached.

3. Gather the dough together and gently knead a few times in the bowl, then divide it in half and form into 2 disks. Wrap each one tightly in parchment paper and refrigerate for at least 2 hours, or up to overnight.

4. Make the filling: Combine the chocolate and butter in a microwave-safe bowl and microwave for 20-second intervals, stirring after each one, until melted. Remove from the microwave and vigorously stir the sugar, salt, and egg into the warm chocolate mixture until the sugar begins to dissolve. Add the flour and stir until smooth and glossy, then fold in the chocolate chips. Cover and refrigerate for 15 to 30 minutes before filling the cookies.

5. Assemble and bake the cookies: Line two large baking sheets with parchment paper. Remove one dough disk from the fridge. (Keep the other one chilled.) On a lightly floured surface, roll the dough out to a 1/8-inch (3 mm) thickness.

6. Use a 3-inch (7.5 cm) round cookie cutter to stamp out as many rounds of dough as possible, then use a thin metal spatula or bench scraper to transfer them to one of the prepared baking sheets. Gather the scraps, reroll, and cut out additional rounds.
7. Spoon 1 rounded teaspoon of the filling into the center of each round. Fold the left side over on an angle, followed by the right side. Fold the bottom flap up, tucking one end under the side flap to make a pocket (the filling should still be visible in the center). Lightly pinch the corners together, if desired. Repeat the process with the remaining dough and filling.
8. Refrigerate the cookies on the baking sheets for about 15 minutes. (This will help them keep their shape while baking.) Meanwhile, preheat the oven to 350°F (180°C).
9. Bake the cookies until they are gently puffed and the filling is set, 16 to 20 minutes. Let cool on the baking sheets for 5 minutes, then transfer to wire racks to cool completely.
10. Store the cookies in an airtight container in the fridge for up to 1 week or in the freezer for up to 3 months.

ALMOND CROISSANT RUGELACH

Makes 32 cookies

One of the things I love most about American rugelach's butter and cream cheese dough is how it puffs and crisps up in the oven, ending up almost as flaky as a croissant. In this spin on the classic Ashkenazi cookie, I leaned all the way into the French pastry vibes to create rugelach that taste remarkably similar to almond croissants. The rich frangipane-inspired filling is flavored with an irresistible trio of almond extract, vanilla extract, and ground cinnamon. (For more about the history of rugelach, see page 75.)

FOR THE DOUGH

16 tablespoons (2 sticks / 227 g) unsalted butter, softened

8 ounces (225 g) cream cheese, softened

¼ cup (50 g) granulated sugar

½ teaspoon vanilla extract

½ teaspoon kosher salt

2 cups (280 g) all-purpose flour, plus more for rolling

FOR THE FILLING

1½ cups (150 g) almond flour

8 tablespoons (1 stick / 113 g) unsalted butter, softened

1 cup (120 g) confectioners' sugar

1 teaspoon ground cinnamon

1 teaspoon vanilla extract

¾ teaspoon almond extract

¼ teaspoon kosher salt

TO FINISH

1 large egg, beaten

Granulated sugar for sprinkling

1. Make the dough: In the bowl of a stand mixer fitted with the paddle attachment (or using a handheld electric mixer and a large bowl), beat the butter, cream cheese, sugar, vanilla, and salt on medium speed until light and fluffy, about 2 minutes. Add the flour in two additions, beating at low speed and scraping down the sides of the bowl as necessary, until a soft dough forms.

2. Transfer the dough to a work surface and knead it a few times to bring it together. Divide it in half, shape into 2 disks, wrap each one well in parchment paper, and refrigerate for at least 2 hours, and up to 1 day.

3. Make the filling: Combine the almond flour, butter, confectioners' sugar, cinnamon, vanilla extract, almond extract, and salt in the bowl of a food processor and pulse, scraping down the sides as necessary, until a smooth paste forms.

4. Preheat the oven to 350°F (180°C). Line two large baking sheets with parchment paper.

5. Remove one of the dough disks from the fridge (keep the remaining dough chilled). On a lightly floured surface, roll the dough into a large circle that is ⅛ inch (3 mm) thick. Trim the dough to an approximately 12-inch (30 cm) round. Spread about half of the almond filling evenly over it, leaving a ¼-inch (6 mm) border all around.

6. Using a pizza cutter or sharp knife, cut the round into 4 equal wedges, then cut each wedge into 4 wedges (ending up with 16 wedges). Starting from the outer edge, roll each wedge up on itself. Gently curve the rugelach into crescent shapes and place seam side down on the prepared baking sheets. Repeat the filling and rolling process with the remaining dough and filling.
7. Brush the top of each cookie with a little of the beaten egg (you will not use all of it), then sprinkle generously with sugar.
8. Bake, rotating the baking sheets back to front and top to bottom halfway through baking, until the rugelach are deep golden brown and the tops are flaky and puffed, 25 to 30 minutes. Remove from the oven and immediately transfer the cookies to wire racks to cool.
9. Store the rugelah in an airtight container in the fridge for up to 1 week or, well wrapped, in the freezer for up to 6 months.

RUGELACH'S CENTRAL EUROPEAN PREDECESSOR

Did you know that rugelach—the pastry spirals swirled with jam, chopped nuts, or chocolate that I (and countless other Jewish Americans) grew up eating on holidays and after synagogue services—are an American invention? Well, at least sort of. Rugelach are one of the most recognizably Ashkenazi Jewish cookies, but they are actually a descendent of kipfel—a genre of crescent-shaped cookies and pastries that originated in Austria.

According to *Crumbs: Cookies and Sweets from Around the World*, by Ben Mims, "Popular lore states that the crescent shape, or *kipfel*, found in so many Austrian baked goods is because of a culinary tribute to the victory over Ottoman soldiers at the siege of Vienna." (The shape is a nod to the crescent on the Turkish flag.) Kipfel recipes come in many forms, from yeasted pastries to buttery shortbreads—but they all share the signature half-moon-like shape.

Many Jewish Austrians baked dairy-free versions of kipfel that could be enjoyed with kosher meat meals, although dairy versions made with curd cheese were also popular. When some of these Central European Jews emigrated to America in the mid-to-late nineteenth century, their recipes for kipfel came along. Many of the earliest American Jewish cookbooks, including *Aunt Babette's Cook Book*, from 1889, and *The Settlement Cook Book*, from 1901, included recipes for kipfel—some yeasted, some not.

In America, kipfel recipes evolved to include sour cream, and later cream cheese in place of sour cream, in the dough. These enrichments made the pastry rich and tender without yeast and an extended rising time. (Israeli-style rugelach recipes are typically yeasted and do not contain cream cheese.) Over time, the dessert was renamed rugelach—which roughly translates from Yiddish as "little corners." According to Gil Marks's *Encyclopedia of Jewish Food*, "The first record of the word *rugelach* was only in 1941 in *The Jewish Home Beautiful* by Betty D. Greenberg and Althea O. Silverman, in a recipe entitled 'Crescents or Rugelach.'" Within a generation, writes Marks, "the name *rugelach* would almost totally supplant *kipfel*" in America.

Some American recipes for rugelach also tinkered with the shape. Filling and forming individual crescent-shaped cookies takes time, so home cooks improvised by rolling the filled dough up into a log and cutting out plump pinwheel rounds. This change in shape only further divorces rugelach from its kipfel predecessor—but the lineage remains. Despite the bit of extra effort it takes, I prefer the look of individually formed rugelach, so both the Almond Croissant Rugelach (page 72) and the Prune and Chocolate Rugelach (page 76) follow that method.

PRUNE AND CHOCOLATE RUGELACH

Makes 32 cookies

Over the decades, prunes have gained an undeserved reputation as a stodgy, old-fashioned ingredient. I am here to declare that they are one of the most exceptional dried fruits around—all lusciously soft texture and jammy-sweet flavor. Prune jam, often referred to as *lekvar*, is one of the unsung heroes of Ashkenazi Jewish baking, showing up in cakes, cookies, and pastries. (See page 190 for more about lekvar.) In this riff on classic rugelach, the dough is spread with a thick prune jam and sprinkled with dark chocolate chips. The cookies bake up golden and irresistably flaky—a bite-size sweet destined to win over any prune skeptic.

FOR THE FILLING

2 cups (310 g) pitted prunes

1¼ cups (295 ml) water

Grated zest and juice of 1 large orange

1 teaspoon ground cinnamon

½ cup (100 g) granulated sugar

1 cup (180 g) mini semisweet chocolate chips

FOR THE DOUGH

16 tablespoons (2 sticks / 227 g) unsalted butter, softened

8 ounces (225 g) cream cheese, softened

¼ cup (50 g) granulated sugar

½ teaspoon vanilla extract

½ teaspoon kosher salt

2 cups (280 g) all-purpose flour, plus more for rolling

TO FINISH

1 large egg, beaten

Granulated sugar for sprinkling

1. Make the filling: Combine the prunes, water, orange zest, orange juice, and cinnamon in a medium saucepan and bring to a boil over medium heat, stirring occasionally, then reduce the heat to low, cover the pan, and cook, stirring occasionally, until the prunes have softened and only a few tablespoons of syrupy liquid remain, 15 to 20 minutes.

2. Remove from the heat and immediately stir in the sugar to dissolve. Using an immersion blender, blend the mixture into a thick puree. (Or transfer the mixture to a food processor and pulse until smooth.) Set aside to cool while you make the dough. (*The cooled filling can be stored, covered, in the fridge for up to 1 week. Bring to room temperature before using.*)

3. Make the dough: In the bowl of a stand mixer fitted with the paddle attachment (or using a handheld electric mixer and a large bowl), beat the butter, cream cheese, sugar, vanilla, and salt on medium speed until smooth and creamy, about 2 minutes. Add the flour in two additions, beating at low speed and scraping down the sides of the bowl as necessary, until a soft dough forms.

4. Transfer the dough to a work surface and knead it a few times to bring it together. Divide it in half, shape into 2 disks, wrap each one well in parchment paper, and refrigerate for at least 2 hours, and up to overnight.

5. Preheat the oven to 350°F (180°C). Line two large baking sheets with parchment paper.

6. Remove one of the dough disks from the fridge (keep the remaining dough chilled). On a lightly floured surface, roll it into a large circle that is ⅛ inch (3 mm) thick. Trim the dough to an approximately 12-inch (30 cm) round. Spread ½ cup (140 g) of the prune filling evenly over it, leaving a ¼-inch (6 mm) border all around. Sprinkle half of the chocolate chips evenly over the filling.
7. Using a pizza cutter or sharp knife, cut the round into 4 equal wedges, then cut each wedge into 4 wedges (ending up with 16 wedges). Starting from the outer edge, roll each wedge up on itself. Gently curve each rugelach into a crescent shape and place seam side down on the prepared baking sheets. Repeat the process with the remaining dough and filling.
8. Brush the top of each cookie with a little of the beaten egg (you will not use all of it), then sprinkle generously with sugar.
9. Bake the rugelach, rotating the baking sheets back to front and top to bottom halfway through baking, until they are deep golden brown and the tops are flaky and puffed, 25 to 30 minutes. Remove from the oven and immediately transfer the cookies to wire racks to cool.
10. Store the rugelach in an airtight container in the fridge for up to 1 week or, well wrapped, in the freezer for up to 6 months.

FLAKY DATE ROLL-UP COOKIES

Makes about 36 cookies

I was inspired to create these cookies while flipping through a 1950s-era issue of *Woman's Day* magazine. The December cookie spread included a recipe for Date Cream Cheese Roll-Ups that, upon closer inspection, were made with a dough identical to a traditional American rugelach dough. (For more on rugelach, see page 75.) Instead of cutting the dough into crescents, spreading the cookies with a sweet filling, and rolling them up into crescents, though, the dough was cut into strips and each one rolled up around a whole dried date. Genius! Baked following the original recipe, the cookies tasted predictably old-fashioned—a relic of another era's palate. (Our modern tastebuds have grown accustomed to more interesting and complex flavors.) So I tinkered with the recipe, adding sugar and vanilla extract to the dough and sprinkling the tops with cinnamon-sugar. The petite roll-up cookies are crisp and flaky with sweet, chewy centers—a perfect treat to pair with your afternoon tea or coffee and a fun retro addition to any Hanukkah cookie platter.

FOR THE COOKIES

8 tablespoons (1 stick / 113 g) unsalted butter, softened

4 ounces (113 g) cream cheese, softened

½ cup (50 g) granulated sugar

½ teaspoon vanilla extract

¼ teaspoon kosher salt

1 cup (140 g) all-purpose flour, plus more for rolling

About 18 large pitted Medjool dates, halved lengthwise

TO FINISH

2 tablespoons granulated sugar

1 teaspoon ground cinnamon

1 large egg, beaten

NOTE: Medjool dates can be quite sticky and squishy, which makes them especially good in these cookies, but also tricky to cut. To make the process easier, use a very sharp knife sprinkled with a little flour.

1. Make the dough: In the bowl of a stand mixer fitted with the paddle attachment (or using a handheld electric mixer and a large bowl), beat the butter, cream cheese, sugar, vanilla, and salt on medium speed until smooth and creamy, about 2 minutes. Add the flour in two additions, beating at low speed and scraping down the sides of the bowl as necessary, until a soft dough forms.

2. Transfer the dough to a floured work surface and knead it a few times to bring it together. Divide it in half and shape into 2 disks, wrap well in parchment paper and refrigerate for at least 2 hours, and up to overnight.

3. Preheat the oven to 350°F (180°C). Line two large baking sheets with parchment paper.

4. Remove one of the dough disks from the fridge and, on a floured surface, roll it into a large rectangle that is ⅛ inch (3 mm) thick. Trim off any ragged edges. Use a fluted pastry wheel or a sharp knife to cut the dough into 3 × 1-inch (7.5 × 2.5 cm) strips. Place a date half at one end of each strip and roll up the dough around the date. Transfer the cookies, seam side down, to one of the baking sheets.

5. Repeat the process with the remaining dough and dates.

6. In a small bowl, mix the sugar and cinnamon together. Brush the tops of each cookie with a little beaten egg (you will not use all of it), then sprinkle generously with the cinnamon-sugar.
7. Bake, rotating the baking sheets back to-front and top to bottom halfway through, until the cookies are deep golden brown and the tops are flaky and puffed, 25 to 30 minutes. Remove from the oven and transfer the cookies to wire racks to cool. Serve slightly warm or at room temperature.
8. Store the cookies in an airtight container in the fridge for up to 1 week or, well wrapped, in the freezer for up to 6 months.

HAZELNUT CRESCENTS

Makes about 48 cookies

All across Central Europe, home bakers served crescent-shaped cookies made with ground nuts (called *nusskipferlin*, or “nut crescents” in Yiddish) to delighted family and friends. The individual recipes varied widely: Some were made with a puffy yeasted dough, others with a buttery cookie dough. Walnuts were commonly used, but almond and hazelnut versions were also popular. Sometimes the cookies were filled with ground nuts, other times the nuts were mixed directly into the batter. This version is light and sweet with a crumbly, shortbread-like texture; a delicate but distinct hazelnut flavor; and a final dusting of confectioners’ sugar and cocoa powder. They make a wonderful treat to enjoy with an afternoon coffee or tea, or a simple but satisfying dessert.

FOR THE COOKIES

16 tablespoons (2 sticks / 227 g) unsalted butter or vegan butter, softened

1 cup (120 g) confectioners’ sugar, sifted

1 teaspoon vanilla extract or vanilla bean paste

1¾ cup (245 g) all-purpose flour

1 cup (85 g) hazelnut flour

¾ teaspoon kosher salt

TO FINISH

½ cup (60 g) confectioners’ sugar, sifted

2½ tablespoons unsweetened cocoa powder

1. In the bowl of a stand mixer fitted with the paddle attachment (or using a handheld electric mixer and a large bowl), beat the butter and confectioners’ sugar together at medium speed until light and fluffy. Beat in the vanilla.

2. Add the flour, hazelnut flour, and salt and beat at low speed, scraping down the sides of the bowl as necessary, until a soft dough forms. Bring the dough together in your hands and divide it in two. Form each piece of dough into a disk, wrap well in parchment paper, and refrigerate for at least 1 hour, or up to overnight.

3. Preheat the oven to 350°F (180°C). Line two large baking sheets with parchment paper.

4. Remove one disk of dough from the refrigerator (keep the other one chilled) and roll it under your palms into a long rope about ¾ inch (2 cm) thick. If you chilled the dough overnight, it might need to sit at room temperature for a few minutes before rolling.

5. Cut the rope into 2-inch- (5 cm) long pieces. Gently curve each piece into a crescent-moon shape and arrange on the baking sheets, leaving about 1 inch (2.5 cm) between the cookies, since they will puff up during baking. Repeat with the remaining dough.

6. Bake, rotating the baking sheets back to front and top to bottom halfway through, until the crescents are puffed and just barely golden, 15 to 17 minutes. (The tops of the cookies should still be quite pale, but the bottoms will be a few shades darker.) Remove from the oven and set the baking sheets on wire racks to cool for about 5 minutes.

7. Finish the cookies: Whisk together the confectioners' sugar and cocoa powder in a small bowl. Using a fine-mesh sieve, dust the warm cookies with about half of the confectioners' sugar mixture, then transfer the cookies to the racks to cool completely. (Set the remaining confectioners' sugar mixture aside.)
8. When the cookies are cooled, dust them with the remaining confectioners' sugar mixture. Store the cookies in an airtight container at room temperature for up to 3 days or in the fridge for up to 1 week; or wrap them well and freeze for up to 6 months.

POPPY SEED AND WALNUT ROLL COOKIES

Makes about 30 cookies

According to Israeli-born food writer and chef Vered Guttman, Israelis hold a deep fondness for poppy seed pastries thanks to the Eastern European immigrants who introduced them to the country. "In bakeries, you will find poppy seed cakes and yeasted pastries stuffed with poppy seeds, but these rolled cookies would usually be baked at home," she said.

For decades after Israel's founding, when resources were tight throughout the country, home cooks baked many sweet and savory pastries—including these poppy seed rolls—from a simple, inexpensive dough made from self-rising flour, sour cream, and margarine. The dough was called *shekem*, which is an acronym for shamenet (sour cream), kemach (flour), and margarina (margarine). It was rolled out thin and spread with ground poppy seeds that had been simmered in milk with sugar. This variation uses a slightly more sophisticated dough and adds a bit of honey and ground walnuts to the filling for extra sweetness, body, and flavor. After the filling is spread over the dough, it is rolled up into a log and baked before being sliced into individual cookies, revealing a spiral of poppy seeds inside. The cookies are delicate, crumbly, and filled with satisfying poppy seed flavor.

FOR THE FILLING

½ cup (70 g) poppy seeds

¾ cup milk or nondairy milk

¼ cup (50 g) granulated sugar

2 tablespoons mild honey

⅓ cup (35 g) walnut halves, very finely chopped

1 tablespoon unsalted butter or vegan butter

1½ teaspoons vanilla extract

1 packed teaspoon grated lemon zest

NOTE: The delicate dough for these cookies requires an extended chill in the refrigerator, so plan accordingly.

1. Make the filling: Working in batches if necessary, pour the poppy seeds into a spice grinder or coffee grinder and pulse until finely ground. The seeds should be fluffy and have the texture of slightly damp soil.

2. Combine the ground poppy seeds, milk, sugar, and honey in a medium saucepan and bring to a boil over medium-high heat, then turn the heat down to medium-low and cook, stirring occasionally, until the mixture thickens and most of the milk has evaporated, 6 to 8 minutes.

3. Remove from the heat and immediately stir in the walnuts, butter, vanilla, and lemon zest. Let cool completely before using. (*The filling can be made up to 3 days in advance and stored, covered, in the fridge.*)

4. Make the dough: Combine the flour, confectioners' sugar, baking powder, salt, and butter in a food processor and pulse, scraping down the sides of the bowl as necessary, until the mixture is dry and crumbly. Add the egg, egg yolk, and cold water and pulse until the dough is beginning to clump together. If the dough is too dry to hold together when pinched, add more water, 1 teaspoon at a time, until you reach the desired consistency. (Be careful not to add too much water.)

recipe continues

FOR THE DOUGH

2¾ cups (385 g) all-purpose flour, plus more for rolling

1 cup (120 g) confectioners' sugar, sifted, plus more for dusting

½ teaspoon baking powder

½ teaspoon kosher salt

16 tablespoons (2 sticks / 227 g) cold unsalted butter or vegan butter, cut into pieces

1 large egg

1 large egg yolk

2 tablespoons cold water, plus more if needed

5. Turn the dough out, gather it together, and form it into a disk. Wrap it tightly in parchment paper and refrigerate for at least 4 hours, and up to overnight.

6. When ready to bake, line a large baking sheet with parchment paper and set aside. Lay a second piece of parchment paper (about the size of the baking sheet) on a work surface and dust generously with flour. Cut off about one-third of the dough (keep the rest refrigerated), place it on the floured parchment paper, flour the dough, and top with another piece of parchment. Use a rolling pin to roll the dough into a large rectangle approximately ⅛ inch (3 mm) thick, then carefully peel back the top layer of parchment.

7. Spoon about one-third of the poppy seed filling over the dough and use an offset spatula or butter knife to spread it into a thin, even layer. Starting from one of the long sides and using a bench scraper or metal spatula to help nudge the dough along, carefully roll the dough up like a jelly roll. (The dough is quite delicate at this stage, so flour your hands and the dough as necessary. It is okay if it tears a bit while rolling.) Trim off and discard about ½ inch (12 mm) from each end of the log, then carefully transfer the log to one side of the baking sheet. Repeat the rolling and filling process twice with the remaining dough and filling, leaving about 1 inch (2.5 cm) of space between the logs on the baking sheet. Transfer the baking sheet to the refrigerator and chill the logs for 30 minutes.

8. Preheat the oven to 350°F (180°C).

9. Use a sharp knife to slice the logs into 1-inch- (2.5 cm) wide pieces, but do not fully separate them. Bake the logs, rotating the baking sheet back to front halfway through baking, until golden brown, 25 to 30 minutes. Transfer the baking sheet to a wire rack and let the logs cool completely.

10. Slice the cooled logs all the way through and separate the slices. Just before serving, use a fine-mesh sieve to dust the cookies with more confectioners' sugar.

11. Store the cookies in an airtight container at room temperature for up to 3 days or in the fridge for up to 1 week or, well wrapped, in the freezer for up to 6 months.

THE EVOLUTION OF VEGAN BUTTER

American Jews who follow the kosher laws have long embraced nondairy butter substitutes. From vegetable shortenings like Crisco, which was introduced in the early twentieth century and enthusiastically employed by the Jewish community, to the margarine touted in the 1980s and 1990s as the "healthier" alternative to butter, these dairy-free fats allowed kosher keepers to serve a wide variety of cakes and cookies after meat meals without breaking the prohibition against consuming meat and dairy at the same meal.

For a long time, I was deeply skeptical about using margarine—and for good reason. Most brands were (and some still are) full of hydrogenated oils, trans fats, preservatives, and artificial flavors. Thankfully, the past decade has witnessed a flourishing of plant-based products that cater to vegetarian, health-conscious, and dairy-free consumers. That includes a proliferation of vegan butter brands that eschew artificial ingredients and cheap oils and embrace cleaner ingredients ranging from aquafaba and avocado oil to cultured cashew cream.

Vegan butter, which is increasingly available in mainstream supermarkets, has elevated the dairy-free kosher baking experience. That said, not all vegan butters are created equal. Some are formulated for easy spreading on toast or bagels, while others are designed to mimic butter's structure and flavor in baking. At the store, look for vegan butter brands that are explicitly baking friendly. And if you don't already have a favorite, try a few brands until you find one that works best in your kitchen.

CHERRY-COCONUT FLAKE MACAROONS

Makes about 24 cookies

Coconut flakes, which are sometimes, rather confusingly, marketed under the name coconut chips, are shredded coconut's larger, meatier cousin. They bring big tropical vibes and a satisfying texture to baked goods that I think deserves way more attention than they get. In this variation on a traditional coconut macaroon, coconut flakes play the starring role. The cookies are chewy, toasty, and satisfying, with a hint of almond flavor and a generous amount of dried cherries to offset that sweetness. Made without flour, they are a natural fit for the Passover seder. I also bake them up to share with friends on Purim, and I like to keep some in the freezer for unexpected visitors.

- 3 large egg whites
- ⅔ cup (130 g) granulated sugar
- ¼ teaspoon kosher salt
- 1 teaspoon vanilla extract or vanilla bean paste
- ½ teaspoon almond extract
- 3½ cups (175 g) unsweetened coconut flakes
- ¾ cup (100 g) dried cherries, roughly chopped

1. Preheat the oven to 325°F (165°C). Line two large baking sheets with parchment paper.
2. Stir together the egg whites, sugar, salt, vanilla extract, and almond extract in a medium saucepan until combined. Set the pan over medium-low heat, stir in the coconut flakes, and cook, stirring frequently, until the mixture thickens slightly and turns sticky, 5 to 6 minutes. Remove from the heat and stir in the dried cherries, then set aside to cool slightly.
3. Using a 1½-tablespoon cookie scoop, scoop small mounds of the batter onto the prepared baking sheets, leaving about 1 inch (2.5 cm) between them. Bake, rotating the baking sheets top to bottom and back to front halfway through, until the macaroons are golden brown but still soft, 18 to 22 minutes.
4. Remove from the oven and let the macaroons cool on the baking sheets for 5 minutes, then use a thin metal spatula to carefully transfer them to wire racks to cool completely. The macaroons will continue to firm up as they cool.
5. Store the macaroons in a single layer, in an airtight container in the fridge for up to 3 days or, well wrapped, in the freezer for up to 6 months.

LEMON CURD MACAROON THUMBPRINTS

Makes about 15 macaroons

Coconut macaroons, made from dried shredded coconut, are one of the most popular Passover desserts in America. The first American Jewish cookbook, *Jewish Cookery*, published in 1871, includes a recipe for "cocoanut" macaroons. And kosher food companies like Streits and Manischewitz helped ensure that packaged coconut macaroons made their way into the cupboards of virtually every Jewish household in the country. Free of both dairy (making them suitable to serve after a kosher meat meal) and chametz (the five grains forbidden during Passover), they offer a sweet, uncomplicated seder dessert and a treat all holiday long. This variation on the classic caps the nests of floral coconut with sunny crowns of mouth-puckering lemon curd. The cookies are crisp and chewy and the curd is custard-smooth. They are destined to become the runaway hit of your next seder's dessert table.

FOR THE LEMON CURD

1 large egg

1 large egg yolk

⅓ cup (65 g) granulated sugar

¼ cup (60 ml) strained fresh lemon juice (from 2 medium lemons)

⅛ teaspoon kosher salt

3 tablespoons unsalted butter or vegan butter, cut into pieces and softened

FOR THE MACAROONS

3 large egg whites

⅔ cup (130 g) granulated sugar

¼ teaspoon kosher salt

1 teaspoon vanilla extract or vanilla bean paste

2¼ cups (180 g) unsweetened dried shredded coconut

NOTE: This recipe makes more lemon curd than you need for filling the macaroons, but it keeps well. Spread the leftover curd on matzo with butter, or spoon it onto yogurt and granola.

1. Make the lemon curd: Bring about 2 inches (5 cm) of water to a boil over high heat in the bottom of a double boiler. (Or use a heat resistant bowl set over a medium saucepan of water.) Once the water boils, reduce the heat to medium-low to keep the water at a low simmer.

2. Combine the egg, egg yolk, sugar, lemon juice, and salt in the bowl and whisk constantly until the sugar dissolves, then continue whisking until the mixture thickens enough to coat the back of a spoon, 5 to 7 minutes.

3. Remove the pan from the heat and immediately whisk the softened butter into the lemon juice mixture. Transfer the curd to a jar or a bowl and place a piece of parchment paper directly on the surface of the curd to prevent a skin from forming. The curd will continue to thicken as it cools. Once it is cool, cover and refrigerate until chilled, about 3 hours. (*The curd can be refrigerated for up to 1 week.*)

4. Make the macaroons: Preheat the oven to 325°F (165°C). Line two large baking sheets with parchment paper.

5. Stir together the egg whites, sugar, salt, and vanilla in a medium saucepan until combined. Set the pan over medium-low heat, stir in the coconut, and cook, stirring frequently, until the mixture thickens slightly and turns sticky, 5 to 6 minutes. Remove from the heat and let cool slightly.

recipe continues

6. Using a 1½-tablespoon cookie scoop, scoop small mounds of the batter onto the prepared baking sheets, leaving 1 inch (2.5 cm) space between them. Use your index finger or thumb to press an indentation into the center of each macaroon, creating a small nest. (Wet your finger with water to prevent sticking.) Bake, rotating the baking sheets top to bottom and back to front halfway through baking, until the macaroons are golden brown but still soft, 18 to 20 minutes.
7. Remove from the oven and let the macaroons cool on the baking sheets for 2 to 3 minutes, then use a thin metal spatula to carefully transfer them to wire racks to cool completely. The macaroons will continue to firm up as they cool.
8. Shortly before serving, spoon about ½ teaspoon of the lemon curd into the indentation in each macaroon. Serve at room temperature.
9. Store the macaroons in a single layer in an airtight container in the fridge for up to 3 days.

PISTACHIO MACAROONS

Makes about 18 cookies

In the weeks leading up to Passover, American supermarkets that serve Jewish communities begin to stock containers of coconut macaroons—one of the holiday's most popular flour-free desserts. But long before there were coconut macaroons, there were marunchinos—Sephardi cookies made from sweetened ground almonds lightened with whipped egg whites. Hailing from the Jewish communities living in pre-Inquisition Spain, marunchinos are the precursor to any macaroons enjoyed today. (See page 92 for more about the Sephardi cookies.) This variation swaps ground pistachios for the almonds, giving the cookies a distinctly fresh, pistachio-forward flavor. Enjoy them as is, or play with the flavor profile by drizzling a little rosewater or orange blossom water into the batter or topping the baked cookies with melted dark chocolate.

2 cups (200 g) roasted unsalted pistachios

½ teaspoon kosher salt

1 cup (120 g) confectioners' sugar, sifted

2 large egg whites

1 teaspoon vanilla extract

1. Preheat the oven to 325°F (165°C). Line two large baking sheets with parchment paper.
2. Combine the pistachios and salt in a food processor and pulse, scraping down the sides of the bowl as necessary, until finely ground and powdery, with a few slightly larger pieces.
3. Transfer the ground pistachios to a medium bowl. Add the confectioners' sugar, egg whites, and vanilla and stir to combine.
4. Mound rounded tablespoons of the batter onto the baking sheets, leaving 2 inches (5 cm) between them. Bake, rotating the baking sheets top to bottom and back to front halfway through baking, until golden, 20 to 25 minutes.
5. Set the baking sheets on wire racks to cool for 2 to 3 minutes, then use a thin metal spatula to transfer the cookies to the racks to cool completely.
6. Store the macaroons, well wrapped, in the fridge for up to 1 week or in the freezer for up to 6 months.

NOTE: If you can only find salted pistachios, reduce the salt in the recipe to ⅛ or ¼ teaspoon, depending on how salty the nuts are.

MACAROONS: THE SEPHARDI HISTORY BEHIND A UBIQUITOUS ASHKENAZI COOKIE

As is true for many Ashkenazi American Jews, my week of Passover is defined by spreading cream cheese on matzo instead of bagels, missing my favorite pastas, and eating an abundance of store-bought coconut macaroons. These macaroons, which were for decades sold in cylindrical cans (recently many companies have rebranded with more modern packaging), are distressingly sweet and cloying. To be honest, I never liked them very much when I was growing up, but the Passover dessert pickings were slim in the 1980s and '90s, so I made it work. As an adult, I have learned that baking coconut macaroons from scratch (see the recipes on pages 86, 89, and 91) results in significantly more delicious cookies.

I also learned that coconut macaroons are a surprisingly recent variation of a much older Sephardi cookie. The techniques of leavening baked goods with whipped egg whites and making cookies and cakes from ground almonds and other nuts date back to the Moorish and Jewish kitchens of pre-Inquisition Spain. There, Jewish families baked sweet almond flour and egg white cookies called *marunchinos*. (See the headnote on page 91.)

These techniques eventually spread around the region—thanks in large part to Jewish exiles from Spain who brought their recipes with them—and gave rise to a variety of other almond flour–based cookies, including Italian amaretti and, likely, French macarons.

Because of their Passover-friendly status, almond flour cookies were eventually adopted by Ashkenazi communities as well. *The Jewish Manual*, a cookbook published in the 1840s in England, mentioned almond macaroons. And the first American Jewish cookbook, *Jewish Cookery*, which was published in 1871, contained recipes for both almond and "cocoanut" macaroons.

The inclusion of the tropical tree fruit in an American Jewish cookbook might seem surprising, but coconut was a fashionable ingredient in late nineteenth-century America. Over time, the coconut version became the most common type of macaroon on Passover—a status it continues to hold today.

STRAWBERRY CLOUD MERINGUES

Makes about 30 meringues

My mom made meringues every year at Passover, and they were always the highlight of the holiday for me. I loved watching her pipe the sweetened whipped egg whites into dainty little kisses on the baking sheets before dehydrating them in a low oven until they were impossibly light and crisp. She typically made cocoa meringues, no doubt to satisfy my chocolate-obsessed sweet tooth. Now that I am grown up and my palate has expanded, I actually prefer these strawberry meringues, which swirl strawberry jam into the tops of vanilla meringues: the jam's fruit-forward tartness balances the cookies' extravagant sweetness. These crackly-chewy bites of heaven are destined to become both a Passover and year-round favorite in your household.

3 large egg whites, at room temperature

¼ teaspoon cream of tartar

½ teaspoon vanilla extract or vanilla bean paste

⅔ cup (130 g) granulated sugar

About 3 tablespoons strawberry jam

1. Preheat the oven to 225°F (105°C). Line two large baking sheets with parchment paper.
2. Combine the egg whites, cream of tartar, and vanilla in the bowl of a stand mixer fitted with the whisk attachment (or use a handheld electric mixer and a large bowl) and beat until the mixture is foamy with soft peaks, 1 to 2 minutes.
3. Beating constantly, gradually add the sugar, a tablespoon or two at a time, until the mixture is thick and glossy and holds firm peaks, 3 to 5 minutes.
4. Working in batches if necessary, spoon the mixture into a pastry bag fitted with a large round tip. (Alternatively, spoon it into a large zip-top plastic bag, then cut a small corner off the bottom of the bag.) Pipe 2-inch (5 cm) meringues onto the baking sheets, leaving about 2 inches (5 cm) between them.
5. Spoon about ¼ teaspoon of jam into the center of each meringue, then use a toothpick to gently swirl the jam and a bit of the meringue on top together. (Most of the meringue should still be white.)
6. Bake until the meringues are firm to the touch and release easily from the parchment paper, 1½ to 2 hours. Turn off the oven and let the meringues rest in the oven's residual heat for 2 hours, then remove and transfer to wire racks to cool completely.
7. Store the meringues, well wrapped, in the freezer for up to 3 months.

FLOURLESS CHOCOLATE WALNUT COOKIES

Makes about 24 cookies

Fudgy, crisp, and chewy-centered—what more can one ask for from a cookie? How about one that is also naturally gluten-free, dairy-free, and Passover friendly? One of my volunteer recipe testers described their texture as "meringue meets brownie," and I think she got it exactly right. My original inspiration for these wonder cookies was a recipe developed in the 1990s by famed French pastry chef François Payard. Later, when reading Anne Byrn's cookbook *Baking in the American South*, I discovered that a strikingly similar cookie was sold for decades at Gottlieb's, a bakery founded in downtown Savannah in 1884 by a Russian Jewish immigrant named Isadore Gottlieb. (The primary difference between the two is that Gottlieb's Chocolate Chewies used pecans instead of walnuts.) Regardless of the cookies' original provenance, their crackly tops and gooey centers make them utterly addictive on Passover and all year round. My version adds a glug of fruity olive oil and a bit of potato starch to the batter, which lends complexity and depth to the otherwise very sweet cookies.

- 2 cups (200 g) walnut halves, roughly chopped
- 3 cups (360 g) confectioners' sugar, sifted
- ½ cup (40 g) unsweetened cocoa powder, sifted
- ¼ cup (35 g) potato starch or cornstarch, sifted
- ½ teaspoon kosher salt
- 3 large egg whites, at room temperature
- ¼ cup (60 ml) extra-virgin olive oil
- 2 teaspoons vanilla extract

1. Preheat the oven to 325°F (160°C). Line two large baking sheets with parchment paper. (Do not use silicone baking mats, or the cookies may stick.)
2. Combine the walnuts, confectioners' sugar, cocoa powder, potato starch, and salt in the bowl of a stand mixer fitted with the paddle attachment (or use a handheld electric mixer and a large bowl) and blend briefly.
3. Add the egg whites, olive oil, and vanilla to the bowl and beat at low speed, scraping down the sides as necessary, until slightly thickened, about 2 minutes.
4. Using a 1½-tablespoon cookie scoop, scoop the batter onto the prepared baking sheets, leaving about 1 inch (2.5 cm) between the cookies. (The batter will be quite sticky, so rinse and dry the cookie scoop as needed.)
5. Bake, rotating the baking sheets top to bottom and back to front halfway through baking, until the cookies are glossy and slightly cracked, 16 to 18 minutes. (They will still feel soft but will firm up as they cool.) Remove from the oven and let the cookies cool on the baking sheets for 10 minutes, then carefully transfer to wire racks to cool completely.
6. Store the cookies in an airtight container at room temperature for up to 3 days, in the fridge for up to 1 week, or in the freezer for up to 6 months.

CRANBERRY-APRICOT ALMOND COOKIES

Makes about 20 cookies

While researching my cookbook *Portico: Cooking and Feasting in Rome's Jewish Kitchen*, I fell in love with the amaretti I tasted at Pasticceria il Boccione—the 200-year-old kosher bakery in the heart of Rome's Jewish Quarter. Just like Boccione's amaretti, these almond flour cookies are lightly crisp outside and give way to decadently chewy centers. But the addition of sweet-tart cranberries and jammy chopped dried apricots makes them even more addictive. I almost always bake up a batch for Passover, and they make a festive addition to the Hanukkah cookie boxes I deliver to friends and family.

- 2 cups (200 g) almond flour
- ⅔ cup (135 g) granulated sugar
- ½ teaspoon kosher salt
- ⅓ cup (60 g) finely chopped dried apricots (about 8 medium apricots)
- ⅓ cup (40 g) sweetened dried cranberries, roughly chopped if large, plus more whole dried cranberries for decoration
- 3 large egg whites
- ¾ teaspoon almond extract
- 1 packed teaspoon grated lemon zest

1. Preheat the oven to 325°F (160°C). Line two large baking sheets with parchment paper.
2. Whisk together the almond flour, sugar, salt, apricots, and cranberries in a large bowl. Whisk together the egg whites, almond extract, and lemon zest in a medium bowl until just slightly foamy. Pour the egg white mixture over the almond flour mixture and stir until a soft dough forms.
3. Scoop out tablespoons of the dough, roll them into balls, and place on the baking sheets about 1 inch (2.5 cm) apart. Lightly moisten your hands if the mixture is sticking.
4. Using the tip of your finger, gently press each cookie to flatten it slightly, then press a dried cranberry into the center of each one for decoration.
5. Bake, rotating the baking sheets back to front and top to bottom halfway through baking, until the cookies are very lightly golden on top and a few shades darker on the bottom, 25 to 30 minutes. The cookies will still feel soft, but they will continue to firm up as they cool.
6. Remove the baking sheets from the oven and let the cookies cool for 5 minutes, then transfer to wire racks to cool completely.
7. Store the cookies in an airtight container at room temperature for up to 3 days or in the fridge for up to 1 week or, well wrapped, in the freezer for up to 6 months.

PASSOVER JAM THUMBPRINTS

Makes about 18 cookies

Thumbprint cookies may or may not have a Jewish pedigree. Some sources suggest Swedish origins, where the cookies are called *hallongrotta*, or "raspberry caves." Others point to Eastern Europe, particularly Poland, where they would have filled cookie jars in Jewish and non-Jewish homes alike. But regardless of where they were first baked, the jam-filled cookies, with their trademark "thumbprint" indentations, have long been a comforting favorite in Ashkenazi households. This Passover-friendly version combines almond flour and a bit of potato starch, yielding a chewy, not-too-sweet cookie that holds its shape in the oven and provides a tasty base for jam. Strawberry, raspberry, and apricot jams are all wonderful options for filling the cookies, but you can use whatever type you prefer.

2½ cups (250 g) almond flour

2 tablespoons potato starch

¾ cup (90 g) confectioners' sugar, sifted, plus (optional) more for dusting

¼ teaspoon kosher salt

2 large egg whites

½ packed teaspoon grated lemon zest

1 teaspoon vanilla extract or vanilla bean paste

About ¼ cup (70 g) jam for filling

1. Preheat the oven to 350°F (180°C). Line a large baking sheet with parchment paper.
2. Whisk together the almond flour, potato starch, confectioners' sugar, and salt in a large bowl. Whisk together the egg whites, lemon zest, and vanilla in a medium bowl until just slightly foamy. Pour the egg white mixture over the almond flour mixture and stir until fully combined.
3. Scoop out tablespoons of the dough, roll them into balls, and place on the baking sheets about 1 inch (2.5 cm) apart. Wash and dry your hands periodically if the mixture is sticking.
4. Use your index finger to make a deep indentation in the center of each cookie (see Note). Spoon about ½ teaspoon of jam into the indentations (take care not to overfill them)
5. Bake, rotating the baking sheet back to front halfway through, until the cookies are lightly golden on top and a few shades darker on the bottom, 15 to 17 minutes. Remove the baking sheet from the oven and let the cookies cool for 5 minutes, then transfer to wire racks to cool completely.
6. Just before serving, if desired, use a fine-mesh sieve to lightly dust the tops of the cookies with confectioners' sugar.
7. Store the cookies in an airtight container at room temperature for up to 3 days or in the fridge for up to 1 week or, well wrapped, in the freezer for up to 6 months.

NOTE: Despite their name, you will get more control of the depth and size of the indentations in these cookies if you use your index finger instead of your thumb.

FIG-AND-LEMON-SCONE COOKIES

Makes about 24 cookies

Many weekdays, shortly before school pickup time, you will find me at my favorite Brooklyn coffee shop, which just happens to be located around the corner from my kids' school. I go there for an afternoon coffee but also for their incredible fig and lemon scones. They are bronzed and caramelized at the edges, flaky-tender inside, and packed with sunny lemon zest and jammy bites of dried fig. While they are not a traditional Jewish pastry, their flavors feel directly pulled from the shores of the Mediterranean. I love those scones so much, I turned them into a cookie–dropping bite-size mounds of the dough onto baking sheets and sprinkling the tops with crunchy turbinado sugar. They are the ideal bite-size treat to keep on hand for anytime you need a little something sweet.

2 cups (280 g) all-purpose flour

⅔ cup (135 g) granulated sugar

1½ teaspoons baking powder

½ teaspoon kosher salt

1 tablespoon grated lemon zest

12 tablespoons (1½ sticks / 170 g) cold unsalted butter or vegan butter, cubed

10 dried brown figs, stems trimmed and chopped into ½-inch (12 mm) pieces

⅓ cup (80 ml) heavy cream or nondairy milk, plus more as needed and for brushing

1 large egg, lightly beaten

1 teaspoon vanilla extract or vanilla bean paste

Turbinado sugar for sprinkling

1. Preheat the oven to 400°F (200°C). Line two large baking sheets with parchment paper.
2. Combine the flour, sugar, baking powder, salt, and lemon zest in a large bowl and stir to fully mix. Add the butter cubes and, using your fingers and working quickly, pinch the butter into the flour mixture until the butter is in pieces the size of small peas. Add the figs and stir to incorporate.
3. Whisk together the cream, egg, and vanilla in a small bowl. Make a well in the center of the flour mixture and pour in the cream mixture. Using a silicone spatula, mix and press the wet and dry ingredients together until just combined, being careful not to overmix. The dough should still be a little shaggy. If it appears very dry, blend in more cream, 1 teaspoon at a time, until the desired consistency is reached.
4. Use a 1½-tablespoon cookie scoop to scoop slightly rounded mounds of dough onto the baking sheets, leaving about 1 inch (2.5 cm) between the cookies. Use a pastry brush to dot the tops of each cookie lightly with additional cream and sprinkle each with a little turbinado sugar.
5. Bake, rotating the baking sheets back to front and top to bottom halfway through, until the cookies are lightly golden on top and darker around the edges, 15 to 18 minutes. Transfer the cookies to wire racks to cool, and serve slightly warm or completely cooled.
6. Store the cookies in an airtight container in the fridge for up to 1 week or, well wrapped, in the freezer for up to 6 months. If desired, warm the cookies briefly in the oven or toaster oven before serving.

NOTE: If you do not have turbinado sugar, sprinkle the tops of the cookies with granulated sugar.

WHITE CHOCOLATE TAHINI COOKIES

Makes about 24 cookies

Providence, Rhode Island, is home to Oak Bakeshop—a self-described “Jew-ish” bakery and café founded in 2022 by husband-and-wife team Lori and Paul Kettelle. The bakery’s menu features Ashkenazi and Middle Eastern–inspired pastries (think hamantaschen, rugelach, knishes, and Jerusalem bagels) along with American favorites like cinnamon buns and banana bread. “We wanted to create a place that when you walk in, it felt like it had always been there,” Lori told me. These tahini and almond flour–based cookies are a constant on the menu—a recipe the Kettelles developed early on to offer something that other bakeries didn’t have. My slightly adapted version of their recipe bakes up chewy with caramelized edges and a nutty flavor. A coating of sesame seeds adds crunch and contrast, while the white chocolate chips folded in provide pops of sweetness.

¾ cup (230 g) mild honey
2 tablespoons light brown sugar
½ cup (120 g) well-stirred tahini
1 large egg
1½ teaspoons vanilla extract
2½ cups (250 g) almond flour
¾ teaspoon kosher salt
1 cup (180 g) white chocolate chips
About 2 cups (200 g) sesame seeds for rolling

NOTE: To make these cookies dairy-free, use vegan or parve white chocolate chips.

1. Preheat the oven to 350°F (180°C). Line two large baking sheets with parchment paper.
2. Combine the honey, brown sugar, tahini, egg, and vanilla in the bowl of a stand mixer fitted with the paddle attachment (or use a handheld electric mixer and a large bowl) and beat on medium speed until fully combined. Add the almond flour and salt and beat on low to combine, then beat in the white chocolate chips.
3. Spread a generous amount of the sesame seeds on a plate. Using a 1½-tablespoon cookie scoop, scoop out the dough and roll into balls. (The dough may be sticky, so wash and dry your hands as needed.) Roll the balls in the sesame seeds, covering them on all sides, and place on the baking sheets, leaving about 1 inch (2.5 cm) between the cookies. Gently press down on the cookies to flatten them a bit.
4. Bake, rotating the baking sheets back to front and top to bottom halfway through, until the cookies are lightly puffed and golden, 10 to 12 minutes. The cookies will still feel soft on top but will firm up as they cool.
5. Remove from the oven and let the cookies cool on the baking sheets for 5 minutes, then transfer to wire racks to cool completely.
6. The cookies can be stored in an airtight container at room temperature for up to 3 days or in the fridge for up to 1 week. They do not freeze well.

CITRUSY COOKIE TWISTS

About 24 cookies

When it comes to Syrian Jewish cuisine, cookbook authors Jennifer Abadi (*A Fistful of Lentils*) and Poopa Dweck (*Aromas of Aleppo*) are my go-to experts. When both of their cookbooks mentioned that these treats are a staple of Syrian Jewish cookie jars, I knew I had to include a recipe for them. Called ka'ak b'sukar (which loosely translates from Arabic as "sugary biscuit"), the lightly golden twisted braids are at once delicate and snappy, with a sunny, citrusy flavor. A light coating of sugar lends the cookies extra sparkle and crunch. Serve them with coffee or tea for unparalleled after-dinner dipping. (For more about the wide variety of Middle Eastern ka'ak, see page 106.)

- 2½ cups (350 g) all-purpose flour, plus more for forming
- ½ teaspoon kosher salt
- ½ teaspoon baking powder
- ½ cup (120 ml) neutral vegetable oil
- 1 cup (200 g) granulated sugar, plus more for rolling
- 2 large eggs
- 2 teaspoons vanilla extract or vanilla bean paste
- 2 packed teaspoons grated lemon zest
- 1½ packed teaspoons grated orange zest

1. Whisk together the flour, salt, and baking powder in a medium bowl.
2. Whisk together the oil, sugar, eggs, vanilla, lemon zest, and orange zest in a large bowl until fully combined and glossy.
3. Add the flour mixture in two stages, stirring with a sturdy spoon until you have a thick, slightly tacky dough. Cover the bowl and refrigerate for 1 hour.
4. Preheat the oven to 350°F (180°C). Line two large baking sheets with parchment paper.
5. Spread a generous layer of sugar on a large plate. Using lightly floured hands, pinch off about ¼ cup (60 g) of the dough and roll it into a rope about 12 inches (30 cm) long and ½ inch (12 mm) thick. Fold the rope lengthwise in half, then gently twist the length of the rope to make a corkscrew. Cut the rope crosswise into approximately 3-inch- (7.5 cm) long pieces, Then dip each piece in the sugar to coat on both sides and arrange on one of the baking sheets, about 1 inch (2.5 cm) apart. Repeat with the remaining dough, using more sugar as needed
6. Bake, rotating the baking sheets back to front and top to bottom halfway through baking, until the bottoms of the cookies are very lightly golden and crisp but the cookies are still pale on top, 12 to 15 minutes. Remove from the oven and let the cookies cool on the baking sheets for about 1 minute, then transfer to wire racks to cool. The cookies will continue to firm up as they cool.
7. Store the cookies in an airtight container at room temperature for up to 3 days or in the fridge for up to 1 week or, well wrapped, in the freezer for up to 3 months.

KA'AK: THE MIDDLE EASTERN BISCUIT WITH ENDLESS VARIATIONS

Years ago, while I was doing research for my book *The Jewish Cookbook*, I got invited to cook alongside my friend's mother, a Syrian Jew and accomplished home cook living in South Brooklyn. I arrived at her home with the ingredients needed to make zucchini stuffed with allspice-scented ground beef and rice. But before we started chopping, she poured me a cup of coffee and set out a plate of homemade ka'ak—crunchy, barely sweetened ring-shaped biscuits covered in sesame seeds. I had never tried them before and was so smitten I asked if our cooking lesson might include them as well. She generously obliged.

Since that afternoon, I have learned that ka'ak is less of a particular recipe and more of a genre of diverse pastries. There are hard and crunchy biscuits like the ones I enjoyed in Brooklyn; softer yeasted rings (the Arabic name for these elongated sesame seed–covered Jerusalem bagels is *ka'ak al-quds*); and delicately braided wreaths made from sweetened almond paste. There are also savory versions that are served as a snack and sweet dessert versions flavored with anise, fennel, or citrus. Many ka'ak are ring-shaped, but some recipes turn out twisted breadsticks or elaborately decorated cookies that have been pressed in a wooden mold.

Ka'ak have roots in ancient Egypt and Iraq, and they are mentioned in both the Babylonian Talmud and medieval Arabic cookbooks. Today they are widely enjoyed throughout the Middle East and North Africa—and wherever the Jewish communities that originally hailed from those regions resettled. Within Middle Eastern and Maghrebi Jewish communities, ka'ak are served on Shabbat morning, at virtually every holiday, and at weddings and other festive celebrations.

As I learned that day in Brooklyn, ka'ak are the ultimate treat for entertaining. In *The Book of Jewish Food*, Cairo-born author Claudia Roden recalls that her mother kept a box of ka'ak on hand all the time to serve with mezze. Roden writes that her mother also "filled plastic bags for us to take home after her Friday-night dinners." While there are likely enough ka'ak recipes to devote an entire recipe booklet to them, in this book, I've included only one of my absolute favorites: Citrusy Cookie Twists (page 104) from Syria, called ka'ak b'sukar. Meanwhile, the rounded Italian Anise Seed Cookies (page 107) are not technically in the ka'ak family, but they share a lot of the same attributes and are likely cousins.

ITALIAN ANISE SEED COOKIES

Makes about 24 cookies

In Venice's historic Jewish ghetto neighborhood, the kosher bakery, Panificio Volpe Giovanni, turns out traditional Venetian Jewish sweets—including these anise seed cookies, called *azzime dolci* ("sweet matzo"). The cookies were traditionally baked for Passover, using a special flour that had been checked for any possible contact with water or contaminants. And, like regular matzo, they were prepared and baked quickly to prevent leavening. Today they are primarily sold to tourists hoping to experience a taste of the past. The crisp, delicate cookies are flavored with whole anise seeds, which gives them a distinct, but not overpowering, licorice flavor and aroma. They make a delightful companion to an espresso.

2¼ cups (315 g) all-purpose flour, plus more if needed

½ teaspoon kosher salt

½ cup (120 ml) light olive oil or neutral vegetable oil

1 cup (200 g) granulated sugar

2 large eggs

1 teaspoon vanilla extract or vanilla bean paste

2 packed teaspoons grated lemon zest

2½ tablespoons whole anise seeds

Sanding sugar or turbinado sugar for topping

NOTE: If you cannot find anise seeds, fennel seeds make a fitting substitute.

1. Preheat the oven to 350°F (180°C). Line two baking sheets with parchment paper.
2. Whisk together the flour and salt in a medium bowl; set aside.
3. Whisk the oil, granulated sugar, eggs, vanilla, lemon zest, and anise seeds together in a large bowl until fully combined.
4. Add the flour mixture in two stages, stirring with a sturdy spoon until you have a thick, slightly tacky dough. If the dough is too soft or sticky to roll out with floured hands, add a little more flour, 1 tablespoon at a time, until you reach the desired consistency.
5. Pinch off rounded tablespoons of the dough, roll them into balls, and place on the baking sheets, leaving 1 inch (2.5 cm) between the cookies.
6. Lightly flour the bottom of a glass and use the glass to flatten the dough balls to about ¼ inch (6 mm) thick (reflour the glass as necessary). Use the tips of your fingers to press decorative indentations all around the edges of each cookie. Sprinkle the tops of the cookies with a little sanding sugar.
7. Bake, rotating the baking sheets back to front and top to bottom halfway through baking, until the cookies are lightly golden and firm to the touch, 16 to 18 minutes. Remove from the oven and transfer the cookies to wire racks to cool. The cookies will continue to crisp up as they cool.
8. Store the cookies in an airtight container at room temperature for up to 3 days or in the fridge for up to 1 week or, well wrapped, in the freezer for up to 6 months.

STRAWBERRY SUMAC LINZER COOKIES

Makes about 24 sandwich cookies

Chef Katreena Kanney grew up in South Jersey with a Russian Jewish (by way of the Bronx) dad who introduced her to the delights of pastrami sandwiches and black-and-white cookies. "We were very into the Jewish deli scene," she said. These days Kanney is the pastry chef at K'far—chef Michael Solomonov's Israeli-inspired bakery and café, which has locations in Philadelphia and Brooklyn. In the K'far kitchen, Kanney, who is entirely self-taught, brings her innovative approach to the marzipan challah Danishes, brown sugar and ricotta kubaneh toasts, and every other pastry on the menu. For her Strawberry Sumac Linzer Cookies, she updated the Austrian dessert by spiking strawberry jam with lemon juice and mouth-puckering ground sumac. "Sometimes I also like to add a little cardamom to the confectioners' sugar topping for an added pop of flavor," she says. Kanney's linzers have all the whimsical peekaboo-jam appeal of the classic cookie, but with a little extra magic.

FOR THE JAM

16 ounces (454 g) strawberry jam
1½ tablespoons fresh lemon juice
3 tablespoons ground sumac
¼ teaspoon kosher salt

FOR THE COOKIES

2 cups (280 g) all-purpose flour, plus more for rolling
1 cup (100 g) almond flour
¾ teaspoon kosher salt
½ teaspoon ground cinnamon
16 tablespoons (2 sticks / 227 g) unsalted butter or vegan butter, softened
1 cup (200 g) granulated sugar
1 packed teaspoon grated lemon zest
1 large egg
2 teaspoons vanilla extract or vanilla bean paste
½ teaspoon almond extract
Confectioners' sugar for dusting

1. Make the jam: Combine the strawberry jam, lemon juice, sumac, and salt in a medium saucepan and bring to a bubble over medium heat, then reduce the heat to low and cook, stirring often, until the mixture coats the back of a spoon, 10 to 15 minutes. Remove from the heat, transfer the jam to a bowl, and set aside to cool. (The jam will continue to thicken as it cools.)

2. Once the jam is cool, cover the bowl and refrigerate until needed. (*The jam can be stored in the fridge for up to 1 week. Let it come to room temperature before using.*)

3. Make the cookies: Whisk together the all-purpose flour, almond flour, salt, and cinnamon in a medium bowl.

4. In the bowl of a stand mixer fitted with the paddle attachment (or using a handheld electric mixer and a large bowl), beat the butter, sugar, and lemon zest at medium speed until light and fluffy, about 2 minutes. Add the egg, vanilla extract, and almond extract and beat to combine.

5. Add the flour mixture in two stages, beating at low speed and scraping down the sides of the bowl as necessary, until a soft dough forms. Transfer the dough to a lightly floured work surface and knead briefly with lightly floured hands to bring it together. Divide the dough in half, shape into 2 disks, wrap well in parchment paper, and refrigerate for at least 2 hours, or up to overnight.

6. Preheat the oven to 350°F (180°C). Line two large baking sheets with parchment paper.
7. Remove one disk of dough from the refrigerator (keep the other disk chilled) and roll it out on a lightly floured surface to a ¼-inch (6 mm) thickness. Using a 2½-inch (6 cm) round cookie cutter, stamp out as many circles as you can and transfer them to the baking sheets. (You do not need to leave much space between the cookies, as they barely spread while baking.) Using a 1-inch (2.5 cm) round cookie cutter, or the end of a large round piping tip, stamp out holes in the center of half of the cookies. (These cookies will be the tops of the cookie sandwiches.) Repeat the rolling and stamping process with the remaining dough.
8. Bake the cookies, rotating the baking sheets back to front and top to bottom halfway through baking, until they are just set and barely golden around the edges, 10 to 12 minutes.
9. Remove from the oven and let the cookies cool for 5 minutes on the baking sheets, then transfer to wire racks to cool completely.
10. Assemble the cookie sandwiches: Spread a rounded teaspoon of jam onto the flat, bottom side of each full cookie round, then arrange the cookies jam side up on a serving platter. Use a fine-mesh sieve to lightly dust the tops of the ring cookies with confectioners' sugar and place on top of the jam-filled cookies, creating a sandwich with jam peeking out of the centers.
11. Store the cookies in an airtight container in the fridge for up to 5 days or, well-wrapped, in the freezer for up to 6 months.

ORANGE BLOSSOM BUTTER COOKIES

Makes about 24 cookies

Many Middle Eastern and North African cuisines include some form of shortbread, called *ghraybeh* in Arabic, in their dessert repertoires. The exact formulas and flavorings vary from recipe to recipe, but they all transform a simple mix of flour, sugar, and clarified butter into supremely tender, melt-in-the-mouth cookies. (The name ghraybeh fittingly translates as "swoon"—they are indeed swoon-worthy.) In *The Book of Jewish Food*, the Egyptian-born author Claudia Roden recalls that, "Everybody always had a tin of these . . . in the house to offer with coffee." They are also served on Purim and other joyful occasions.

¾ cup (170 g) clarified butter (ghee), softened but not melted

1¼ cups (150 g) confectioners' sugar, sifted

1 tablespoon orange blossom water

1½ cups (210 g) all-purpose flour

¼ teaspoon kosher salt

About 24 roasted pistachios for decoration

NOTE: Since so much of the flavor for these cookies comes from the clarified butter, I do not recommend substituting vegan butter. You can, however, substitute 12 tablespoons (1½ sticks / 170 g) unsalted butter.

1. Preheat the oven to 325°F (160°C). Line two large baking sheets with parchment paper.
2. Combine the clarified butter and confectioners' sugar in the bowl of a stand mixer fitted with the paddle attachment (or use a handheld electric mixer and a large bowl). Beat at medium speed until pale and fluffy, 2 to 3 minutes, then beat in the orange blossom water.
3. Whisk together the flour and salt in a small bowl. Add the flour mixture to the butter mixture in two stages, beating at low speed and scraping down the sides of the bowl as necessary, until just combined.
4. Scoop out tablespoons of the dough, roll into balls, and place on the baking sheets, leaving about 2 inches (5 cm) between the cookies. If the dough is too soft to roll, place the bowl in the refrigerator for about 20 minutes, then proceed. Press a pistachio into the center of each cookie.
5. Bake, rotating the baking sheets back to front and top to bottom halfway through baking, until the cookies are just firm to the touch but still pale, 15 to 17 minutes. (If you touch one, it should leave a powdery residue on your fingertip.) Remove from the oven and let the cookies cool on the baking sheets for 5 minutes, then transfer to wire racks to cool completely.
6. Store the cookies in an airtight container at room temperature for up to 3 days, in the fridge for up to 2 weeks, or in the freezer for up to 6 months.

CRISP SEPHARDI SPONGE COOKIES

Makes about 24 cookies

In the historic Sephardi community of Curaçao, these Dutch-inspired cookies, called *pan-levi*, are baked for virtually every Jewish holiday. They are also served with hot chocolate (page 277) at a baby boy's b'rit milah (circumcision ceremony). Older recipes flavor the cookies with mace, but a version I found in *Recipes from the Jewish Kitchens of Curaçao*, which was published in 1982 by the Mikvé Israel-Emanuel Synagogue, uses cinnamon and vanilla. I also like to add a heap of lime zest to the batter. While that is not traditional to this cookie, limes show up often in recipes from Curaçao and add brightness here. Panlevi are crisp, sturdy, and gently sweet—an ideal companion for hot chocolate. When serving them without a drink for dipping, I like to frost the cookies with a sweet-tart lime glaze; see the recipe below.

FOR THE COOKIES

1¾ cups (245 g) all-purpose flour

1 teaspoon baking powder

1 teaspoon ground cinnamon

¼ teaspoon kosher salt

3 large eggs

1 cup granulated sugar

1 teaspoon vanilla extract or vanilla bean paste

1 packed tablespoon grated lime zest

FOR THE OPTIONAL LIME GLAZE

2 cups (240 g) confectioners' sugar, sifted, plus more as needed

2 tablespoons fresh lime juice

1 tablespoon milk or nondairy milk, plus more as needed

½ teaspoon vanilla extract or vanilla bean paste

Finely grated lime zest, for topping (optional)

1. Make the cookies: Preheat the oven to 350°F (180°C). Line two large baking sheets with parchment paper.

2. Whisk together the flour, baking powder, cinnamon, and salt in a medium bowl. Whisk together the eggs, sugar, vanilla, and lime zest in a large bowl until fully combined.

3. Add the dry ingredients to the wet and stir until just combined. Using a 1½-tablespoon cookie scoop, scoop out the dough and drop onto the prepared baking sheets, leaving 1 inch (2.5 cm) between the cookies.

4. Bake the cookies, rotating the baking sheets back to front and top to bottom halfway through, until the tops are set and very lightly golden, 10 to 12 minutes. Turn off the oven and let the cookies sit in the ambient heat for 10 minutes, then remove from the oven and transfer the cookies to wire racks to cool. The cookies will continue to crisp up as they cool.

5. If desired, make the glaze: Whisk together the confectioners' sugar, lime juice, milk, and vanilla in a medium bowl until smooth. If the glaze is either too runny or thick to spread, stir in a little more milk or confectioners' sugar, as needed. Spread the glaze on the tops of the cooled cookies and place the cookies glazed side up back on the racks to set. While the glaze is still wet, sprinkle the top of each cookie with a little bit of lime zest, if desired.

6. The cookies can be stored in an airtight container at room temperature for up to 3 days or in the fridge for up to 1 week or, well wrapped, in the freezer for up to 6 months.

Crisp Sephardi Sponge Cookies (page 111) and Sipping Chocolate (page 277)

SNACKING CAKES & CELEBRATION CAKES

BACK POCKET APPLE CAKE

Makes one 9 × 13-inch (23 × 33 cm) cake

Apple cakes (called apfelkuchen in German and Yiddish), made with heaping amounts of the sweet-tart autumn fruit, are a standard Ashkenazi dessert for Rosh Hashanah and a welcome treat anytime—especially during apple season. I firmly believe that all Jewish home cooks (and everyone else too) should have a great apple cake recipe in their back pockets. This version, which is inspired by the apple cake my mom made when I was growing up, is excellent. The crumb is light and tender and threaded through with juicy bites of fruit. And the apples are accented with orange zest—a simple tweak that adds abundant flavor.

FOR THE APPLE LAYER

5 medium baking apples, peeled, cored, and cut into ¾-inch (2 cm) pieces (about 5 cups / 550 g)

½ packed cup (100 g) light brown sugar

1½ teaspoons ground cinnamon

Grated zest of 1 medium orange

½ cup (50 g) walnut halves, roughly chopped (optional)

FOR THE CAKE

2 cups (280 g) all-purpose flour

2 teaspoons baking powder

1½ teaspoons ground cinnamon

½ teaspoon kosher salt

3 large eggs

1¼ cups (250 g) granulated sugar

¾ cup (180 ml) neutral vegetable oil

¼ cup (60 ml) orange juice

1½ teaspoons vanilla extract

Confectioners' sugar for dusting (optional)

1. Preheat the oven to 350°F (180°C). Grease a 9 × 13-inch (23 × 33 cm) baking dish.
2. Make the apple layer: Combine the apples, brown sugar, cinnamon, orange zest, and walnuts, if using, in a medium bowl. Mix well to coat the apples with the brown sugar mixture and set aside.
3. Make the cake: Whisk together the flour, baking powder, cinnamon, and salt in a medium bowl.
4. Whisk together the eggs, sugar, oil, orange juice, and vanilla in a large bowl until combined. Add the flour mixture in two stages, stirring and scraping down the sides of the bowl as necessary, until just combined.
5. Spread about half of the batter over the bottom of the baking dish. (It will be a thin layer.) Spoon the apple mixture (and its juices) evenly over the top, then dollop and spread the remaining batter over the apples. It may seem like too many apples and they may not be fully covered with batter, but the cake will rise during baking and even out the layers.
6. Bake until a tester inserted into the center of the cake comes out clean, 40 to 45 minutes. If the top is browning too quickly and the cake isn't cooked through yet, loosely drape the top with foil. Remove the cake from the oven and set the baking dish on a wire rack to cool completely.
7. If desired, just before serving, use a fine-mesh sieve to lightly dust the top of the cake with confectioners' sugar. Store any leftovers, covered, in the fridge for up to 1 week or, well-wrapped, in the freezer for up to 6 months.

APPLE SHARLOTKA

Makes one 9-inch (23 cm) round cake

Jessica Quinn and her wife, Trina, co-run Dacha 46, an Eastern European Jewish pop-up restaurant in Brooklyn. Together they delight diners with piles of pelmeni (Russian dumplings), ruby-red borscht, and a wide variety of cakes and pastries. Many of the pastry recipes are inspired by Jessica's family, which immigrated to New York City from the former Soviet Union and spent holidays cooking together or visiting one of the lavish Eastern European banquet halls that lined the boardwalk in Brooklyn's Brighton Beach. "Desserts were always a big focus—elaborate layer cakes, buttery walnut-shaped cookies called *oreshki*, and sponge cakes," she said. This sponge cake, which Jessica's family served on Rosh Hashanah and most holiday dinners, is made from a simple batter of whipped eggs, flour, and sugar that gets layered with sliced apples. It bakes up moist and airy, with chunks of tender apple threaded throughout. Jessica suggests serving the cake the traditional way, with strong black tea that has been swirled with spoonfuls of store-bought sour cherry jam.

- 1 cup (140 g) all-purpose flour
- ¾ teaspoon baking powder
- ¼ teaspoon kosher salt
- 4 large eggs, at room temperature
- 1¼ cups (250 g) granulated sugar
- Grated zest of 1 medium lemon
- 1½ teaspoons vanilla extract or vanilla bean paste
- 4 medium baking apples (about 1½ pounds / 680 g), peeled, quartered, cored, and thinly sliced lengthwise
- Confectioners' sugar for dusting

1. Preheat the oven to 350°F (180°C). Grease a 9-inch (23 cm) round springform cake pan.
2. Sift together the flour, baking powder, and salt in a small bowl and set aside.
3. Combine the eggs, sugar, lemon zest, and vanilla in the bowl of a stand mixer fitted with the whisk attachment (or use a handheld electric mixer and a large bowl). Beat at medium-high speed until the mixture is thick, voluminous, and light in color, 7 to 10 minutes.
4. Sift the flour mixture over the egg mixture and gently fold together with a silicone spatula, taking care not to deflate the eggs. (The flour tends to sink to the bottom of the bowl, so make sure to incorporate all of it.)
5. Spoon about one-third of the batter into the cake pan and gently smooth the top. Arrange a layer of apple slices in an overlapping spiral pattern on top of the batter. Repeat the layering process with another third of the batter and a second layer of apples, and finish with a final layer of batter on top. It may seem like too many apples for the batter, but the cake will rise during baking and even out the layers.

recipe continues

6. Bake until the top of the cake is golden brown and a cake tester inserted into the center comes out clean, 45 to 55 minutes. If the top of the cake is browning too quickly toward the end of baking, loosely tent it with foil. Remove the cake from the oven and set the pan on a wire rack to cool completely.

7. Gently unmold the cooled cake and transfer it to a serving plate. Just before serving, use a fine-mesh sieve to generously dust the top of the cake with confectioners' sugar. Any leftovers can be stored, covered, in the fridge for up to 3 days.

SOUR CHERRY COFFEE CAKE

Makes one 8-inch (20 cm) square cake

German and Austrian Jews shared their neighbors' fondness for kaffeekuchen—a genre of simple, sometimes fruit-enriched, often streusel-topped cakes that were meant to be enjoyed with coffee and conversation. When members of these Jewish communities emigrated to America in the late nineteenth and early twentieth centuries, they brought this baking tradition with them. Today Ashkenazi Jews typically serve coffee cakes on Shabbat morning, to break the fast after Yom Kippur, and on Shavuot, when foods made with butter and other dairy products are particularly prized. This variation makes the most of sour cherries' fleeting season in early summer. The combination of mouth-puckering cherries, orange-scented cake, and brown sugar streusel is extraordinary.

FOR THE STREUSEL

½ cup (70 g) all-purpose flour

½ packed cup (100 g) light brown sugar

¼ teaspoon kosher salt

4 tablespoons (½ stick / 57 g) unsalted or vegan butter, softened

FOR THE CAKE

1½ cups (200 g) sour cherries (fresh or thawed frozen), pitted if necessary

1¼ cups (175 g) all-purpose flour, divided

1½ teaspoons baking powder

½ teaspoon kosher salt

4 tablespoons (½ stick / 57 g) unsalted or vegan butter, softened

¾ cup (150 g) granulated sugar

1 packed teaspoon grated orange zest

2 large eggs

1 teaspoon vanilla extract

¼ cup (60 ml) milk or nondairy milk

NOTE: Don't make this cake with jarred or canned sour cherries, as they tend to have a flat or "tinny" flavor that overwhelms the batter.

1. Preheat the oven to 350°F (180°C). Line an 8-inch (20 cm) square cake pan with parchment paper, allowing the parchment to hang over two opposite sides.
2. Make the streusel: Whisk together the flour, brown sugar, and salt in a medium bowl. Add the butter and, using your fingers or a fork, mash them together until they form a crumbly streusel. Set aside.
3. Make the cake: Toss the sour cherries with ¼ cup (35 g) of the flour; set aside. Whisk together the remaining 1 cup (140 g) flour with the baking powder and salt in a medium bowl.
4. In the bowl of a stand mixer fitted with the paddle attachment (or using a large bowl and a handheld electric mixer), beat together the softened butter, sugar, and orange zest until fluffy. Beat in the eggs one at a time, followed by the vanilla extract.
5. Beat half of the flour mixture into the wet mixture, followed by the milk, and then add the remaining flour mixture, beating just to combine and scraping down the sides of the bowl as needed.
6. Remove the cherries from the flour (discarding any excess flour) and gently fold them into the batter. Spread the batter in the prepared pan. Sprinkle the streusel evenly over the top.
7. Bake until a tester inserted into the center of the cake comes out clean, 40 to 50 minutes. Set the cake on a wire rack to cool before slicing. Store leftovers in an airtight container at room temperature for up to 3 days, in the fridge for up to 1 week, or in the freezer for up to 6 months.

BLUEBERRY STREUSEL CAKE

Makes one 9 × 13-inch (23 × 33 cm) cake

Maaryasha Werdiger is a pediatric physiotherapist by training, but several years ago she followed the siren call of bread and pastry. "It started with five bags of flour in the living room, and before long, I had transformed my garage into a bakery with fridges and flour bins and a line of people outside the door each morning," she said. Today Werdiger runs Zelda Bakery—a brick-and-mortar shop located in a suburb of Melbourne, Australia—where she sells everything from baguettes and sourdough loaves to flaky rugelach and babka flavored with crumbled Anzac biscuits (the buttery oatmeal-coconut cookies beloved in Australia).

Zelda's menu also occasionally offers variations on her grandmother's streusel cake—a simple, tender cake threaded through with blueberries and topped with a comforting layer of sweet, buttery crumbs. The streusel cake was a fixture of her family's Shabbat table, and often served to break the fast after Yom Kippur and Tisha B'Av (another fast day on the Jewish calendar). Werdiger said her grandmother doesn't wait for special occasions to serve it. "There's always coffee and a bit of cake around my grandmother's home," she said. "Cake is our love language."

FOR THE STREUSEL

½ cup (70 g) all-purpose flour

½ packed cup (100 g) light brown sugar

½ teaspoon ground cinnamon

¼ teaspoon kosher salt

4 tablespoons (½ stick / 57 g) unsalted butter or vegan butter, softened

NOTE: Fresh blueberries work best for this cake; thawed frozen berries will bleed a lot of purple-blue color into the batter.

1. Preheat the oven to 350°F (180°C). Lightly grease a 9 × 13-inch (23 × 33 cm) baking dish.
2. Make the streusel: Combine the flour, brown sugar, cinnamon, salt, and butter in a medium bowl and rub them together until the mixture resembles coarse bread crumbs; do not overmix. Set aside.
3. Make the cake: Whisk together the flour, baking powder, cinnamon, and salt in a medium bowl.
4. In the bowl of a stand mixer fitted with the paddle attachment (or using a handheld electric mixer and a large bowl), beat together the butter, granulated sugar, and lemon zest at medium speed until fluffy. Beat in the eggs one at a time, followed by the vanilla.
5. On low speed, beat half of the flour mixture into the wet mixture, followed by the orange juice, then add the remaining flour mixture, beating until just combined and scraping down the sides of the bowl as needed. Add the blueberries and use a sturdy spoon or silicone spatula to gently fold them in.

FOR THE CAKE

2 cups (280 g) all-purpose flour

1½ teaspoons baking powder

1 teaspoon ground cinnamon

½ teaspoon kosher salt

8 tablespoons (1 stick / 113 g) unsalted butter or vegan butter, softened

1¼ cups (250 g) granulated sugar

1 packed teaspoon grated lemon zest

3 large eggs

1½ teaspoons vanilla extract

½ cup (120 ml) orange juice

2 cups (300 g) fresh blueberries (see Note)

6. Scrape the batter into the prepared baking dish and smooth the top. Sprinkle the streusel evenly over the top, taking care not to overload the middle of the cake, which could cause the streusel to sink during baking.

7. Bake the cake until it is golden and a tester inserted into the center comes out clean, 35 to 40 minutes. Set the cake on a wire rack to cool completely before slicing.

8. Store any leftovers, covered, at room temperature for up to 3 days or in the fridge for up to 1 week or, well wrapped, in the freezer for up to 6 months.

JAM CAKE

Makes one 8-inch (20 cm) square cake

I have long been inspired by Marcie Cohen Ferris, a professor emeritus at UNC Chapel Hill and author of *Matzoh Ball Gumbo: Culinary Tales of the Jewish South*. Her book, which offers an incomparable trove of history and recipes from Jewish communities across the American South, includes a recipe for a buttermilk-enriched jam cake that her mother baked for Rosh Hashanah. Ferris's mother folded blackberry preserves into the batter, which dyed the baked cake a rich purple. In my interpretation, I stir jam into part of the batter and then swirl the rest of it in for a delicate marbled effect. You can use any jam you like for this cake, but darker jams will yield more pronounced swirls.

1¾ cups (245 g) all-purpose flour
1½ teaspoons baking powder
½ teaspoon kosher salt
1¼ packed cups (250 g) light brown sugar
⅓ cup (80 ml) neutral vegetable oil
2 large eggs
2 packed teaspoons grated lemon zest
1 teaspoon vanilla extract
½ cup (120 ml) buttermilk
⅔ cup (190 g) jam, such as raspberry, blackberry, blueberry, or strawberry
Confectioners' sugar for dusting (optional)

NOTE: To make this cake dairy-free, substitute the buttermilk with ½ cup (120 ml) nondairy milk mixed with 1½ teaspoons lemon juice that has been allowed to stand for 5 minutes.

1. Preheat the oven to 350°F (180°C). Lightly grease an 8-inch (20 cm) square baking pan and line it with parchment paper, allowing the paper to hang over two opposite sides.

2. Whisk together the flour, baking powder, and salt in a medium bowl and set aside. In the bowl of a stand mixer fitted with the paddle attachment (or using a handheld electric mixer and a large bowl), beat the brown sugar, oil, eggs, lemon zest, and vanilla together at medium speed until fully combined, about 1 minute.

3. On low speed, beat in about half of the flour mixture, scraping down the sides of the bowl as necessary. Beat in the buttermilk, followed by the remaining flour mixture.

4. Transfer about one-third of the batter to a second bowl. Add the jam and stir to combine. Spoon the two batters into the prepared pan, alternating big spoonfuls of each one to make a rough checkerboard pattern. (The batter will spread.) Use a butter knife or skewer to make a figure-eight pattern in the pan, swirling both batters together and creating a marbled effect.

5. Bake the cake until it is gently puffed and a tester inserted into the center comes out clean, 40 to 45 minutes. Transfer the cake to a wire rack to cool.

6. Use the overhanging parchment to gently lift the cake out of the pan and transfer it to a cutting board. Serve slightly warm or at room temperature, lightly dusted with confectioners' sugar, if desired.

7. Store leftovers, covered, at room temperature for up to 3 days or in the fridge for up to 1 week, or, well wrapped, in the freezer for up to 3 months.

USING BAKING SODA AND BAKING POWDER DURING PASSOVER

Many years ago, when my husband and I first started cleaning our kitchen for Passover, I got quite the surprise in the supermarket kosher aisle. There, next to the boxes of almond flour and matzo meal, I found containers of baking powder and baking soda being sold for the holiday. Cue the record scratch! Wasn't avoiding leavened foods—and therefore two of the most common leavening agents used in baking—the entire focus of Passover cooking?

Not quite. For countless generations, Jewish bakers relied almost exclusively on whipped egg whites to add lift and lightness to Passover cakes and other desserts. And many of my favorite recipes in this book—like Flourless Fudge Cake with Apricot Sauce (page 156) and Strawberry Cloud Meringues (page 93) still do just that. But, as it turns out, while the act of leavening chametz (the five grains forbidden on Passover: wheat, oats, spelt, barley, and rye) is forbidden, the leavening agents themselves are not.

The word *chametz* means "sour" and refers to the sharp and sour taste that bread gets when it is naturally fermented. Matzo—made from wheat flour and water—must traditionally be prepared and baked within eighteen minutes, which is believed to be the window before leavening from the natural yeasts on the grains begin interacting with the water. Baking soda and baking powder, however, are chemical compounds that are considered categorically different from yeast. You would be hard-pressed to find a rabbi recommending that you simply bake a regular flour-based cake batter within 18 minutes at home and serve that cake at your seder. The baking process takes too much time and leaves too much room for error. But as long as the chemical leavening agents are used with a non-chametz flour (like almond, walnut, or quinoa flour or matzo meal), you are in the clear.

I don't blame you if you feel a little incredulous, but even the store-bought Passover coffee cake mix my husband adores includes baking soda. According to the Orthodox Union, which is considered the gold star for kosher certification, baking soda (technically sodium bicarbonate) does not even require special Passover certification to be used during that week. Baking powder does, since most brands contain cornstarch, which some Ashkenazi Jews avoid on Passover, along with chametz. (The Passover versions swap in Passover-friendly potato starch.)

So go ahead and bake my Best Passover Banana Bread (page 128) and Best Passover Chocolate Zucchini Muffins (page 129), which use baking soda. Your holiday will still be kosher—and a whole lot sweeter.

BEST PASSOVER BANANA BREAD

Makes one 8½ × 4½-inch (22 × 11.5 cm) loaf

I developed this recipe out of love and desperation. I have two wonderful—and also picky—children who are even further limited in their eating options during the week of Passover. (On Passover, leavened foods made with wheat, oats, rye, barley, and spelt are off limits.) In hopes of finding something my kids would truly enjoy eating during the holiday, I adapted one of their favorite year-round treats. The mix of matzo meal and potato starch in the base yields a tender and fluffy loaf that is surprisingly close in texture to the "real thing." I often serve this banana bread, which is generously studded with chocolate chips, for dessert after the seder meal. But it also makes a wonderful breakfast or sweet snack throughout Passover.

- ¾ cup (85 g) matzo meal (not matzo cake meal)
- ⅓ cup (45 g) potato starch
- 1 teaspoon baking soda
- ¼ teaspoon kosher salt
- 2 medium, very ripe bananas
- ½ cup (100 g) granulated sugar
- ¼ packed cup (50 g) light brown sugar
- 2 large eggs
- ⅓ cup (80 ml) neutral vegetable oil
- 1 teaspoon pure vanilla extract
- ¾ cup (135 g) semisweet or bittersweet chocolate chips

1. Preheat the oven to 350°F (180°C). Line an 8½ × 4½-inch (22 × 11.5 cm) loaf pan with parchment paper, allowing the parchment to hang over two opposite sides.
2. Whisk together the matzo meal, potato starch, baking soda, and salt in a medium bowl; set aside.
3. Combine the bananas, granulated sugar, and brown sugar in a large bowl and use a potato masher or a sturdy fork to press them together until the bananas are well mashed. Add the eggs, vegetable oil, and vanilla and stir to fully combine.
4. Add the matzo meal mixture and stir until just combined. Fold in most of the chocolate chips, leaving behind a couple of tablespoons for topping the bread.
5. Scrape the batter into the loaf pan and smooth it with a silicone spatula, then sprinkle the top evenly with the reserved chocolate chips. Bake the cake until it is golden brown and a cake tester inserted into the center comes out clean, 45 to 55 minutes. Remove from the oven and set the loaf pan on a wire rack to cool completely.
6. Once the banana bread is cool, use the overhanging parchment to gently lift it out of the loaf pan and onto a cutting board for slicing.
7. Store any leftovers, covered, at room temperature for up to 3 days or in the fridge for up to 1 week or, well wrapped, in the freezer for up to 6 months.

BEST PASSOVER CHOCOLATE ZUCCHINI MUFFINS

Makes 12 muffins

These muffins are my Passover adaptation of the chocolate zucchini cake my mom baked every summer, when the squash was abundantly in season. A heap of grated zucchini completely disappears into the chocolate batter as it bakes, resulting in a moist, fudgy crumb. The combination of matzo meal and potato starch provides an ideal mix of substance and lightness. These muffins are equally at home served for Passover dessert or as a decadent (but secretly vegetable-packed) breakfast treat.

- 1 large zucchini (about 12 ounces / 340 g), not peeled, ends trimmed
- 2 large eggs
- ⅓ cup (80 ml) neutral vegetable oil
- ¾ packed cup (150 g) light brown sugar
- 1 teaspoon vanilla extract
- ¾ cup (85 g) matzo meal (not matzo cake meal)
- ⅓ cup (45 g) potato starch
- ½ cup (40 g) unsweetened cocoa powder, sifted
- 1 teaspoon baking soda
- ½ teaspoon kosher salt
- 1 cup (180 g) semisweet chocolate chips

1. Preheat the oven to 350°F (180°C). Line a 12-cup muffin tin with paper liners.
2. Shred the zucchini on the large holes of a box grater. (You should end up with about 2 cups grated zucchini.) Gently squeeze most of the water out of the zucchini with your hands (discarding the water) and set aside.
3. Whisk together the eggs, vegetable oil, brown sugar, and vanilla in a large bowl until fully combined. Add the matzo meal, potato starch, cocoa powder, baking soda, and salt and stir to combine.
4. Add the grated zucchini and about three-quarters of the chocolate chips and fold them thoroughly into the batter. Divide the batter equally among the lined muffin cups, then sprinkle the tops of each muffin evenly with a few of the reserved chocolate chips.
5. Bake until a tester inserted into the center of a muffin comes out clean, 20 to 22 minutes. Transfer the muffins to a wire rack to cool completely.
6. Store any leftovers, covered, in the fridge for up to 1 week or, well wrapped, in the freezer for up to 6 months.

VENETIAN PUMPKIN CAKE

Makes one 9-inch (23 cm) square cake

This tender cake, which is called Torta di Zucca Barucca in Italian, originated in Italy's northern Veneto region. My recipe uses canned pumpkin for ease, but it is traditionally made with a beloved local variety of squash called zucca barucca. According to *The Compleat Squash*, by Amy Goldman, "The epithet 'Zucca Barucca' is a play on two words: *verucca*, meaning 'wart,' and the Hebrew word *baruch*, for 'sainted' or 'blessed.'" The wart connection is obvious to anyone who looks at the homely, bumpy-skinned squash. As for the latter, Goldman writes, "Who else but the Italians and Jews would call a squash holy?"

Dishes made with squash were a fixture of Venetian Jewish tables on Rosh Hashanah and were also served to break the fast after Yom Kippur. This Venetian Pumpkin Cake would make a lovely dessert for either holiday, but it is also simple enough to bake as an anytime snacking cake. Some versions of the recipe fold in raisins, candied citron, or almonds, but I prefer a fluffy, unadulterated crumb that lets the essence of autumn shine through.

- 2 cups (280 g) all-purpose flour
- 2 teaspoons baking powder
- 1 teaspoon baking soda
- ½ teaspoon kosher salt
- ¾ packed cup (150 g) light brown sugar
- ⅔ cup (130 g) granulated sugar
- ½ cup (120 ml) neutral vegetable oil
- 2 large eggs, lightly beaten
- One 15-ounce (425 g) can pure pumpkin puree (not pumpkin pie filling)
- 1 teaspoon vanilla extract
- 1½ teaspoons ground cinnamon
- Grated zest of 1 large orange
- Confectioners' sugar for dusting

NOTE: You can swap the canned pumpkin for an equivalent weight of cooked and mashed pumpkin or butternut squash.

1. Preheat the oven to 350°F (180°C). Line a 9-inch (23 cm) square baking pan with parchment paper, allowing the parchment to hang over two opposite sides.
2. Whisk together the flour, baking powder, baking soda, and salt in a medium bowl.
3. Combine the brown sugar, granulated sugar, oil, eggs, pumpkin puree, vanilla, cinnamon, and orange zest in a large bowl and whisk to thoroughly combine. Add the dry ingredients to the wet and fold them together with a sturdy spoon or a silicone spatula until no lumps remain.
4. Transfer the batter to the baking pan and smooth the top. Bake until a tester inserted into the center comes out clean, 30 to 35 minutes.
5. Transfer the cake to a wire rack to cool completely. Once fully cool, use the overhanging parchment to gently lift the cake out of the pan and onto a serving plate.
6. Just before serving, use a fine-mesh sieve to lightly dust the top of the cake with confectioners' sugar. Any leftovers can be stored, covered, at room temperature for up to 3 days or in the fridge for up to 1 week or, well wrapped, in the freezer for up to 6 months.

COCONUT-CARDAMOM SEMOLINA CAKE

Makes one 9-inch (23 cm) round cake

The Cochin Jews trace their 2,500-year-old heritage to the Malabar Coast in southwestern India. Their cuisine is both distinctive and delicious, filled with fresh fish curries, an abundance of spices (for many centuries, Cochin Jews were central to the Malabar spice trade), rice simmered with coconut milk, and a wide variety of desserts. This sweet, fragrant semolina and coconut cake, which is flavored with cardamom and threaded through with nuts and raisins, is invariably served for Rosh Hashanah and at Jewish weddings. According to the cookbook *Spice & Kosher: Exotic Cuisine of the Cochin Jews*, it "is considered a jewel in the community's culinary repertoire." After one slice, it might become the jewel of your Rosh Hashanah table as well.

- ⅔ cup (110 g) clarified butter (ghee) or neutral vegetable oil
- 1½ cups (240 g) fine semolina
- 1 cup (80 g) unsweetened dried shredded coconut
- One 13.5-ounce (380 g) can coconut milk
- 2 large eggs
- 1¼ packed cups (250 g) light brown sugar
- 2 teaspoons baking powder
- ¾ teaspoon ground cardamom
- ⅛ teaspoon ground nutmeg (optional)
- ¼ teaspoon kosher salt
- ¼ cup (35 g) dark or golden raisins
- ½ cup (70 g) roasted unsalted cashews, roughly chopped
- ½ cup (70 g) roasted unsalted almonds, roughly chopped

1. Melt the ghee (or heat the oil) in a medium saucepan over medium heat. Add the semolina and cook, stirring often, until lightly toasted and fragrant, 1 to 2 minutes. Remove from the heat and transfer to a large bowl to cool slightly.
2. Add the coconut, coconut milk, eggs, brown sugar, baking powder, cardamom, nutmeg, if using, and salt to the toasted semolina and whisk or stir well to thoroughly combine. Let the mixture stand for 10 minutes to allow the semolina to hydrate.
3. Meanwhile, preheat the oven to 350°F (180°C). Lightly grease a 9-inch (23 cm) round springform pan or cake pan.
4. Stir the raisins, cashews, and almonds into the batter. Pour the batter into the cake pan and bake until the top is golden and a tester inserted into the center comes out clean, 40 to 45 minutes. Remove from the oven and set the pan on a wire rack to let the cake cool.
5. Serve slightly warm or at room temperature. Any leftovers can be stored, covered, at room temperature for up to 3 days or in the fridge for up to 1 week or, well wrapped, in the freezer for up to 6 months.

ORANGE AND ALMOND CAKE

Makes one 9-inch (23 cm) round cake

In her classic cookbook *The Book of Jewish Food*, Claudia Roden includes a recipe for Gâteau à l'Orange, a Judeo-Spanish cake made from whole oranges that are boiled until soft, then blitzed into a puree and mixed with finely ground almonds, eggs, and sugar. "Orange cakes are typical of all the Mediterranean Jewish communities, even though they are not usually found in the local national cuisines," she writes. "It is something these communities have in common with Spain." In other words, when Jews fled Spain and Portugal in the wake of the Spanish Inquisition, they took their love of citrusy cakes along with them and introduced the cakes to their adopted homelands.

Roden's orange cake recipe is wonderful but ends up closer in texture to a moist pudding. After playing around with the orange-almond profile, I landed on this version, which has a tender crumb and a heady orange aroma. As one volunteer recipe tester described the texture, "It is like a mix between angel food and pound cake—light and airy, with some heft from the almond flour." It makes a fitting end to Shabbat dinner and also satisfies as an anytime snacking cake.

2 cups (200 g) almond flour
½ cup (70 g) all-purpose flour
1 teaspoon baking powder
½ teaspoon kosher salt
4 large eggs, separated, at room temperature
1 cup (200 g) granulated sugar
⅓ cup (80 ml) neutral vegetable oil
1 packed tablespoon grated orange zest
⅓ cup (80 ml) fresh orange juice
½ teaspoon almond extract (optional)
Confectioners' sugar for dusting

1. Preheat the oven to 350°F (180°C). Grease a 9-inch (23 cm) round springform cake pan.
2. Whisk together the almond flour, all-purpose flour, baking powder, and salt in a medium bowl; set aside.
3. In the bowl of a stand mixer fitted with the paddle attachment (or using a handheld mixer and a large bowl), beat the egg yolks and granulated sugar together at medium speed until light and foamy, 1 to 2 minutes. Add the vegetable oil, orange zest, orange juice, and almond extract, if using, and beat to combine.
4. Add the flour mixture in two stages, beating at low speed and scraping down the sides of the bowl as necessary, until just combined.
5. If using a stand mixer, transfer the batter to a clean bowl, wash and thoroughly dry the mixer bowl, and switch to the whisk attachment. If using a handheld mixer, switch to the whisk attachments if you have them, or wash and thoroughly dry the beaters. Add the egg whites to the clean mixer bowl or another large bowl and whip at medium-high speed until firm, glossy peaks form, about 2 minutes. Gently fold the whipped egg whites into the batter until no white streaks remain.

6. Pour the batter into the prepared pan and bake until the top of the cake is golden and a cake tester inserted into the center comes out clean, 30 to 40 minutes. If the top of the cake is browning too quickly toward the end of baking, loosely tent it with foil. Remove the cake from the oven and set the pan on a wire rack to cool completely, then gently unmold the cake and transfer it to a serving plate.

7. Just before serving, use a fine-mesh sieve to dust the top of the cake with confectioners' sugar. Any leftovers can be stored, covered, in the fridge for up to 3 days or, well wrapped, in the freezer for up to 6 months.

YOGURT SEMOLINA LOAF CAKE

Makes one 8½ × 4½-inch (22 × 11.5 cm) loaf

In 2010, I had the good fortune of attending a culinary-focused press trip to Israel led by iconic Jewish food writer Joan Nathan. Our group visited the Fauzi Azar Inn—a guesthouse located inside a historic Ottoman-style mansion in Nazareth's Old City. I was fascinated to learn that the guesthouse was cofounded by an Israeli Jewish man, named Maoz Inon, and a Palestinian Christian woman, named Suraida Shomar Nasser (whose great-grandfather had built the house 200 years earlier). I was also fascinated—and delighted—by breakfast.

Like many hotels in Israel, Fauzi Azar provides a morning meal for its guests—a spread of pita with za'atar, labneh with Galilean olives, and fresh melon from the nearby Arab souk (market). But the standout dish was a syrup-soaked semolina and yogurt cake called *hareesa*. Variations on this cake can be found throughout Mediterranean cuisine (with a variety of names, including *namoura*, *basboosa*, *revani*, *tishpishti*, and *safra*). Nasser, who did most of the inn's baking, steeped her syrup with fresh geranium leaves, but other recipes use orange blossom water, rose water, or citrus. What all these cakes share is a rich and tender texture and a sticky-sweetness that marries perfectly with a glass of strong coffee or tea.

My riff on hareesa bakes the semolina batter in a loaf pan rather than the typical round or square cake pan. I love how the cake bakes up tall and golden, and how the syrup soaks in all the way through. Make this cake the sweet centerpiece at your next brunch, or serve it for dessert after a dairy meal.

FOR THE SYRUP

¾ cup (150 g) granulated sugar

¾ cup (180 ml) water

2 teaspoons orange blossom water

FOR THE CAKE

1 cup (140 g) all-purpose flour

¾ cup (120 g) fine semolina

2 teaspoons baking powder

½ teaspoon kosher salt

8 tablespoons (1 stick / 113 g) unsalted butter, softened

¾ cup (150 g) granulated sugar

1 cup (255 g) full-fat plain yogurt (not Greek)

2 large eggs, separated, at room temperature

1 teaspoon vanilla extract

1. Make the syrup: Combine the sugar and water in a medium saucepan and bring to a boil over medium-high heat, stirring often to dissolve the sugar, then lower the heat to medium and simmer until the syrup is slightly thickened, 2 to 3 minutes. Remove from the heat and stir in the orange blossom water, then set aside to cool.

2. Make the cake: Preheat the oven to 350°F (180°C). Lightly grease an 8½ × 4½-inch (22 × 11.5 cm) loaf pan and line it with parchment paper, allowing the parchment to hang over on the two long sides of the pan.

3. Whisk together the flour, semolina, baking powder, and salt in a medium bowl.

recipe continues

4. In the bowl of a stand mixer fitted with the paddle attachment (or using a handheld electric mixer and a large bowl), beat together the butter and sugar at medium speed until fluffy, 1 to 2 minutes. Add the yogurt, egg yolks, and vanilla and beat to fully combine. The mixture might appear lumpy at this stage, but that is okay. Add the flour and semolina mixture in two stages, beating at low speed and scraping down the sides of the bowl as necessary, until a thick batter forms. If using a stand mixer, transfer the batter to a clean bowl, wash and thoroughly dry the mixer bowl, and switch to the whisk attachment. If using a handheld mixer, switch to the whisk attachments if you have them, or wash and thoroughly dry the beaters.

5. Add the egg whites to the clean mixer bowl or another large bowl and beat at high speed until they hold firm peaks, 1 to 2 minutes. Add a scoop of the beaten egg whites to the batter and gently fold in with a silicone spatula, then fold in the remaining egg whites until no white streaks remain.

6. Transfer the batter to the loaf pan and smooth the top. Bake until the cake is golden and a tester inserted in the center comes out clean, 50 to 55 minutes.

7. Remove the cake from the oven and set the loaf pan on a wire rack. Using a very thin cake tester or skewer, poke holes across the entire surface of the cake. Over the course of several minutes, slowly and evenly ladle the cooled syrup all over the hot cake, allowing it to soak in as you go. Let the cake cool completely (and the syrup to fully penetrate the cake) before slicing and serving.

8. Store any leftovers, covered, at room temperature for up to 3 days.

TRIPLE-POMEGRANATE CAKE

Makes one 9-inch (23 cm) round cake

Pomegranates hold deep symbolic resonance in Jewish tradition. The ruby fruit's seeds evoke abundance and fertility, and they are also said to number the 613 mitzvot (commandments) outlined in the Torah. They are also, of course, stunningly beautiful and delicious. This cake is not a traditional Jewish recipe, but it offers a fitting celebration of pomegranate with a triple dose of the fruit: pomegranate juice, syrupy pomegranate molasses, and a juicy pop of pomegranate seeds on top. Serve it for Rosh Hashanah, Sukkot, or any autumn or early winter Shabbat dinner, when pomegranates are in peak season.

FOR THE CAKE

- 1½ cups (210 g) all-purpose flour
- 1 tablespoon cornstarch
- ½ teaspoon baking powder
- ½ teaspoon baking soda
- ¼ teaspoon kosher salt
- ½ cup (120 ml) neutral vegetable oil
- 1 cup (200 g) granulated sugar
- 2 large eggs
- 2 tablespoons pomegranate molasses
- 1 teaspoon vanilla extract
- ⅓ cup (80 ml) pomegranate juice

FOR THE GLAZE AND TOPPING

- 1½ cups (180 g) confectioners' sugar, sifted
- 2 tablespoons pomegranate juice, plus more if needed
- Pomegranate seeds

1. Make the cake: Preheat the oven to 350°F (180°C). Grease a 9-inch (23 cm) round springform pan or cake pan.
2. Whisk together the flour, cornstarch, baking powder, baking soda, and salt in a medium bowl.
3. Whisk together the oil, sugar, eggs, pomegranate molasses, and vanilla in a large bowl until smooth. Stir half of the flour mixture into the oil mixture, followed by the pomegranate juice, and then the remaining flour mixture.
4. Pour the batter into the pan and smooth the top.
5. Bake the cake until a tester inserted into the center comes out clean, 25 to 30 minutes. Remove from the oven and transfer the pan to a wire rack to cool for 30 minutes, then gently unmold the cake and place it directly on the rack to cool completely.
6. When the cake is fully cooled, make the glaze: Whisk together the confectioners' sugar and pomegranate juice in a medium bowl until a thick but pourable glaze forms. If the glaze is too thick, whisk in more pomegranate juice, 1 teaspoon at a time, until the desired consistency is reached.
7. Pour and spread the glaze evenly over the cake, allowing it to drip down the sides. Sprinkle the top of the cake with pomegranate seeds and let the cake sit until the glaze sets, about 20 minutes, before serving. Store any leftovers, covered, in the fridge for up to 5 days.

CHOCOLATE-FROSTED POPPY SEED CAKE

Makes one 9-inch (23 cm) round cake

Leetal Arazi is half of the team, with her husband, Ron, behind the Brooklyn-based Middle Eastern Foods company NY Shuk. But before she started making some of the best harissa and matbucha on the planet, she was a professional pastry chef in Israel (she is also the granddaughter of a Czechoslovakian Jewish baker). In other words, she knows a top-tier cake when she tastes one. Leetal told me her mom's chocolate-frosted poppy seed cake—a light, fluffy chiffon packed with nutty poppy seeds and frosted with a rich chocolate ganache—was her family's ultimate Shabbat cake. "I would see my mom baking it on Friday afternoon, and we would eat it all weekend long," she said.

I first tasted the cake many years ago when my husband, Yoshie, and I attended a supper club in Brooklyn hosted by Ron and Leetal. After a decadent meal, Leetal surprised me by bringing out the cake—festooned with tall red candles—for my birthday. It was an incredibly kind gesture, especially considering we had only met a few times before. After a piece (or, rather, two pieces) of Leetal's family's magical cake, I was a lifelong fan. I am honored and grateful that she shared the recipe with me.

FOR THE CHOCOLATE FROSTING

1 cup (180 g) bittersweet or semisweet chocolate chips

⅔ cup (160 ml) heavy cream or coconut cream

1. Make the frosting: Place the chips in a medium bowl. Heat the heavy cream in a small saucepan over medium heat until steaming but just shy of boiling, 2 to 3 minutes.

2. Pour the hot cream over the chocolate chips, cover the bowl, and let stand for 5 minutes, then whisk the mixture into a smooth ganache. Let the ganache cool completely, about 2 hours.

3. Make the cake: Working in batches if necessary, pour the poppy seeds into a spice grinder or coffee grinder and pulse until finely ground. The poppy seeds should be fluffy and have the texture of slightly damp soil. Transfer the ground poppy seeds to a bowl, stir in the warmed milk, and let sit until some of the milk has been absorbed, about 30 minutes.

4. Preheat the oven to 350°F (180°C). Line the bottom of a 9-inch (23 cm) round springform cake pan with a round of parchment.

5. Whisk together the flour, baking powder, and salt in a bowl; set aside.

6. In the bowl of a stand mixer fitted with the paddle attachment (or using a handheld mixer and a large bowl), beat the egg yolks, ¾ cup (150 g) of the granulated sugar, the oil, and lemon zest together at medium speed until fully combined, 1 to 2 minutes. Beat in half of the poppy seed–milk

NOTE: For a more celebratory (rather than casual) presentation, double the amount of chocolate ganache and pipe it onto the cake as desired.

FOR THE CAKE

¾ cup (105 g) poppy seeds

1 cup (240 ml) milk or nondairy milk, slightly warmed (see Note)

1½ cups (210 grams) all-purpose flour

1 tablespoon baking powder

⅛ teaspoon kosher salt

5 large eggs, separated, at room temperature

1¼ cups (250 g) granulated sugar, divided

½ cup (120 ml) neutral vegetable oil

1½ packed teaspoons grated lemon zest

mixture, followed by half the flour mixture, beating at low speed and scraping down the sides of the bowl as necessary. Repeat with the remaining milk mixture and flour mixture.

7. If using a stand mixer, transfer the batter to a clean bowl, wash and thoroughly dry the mixer bowl, and switch to the whisk attachment. If using a handheld mixer, switch to the whisk attachments if you have them, or wash and throughly dry the beaters.

8. Add the egg whites to the clean mixer bowl or another large bowl and beat at medium-high speed, slowly adding the remaining ½ cup (100 g) sugar, until firm, glossy peaks form, about 2 minutes. Add the egg whites to the poppy seed batter and gently fold everything together with a silicone spatula until no white streaks remain.

9. Pour the batter into the prepared cake pan, smooth the top, and bake until the cake is golden and a tester inserted into the center comes out clean, 45 to 55 minutes. If the top of the cake is browning too quickly toward the end of baking, loosely tent it with foil. Remove the cake from the oven and set the cake pan on a wire rack to cool completely. Then carefully unmold the cake and transfer it to a serving plate.

10. Frost the cake: Use a handheld electric mixer to beat the cooled ganache at high speed until light and fluffy, 2 to 4 minutes. If the top of the cake is domed, use a serrated knife to gently slice off the dome. Dollop the frosting onto the top of the cooled cake and evenly spread and swoop it over the top.

11. Any leftovers can be stored, covered, at room temperature for up to 3 days or in the refrigerator for up to 1 week.

NOTE: Warm the milk for the cake in a microwave or on the stovetop until it is just barely steaming, not boiling, 30 to 45 seconds.

HONEY CAKE WITH APPLE BUTTER FROSTING

Makes one 8-inch (20 cm) round cake

For many Ashkenazi families, honey cake is a nonnegotiable part of the Rosh Hashanah meal. Like eating apples dipped in honey, it is an edible symbol of hope for a sweet year ahead. (Some families also break the fast on Yom Kippur with honey cake.) The cake's Yiddish name, *lekach*, comes from the German word *lecke*, which means "lick" and likely refers to the sticky honey mixed into the batter. But honey cake might just as well be referred to as spice cake, since it usually contains an array of warming spices. This moist and fluffy take on honey cake is similar to most American-Jewish honey cakes in that I sweeten the batter with both honey and brown sugar and pour in strong brewed coffee to add a slightly bitter counterpoint to the sweetness. But the thick sweet-tart layer of apple butter glaze brings a level of sophistication that will make the cake the star of the dessert table.

FOR THE CAKE

1⅓ cups (185) all-purpose flour
½ teaspoon baking powder
½ teaspoon baking soda
1½ teaspoons ground cinnamon
1 teaspoon ground ginger
½ teaspoon ground allspice
¼ teaspoon ground nutmeg
¼ teaspoon kosher salt
⅓ cup (80 ml) neutral vegetable oil
½ cup (120 ml) mild honey
½ packed cup (100 g) light brown sugar
½ cup (120 ml) brewed coffee (decaf or regular), slightly cooled
1 large egg
1 teaspoon pure vanilla extract

1. Make the cake: Preheat the oven to 350°F (180°C). Grease an 8-inch (20 cm) round springform pan or cake pan.
2. Whisk together the flour, baking powder, baking soda, cinnamon, ginger, allspice, nutmeg, and salt in a medium bowl.
3. Whisk together the oil, honey, brown sugar, coffee, egg, and vanilla in a large bowl until smooth. Add the flour mixture and stir to thoroughly combine. Pour the batter into the pan and smooth the top.
4. Bake the cake until a tester inserted into the center comes out clean, 30 to 35 minutes. Remove from the oven and transfer the pan to a wire rack to cool for 30 minutes, then gently unmold the cake and place on the rack to cool completely.
5. When the cake is fully cooled, make the frosting: Combine the butter, brown sugar, apple butter, milk, and salt in a small saucepan, bring to a boil over medium heat, and let bubble vigorously for 1 minute. Remove from the heat and immediately whisk in the confectioners' sugar and cinnamon.
6. Drizzle and spread the frosting evenly over the cake. If desired, while the frosting is still warm, sprinkle the top of the cake with chopped pecans. Let the cake sit until the frosting sets, about 10 minutes, before serving.
7. Store any leftovers in an airtight container in the fridge for up to 5 days.

FOR THE APPLE BUTTER FROSTING

3 tablespoons unsalted butter or vegan butter

½ packed cup (100 g) light brown sugar

¼ cup (70 g) apple butter

1 tablespoon milk or nondairy milk

⅛ teaspoon kosher salt

1½ cups (180 g) confectioners' sugar, sifted

½ teaspoon ground cinnamon

Chopped toasted pecans for sprinkling (optional)

NOTE: This amount of batter will also make 12 cupcakes. Bake them until a cake tester inserted into the center of a cupcake comes out clean, 18 to 20 minutes.

THE JEWISH AMERICAN BAKERY

It is hard to overstate the importance of the Jewish bakery to American Jewish communities. For several generations, starting in the early twentieth century and continuing for several decades after World War II, the bakery—along with the kosher butcher, the greengrocer, and the fishmonger—was the heart center of a Jewish community's cultural life. The synagogue was for worship and ritual, of course. But at the bakery, as customers jockeyed for a freshly made chiffon cake or a loaf of pumpernickel, gossip was traded, new engagements were celebrated, deaths were mourned, and a strong communal fabric was knit together.

In *Inside the Jewish Bakery: Recipes and Memories from the Golden Age of Jewish Baking*, co-author Stanley Ginsberg recalls his weekly bakery expeditions with his father in 1950s and '60s Brooklyn:

"The bakery was a few doors down and there was always a line on Sunday mornings, mostly men, often with their sons. In the winter especially, a blast of fragrant hot air—an intoxicating bouquet of vanilla, almonds, sugar, chocolate, and citrus—welcomed us in. After what seemed like hours, our dads would order bagels, bialys, onion rolls, and maybe a piece of wonder cake or Russian coffee cake. Then we'd walk home, hand in hand, father and sons."

In the post–World War II era, as members of Jewish communities climbed the social ladder and wartime rationing of butter and sugar eased, Jewish bakeries in New York City and beyond became symbols of progress. Their display cases glistened with towering frosted cakes, oversized black-and-white cookies, pastries decorated with delicate glacé cherries—treats that would have been unthinkable to impoverished shtetl dwellers in Eastern Europe.

But as the years went by, many Jewish bakeries, influenced by the country's fixation with convenience foods, started taking shortcuts—relying on mixes, premade frostings, hydrogenated oils, and artificial colors and flavors. For me, as a child of the 1980s and '90s, my experience of the Jewish bakery was vastly different from Ginsberg's. The hamantaschen, rugelach, and marble cakes my synagogue would order for holidays were often disappointing—dry, overly sweet, and just generally ersatz.

In the final decades of the twentieth century, as demand for traditional Jewish baked goods slowed and supermarkets began to take the place of independent food shops, many of the bakeries that had once anchored communities closed. So, too, closed a chapter of American-Jewish life. But in recent years, a new generation of Jewishly inspired bakeries has begun to appear—places like Elbow Bread in New York City, Loquat Bakery in San Francisco (see page 159), Oak Bakeshop in Providence, Rhode Island (see page 101), and Essen Bakery in Philadelphia (see page 220). Inspired by the recipes of the past but with an eye on the future, these bakeries are reviving the original spirit of the Jewish American bakery.

SPICED CHIFFON CAKE WITH BROWN SUGAR FROSTING

Makes one 10-inch (25 cm) tube cake

Chiffon cakes are a relatively recent addition to the American cake canon. Invented in the late 1920s by an insurance salesman-turned-baking obsessive fittingly named Harry Baker, the moist but featherlight confection became an almost instant sensation. Baker kept his recipe secret for years, finally selling it to General Mills (the parent company of Betty Crocker) in 1947. From there, the chiffon cake's prominence on American dessert tables only grew. Baker's original recipe called for vegetable oil (or "salad oil," as it was often referred to in the mid- twentieth century) rather than butter—a fact that endeared the cake to American Jews, who could serve it after a meat meal without violating the kosher laws. It didn't hurt that chiffon cakes got their airy lightness from whipped egg whites, which gave them a familiar texture similar to that of Passover sponge cakes.

If you flip through a vintage synagogue cookbook's dessert chapter, chances are high you will find some variation (or several) on chiffon cake. This particular chiffon, which comes draped in a luscious brown sugar glaze, has become the star of my Sukkot dessert repertoire. It has the elegance and lofty stature to hold court on a festive table, as well as autumnal spices that make it fitting for a holiday associated with the harvest season.

FOR THE CAKE

1½ cups (210 g) all-purpose flour, sifted

2 teaspoons ground cinnamon

1 teaspoon ground ginger

½ teaspoon ground cloves

¼ teaspoon ground nutmeg

½ teaspoon kosher salt

7 large eggs, separated, at room temperature

1 cup (200 g) granulated sugar

⅓ packed cup (65 g) light brown sugar

½ cup (120 ml) neutral vegetable oil

1½ teaspoons vanilla extract

1 packed teaspoon grated orange zest

½ teaspoon cream of tartar

1. Make the cake: Preheat the oven to 350°F (180°C).
2. Whisk together the flour, cinnamon, ginger, cloves, nutmeg, and salt in a small bowl and set aside.
3. Place the egg yolks in the bowl of a stand mixer fitted with the paddle attachment, or use a handheld electric mixer and a large bowl. Add the granulated sugar and brown sugar and beat at medium speed until the mixture is pale and slightly thickened, about 1 minute. Add the vegetable oil, vanilla, and orange zest and beat until incorporated.
4. Turn the mixer speed down to low and beat in the flour mixture in two stages, scraping down the bowl as necessary. (The batter will be quite thick.) If using a stand mixer, transfer the batter to a clean bowl, wash and thoroughly dry the mixer bowl, and switch to the whisk attachment. If using a handheld mixer, switch to the whisk attachments if you have them or thoroughly wash and dry the beaters.

recipe continues

FOR THE GLAZE

3 tablespoons unsalted butter or vegan butter

½ packed cup (100 g) light brown sugar

3 tablespoons milk or nondairy milk

⅛ teaspoon kosher salt

1 cup (120 g) confectioners' sugar, sifted

1 teaspoon ground cinnamon

5. Combine the egg whites and cream of tartar in the clean mixer bowl or another large bowl and and whip at medium-high speed until glossy peaks form, about 2 minutes. Add a generous dollop of the whipped egg whites to the batter and fold it in to help loosen the batter. Then gently fold in the remaining egg whites until the batter is light and airy, with no remaining white streaks.

6. Scrape the batter into an ungreased 10-inch (25-cm) tube pan and smooth it gently with a spatula. Bake until the cake is golden brown and the top springs back when gently pressed, 45 to 50 minutes. Remove the cake from the oven and invert the pan over a cooling rack; allow the cake to fully cool upside down, about 2 hours.

7. To unmold the cake, gently run a sharp knife around the sides of the pan and the center tube. Gently remove the cake and transfer to a serving platter.

8. Make the glaze: Combine the butter, brown sugar, milk, and salt in a small saucepan, bring to a boil over medium heat, and let bubble vigorously for 1 minute, then remove from the heat and immediately whisk in the confectioners' sugar and cinnamon.

9. Drizzle the glaze evenly over the top of the cake, letting it run down the sides. (If there are any little clumps of confectioners' sugar that didn't dissolve, press the mixture through a fine-mesh sieve before drizzling it over the cake.) Work quickly, as the glaze will set as it cools. Then let the glaze set before serving.

10. Store any leftovers, covered, in the fridge, for up to 3 days. (The unglazed cake can be stored, well wrapped, in the freezer for up to 3 months. Thaw at room temperature for about 2 hours and then proceed with the glazing.)

NOTE: Many chiffon cake recipes call for cake flour, but I have found that sifted all-purpose flour works as well, avoiding the necessity of keeping a second kind of flour on hand.

CHAI-SPICED CHEESECAKE

Makes one 9-inch (23 cm) round cake

In the mid-1800s, German Jewish immigrants brought recipes for kaesekuchen—cakes enriched with a fresh, mild curd cheese—with them to America. A generation later, a New York State dairyman named William Lawrence accidentally doubled the amount of cream in a batch of French-style Neufchâtel cheese he was making and invented cream cheese in the process. Pleased with his decadent creation, he decided to keep making it, and soon cream cheese production took off, changing the American dairy landscape—and American Jewish cheesecake recipes—forever.

My spin on cheesecake employs warming spices—cinnamon, cardamom, ginger, allspice, and nutmeg—to evoke a cup of Indian chai, and maple syrup–sweetened whipped cream to send things over the top. Cheesecake is traditionally served by Ashkenazi Jews on Shavuot, when it is customary to eat dairy foods (see page 21). But you can serve it whenever you want to truly wow your dinner guests.

FOR THE CRUST

1½ cups (165 g) graham cracker crumbs (from about 10 full sheets) (see Note)

3 tablespoons light brown sugar

6 tablespoons (¾ stick / 85 g) unsalted butter, melted

1 teaspoon ground cinnamon

⅛ teaspoon kosher salt

FOR THE FILLING

24 ounces (680 g) cream cheese, softened

½ cup (120 g) sour cream

1 cup (200 g) granulated sugar

2 large eggs

1 teaspoon vanilla extract or vanilla bean paste

1½ teaspoons ground cinnamon

½ teaspoon ground cardamom

½ teaspoon ground ginger

½ teaspoon ground allspice

⅛ teaspoon ground nutmeg

¼ teaspoon kosher salt

1. Preheat the oven to 350°F (180°C). Line the bottom of a 9-inch (23 cm) round springform pan or cake pan with a circle of parchment.

2. Make the crust: Stir together the graham cracker crumbs, brown sugar, melted butter, cinnamon, and salt in a bowl until fully combined. Transfer the crumb mixture to the pan and press over the bottom and partway up the sides of the pan. Place the crust in the freezer while you make the filling.

3. In the bowl of a stand mixer fitted with the paddle attachment (or using a handheld electric mixer and a large bowl), beat the cream cheese at medium speed until creamy. Add the sour cream, sugar, eggs, vanilla, cinnamon, cardamom, ginger, allspice, nutmeg, and salt and continue beating, scraping down the sides of the bowl as necessary, until fully combined.

4. Pour the filling into the crust and smooth the top. Bake until the cake is set around the edges with a slightly jiggly center, 40 to 45 minutes. Set the pan on a wire rack and let the cheesecake fully cool, then cover and refrigerate for at least 4 hours, and up to overnight.

recipe continues

FOR THE TOPPING

¾ cup (180 ml) heavy whipping cream

1 to 2 tablespoons maple syrup or confectioners' sugar

Ground cinnamon for dusting

5. Just before serving, make the topping: Using a whisk or a handheld electric mixer and a medium bowl, beat the whipping cream until soft peaks form. Add 1 tablespoon of the maple syrup and beat until stiff peaks form. Taste and add up to 1 additional tablespoon of maple syrup, if desired.

6. Dollop as much of the of whipped cream onto the cheesecake as you like (serve any leftover whipped cream in a bowl alongside) and use a silicone spatula to spread it evenly over the top. Using a fine-mesh sieve, lightly dust the top of the cheesecake with cinnamon.

7. If using a springform pan, carefully unmold the cake and transfer it to a serving plate to slice. Or serve directly from the cake pan. Any leftovers can be stored in an airtight container in the fridge for up to 5 days.

NOTE: Pulse the graham crackers in a food processor until they are mostly finely ground, with a few larger pieces. You can use either honey or cinnamon graham crackers.

DATE-CARROT CAKE WITH ORANGE BLOSSOM FROSTING

Makes one 9 × 13-inch (23 × 33 cm) cake

I have always been firmly on team carrot cake. The ultimate mid-twentieth century American snacking cake is a squishy, ultramoist vehicle for eating cream cheese frosting—what's not to love? Here I've updated a classic carrot cake recipe with a Middle Eastern flavor profile. I swapped the usual raisins for jammy bits of chopped dates and lifted up the sweet-tangy frosting with orange blossom water and grated orange zest. The result is truly extraordinary. As one volunteer recipe tester put it, "It tasted even better than I imagined!" The cake's flavors continue to develop as it rests, so if possible, bake it a day before serving.

FOR THE CAKE

1¾ cups (245 g) all-purpose flour
2½ teaspoons ground cinnamon
½ teaspoon ground ginger
¼ teaspoon ground cloves
1½ teaspoons baking powder
½ teaspoon baking soda
¾ teaspoon kosher salt
1 cup (125 g) pitted dates, chopped
¾ cup (180 ml) sunflower oil or other neutral vegetable oil
1½ cups (300 g) granulated sugar
3 large eggs
1 teaspoon vanilla extract
¾ pound (340 g) carrots (3 to 4 large carrots), peeled and grated on the large holes of a box grater (see Note)

FOR THE FROSTING

8 ounces (227 g) cream cheese or nondairy cream cheese, softened
8 tablespoons (1 stick / 113 g) unsalted butter or vegan butter, softened
2½ cups (300 g) confectioners' sugar, sifted
¼ teaspoon kosher salt
1½ teaspoons orange blossom water
Grated zest of 1 large orange

1. Make the cake: Preheat the oven to 350°F (180°C). Grease a 9 × 13-inch (23 × 33 cm) baking dish.
2. Whisk together the flour, cinnamon, ginger, cloves, baking powder, baking soda, salt, and chopped dates in a medium bowl.
3. Whisk together the oil, sugar, eggs, and vanilla in a large bowl until smooth. Add the dry ingredients and stir together to combine, then fold in the grated carrots.
4. Pour the batter into the prepared baking dish and smooth the top. Bake until the cake is golden and a tester inserted into the center comes out clean, 35 to 45 minutes. Remove from the oven and set the baking dish on a wire rack to cool completely.
5. Make the frosting: In the bowl of a stand mixer fitted with the paddle attachment (or using a handheld electric mixer and a large bowl), beat the cream cheese and butter together at medium speed until smooth and creamy, 1 to 2 minutes. Add the confectioners' sugar, salt, orange blossom water, and orange zest and beat until creamy.
6. Dollop the frosting onto the top of the cake and use an offset spatula or butter knife to spread and swoop it evenly over the cake. If desired, place the cake in the fridge for 30 minutes to 1 hour before serving to allow the frosting to set a bit.
7. Serve the cake slightly chilled or at room temperature. Store any leftovers, covered, in the fridge for up to 5 days.

NOTE: Save time by shredding the peeled carrots in a food processor fitted with the shredding blade.

FLOURLESS FUDGE CAKE WITH APRICOT SAUCE

Makes one 8-inch (20 cm) round cake

Austria is one of Europe's most esteemed pastry capitals, with a grand tradition of elaborate cakes and confections to its name. The best known of these pastries is the Sachertorte—a ganache-coated chocolate cake that is layered with apricot jam. Less well known is the fact that the cake was developed in the 1800s by a sixteen-year-old Jewish pastry chef named Franz Sacher. Variations of the cake are still served in pastry shops and other establishments across Vienna today, most notably at Hotel Sacher, which was founded by Franz's son, Eduard. Inspired by Sacher's ingenuity, I decided to give my favorite Passover-friendly flourless chocolate cake recipe "the Sachertorte treatment." Today many flourless chocolate cakes are served with a puddle of raspberry coulis, but here, an apricot sauce offers the same sweet-tart counterpoint to the chocolate while recalling the long-ago pastry genius of an Austrian Jewish teenager.

FOR THE CAKE

- 12 ounces (340 g) semisweet chocolate chips (about 2 cups)
- ¾ cup (150 g) granulated sugar
- ½ cup (120 ml) neutral vegetable oil
- ½ teaspoon kosher salt
- 1½ teaspoons vanilla extract
- 5 large eggs, separated, at room temperature
- ¼ cup (20 g) unsweetened cocoa powder, sifted

FOR THE SAUCE

- ¾ cup (210 g) apricot jam
- 1 tablespoon granulated sugar
- 3 tablespoons water
- 1½ teaspoons fresh lemon juice
- Confectioners' sugar for dusting (optional)

1. Make the cake: Preheat the oven to 350°F (180°C). Lightly grease an 8-inch (20 cm) round cake pan and line the bottom with a round of parchment paper.

2. Melt the chocolate chips in a heatproof bowl set over a saucepan of simmering water, stirring often. (Or melt the chocolate in a large microwave-safe bowl, microwaving it for 20-second intervals and stirring after each.) Once the chocolate is melted, remove from the heat and immediately whisk in the sugar, oil, salt, and vanilla.

3. Add the egg yolks and cocoa powder and stir until fully combined. The batter may appear thick and grainy at this stage, that's okay.

4. Add the egg whites to the bowl of a stand mixer fitted with the whisk attachment. Or use a handheld electric mixer and a large bowl. Beat at high speed until the egg whites hold firm peaks, 1 to 2 minutes. Add a generous scoop of the beaten egg whites to the batter and gently fold in with a silicone spatula, then fold in the remaining egg whites.

5. Transfer the batter to the prepared pan and smooth the top. Bake until a tester inserted in the center of the cake comes out clean or has a few moist crumbs sticking to it, 40 to 50 minutes. (Be careful not to overbake.) Remove the pan from the oven and set the cake on a wire rack to cool completely.

NOTE: You can also bake this cake in a 9-inch (23 cm) round cake pan, adjusting the bake time to 30 to 35 minutes.

6. Meanwhile, make the sauce: Combine the apricot jam, sugar, water, and lemon juice in a small saucepan and bring to a low bubble over medium heat, stirring often to dissolve the sugar, then turn the heat down to medium-low and cook, stirring occasionally, until glossy, 3 to 5 minutes. Remove from the heat and set aside to cool a bit.
7. If desired, just before serving, use a fine-mesh sieve to dust the top of the cake with confectioners' sugar. Spread a swoosh of the sauce on each plate and set a slice of cake over it. Store any leftover cake and sauce in airtight containers in the fridge, for up to 5 days.

FLOURLESS CHOCOLATE ESPRESSO CAKE

Makes one 9-inch (23 cm) round cake

Loquat Bakery has made a name for itself in San Francisco with its focus on pastries and sweets inspired by the Jewish diaspora. The bakery's menu mirrors co-owner Tal Mor's own mixed Iraqi, Israeli, and Ukrainian heritage filtered through the lens of his California upbringing. This cake, a variation of the version served at Loquat, began with a flourless chocolate cake Mor's mother always baked for Passover. "Eating it evokes such a deep sense of Jewishness and home for me," he says. Mor brought the recipe to Loquat's pastry chef, Kristina Costa, who maintained all the core elements while adding extra flourishes like an espresso soaking syrup and an orange-scented chocolate ganache. "Kristina's adaptation of it is on another level," Mor says. Decorated with edible flowers, candied orange peel, and chocolate-covered espresso beans, it makes a sophisticated dessert for the Passover seder.

FOR THE ESPRESSO SYRUP

3 tablespoons granulated sugar

3 tablespoons water

3 tablespoons espresso or very strong brewed coffee (regular or decaf)

FOR THE CAKE

2 cups (200 g) almond flour

2 tablespoons unsweetened cocoa powder

¼ teaspoon kosher salt

4 large eggs

½ cup (100 g) granulated sugar

1 tablespoon extra-virgin olive oil

1 tablespoon fresh lemon juice

1 teaspoon instant espresso powder (regular or decaf)

3 ounces (85 g) bittersweet baking chocolate, very finely chopped

NOTE: The chocolate in the cake should be very finely chopped so it will incorporate seamlessly into the batter.

1. Make the espresso syrup: Combine the sugar and water in a small saucepan and bring to a boil over medium-high heat, whisking to dissolve the sugar, then lower the heat to medium and cook, whisking often, until the syrup is slightly thickened, 1 to 2 minutes. Remove from the heat, whisk in the espresso, and set aside to cool completely.

2. Make the cake: Preheat the oven to 325°F (160°C). Grease a 9-inch (23 cm) round springform pan.

3. Whisk together the almond flour, cocoa powder, and salt in a medium bowl and set aside.

4. In the bowl of a stand mixer fitted with the whisk attachment (or using a handheld electric mixer and a large bowl), combine the eggs and sugar and beat at high speed until the mixture is light and billowy, 3 to 5 minutes.

5. Stir together the olive oil, lemon juice, and espresso powder in a small bowl and then, with the mixer running, slowly stream into the egg and sugar mixture. Add the almond flour mixture and beat on low speed, scraping down the sides of the bowl as needed, until just combined. Fold in the finely chopped chocolate with a silicone spatula, being careful to deflate the batter as little as possible.

recipe continues

FOR THE GANACHE AND OPTIONAL DECORATION

4 ounces (113 g) bittersweet baking chocolate, chopped

1 tablespoon unsalted butter or vegan butter

½ packed teaspoon grated orange zest

⅛ teaspoon kosher salt

½ cup (120 ml) heavy cream or coconut cream

Edible flowers, candied orange peel, and/or chocolate-covered espresso beans for decorating (optional)

6. Scrape the batter into the pan and smooth the top. Bake the cake until a tester inserted into the center comes out clean, 25 to 28 minutes. Remove from the oven and set the pan on a wire rack. Gently pour and brush the cooled syrup all over the top of the hot cake, then let cool completely.

7. Make the ganache: Combine the chopped chocolate, butter, orange zest, and salt in a medium bowl. Heat the cream in a small saucepan set over medium heat until steaming but just shy of boiling.

8. Pour the hot cream over the chocolate, cover the bowl, and let stand for 5 minutes, then whisk the mixture together until the chocolate is fully melted and the ganache is completely smooth. Let cool, then refrigerate, covered, until thickened, about 2 hours.

9. Frost and decorate the cake: Remove the chilled ganache from the fridge and use a handheld electric mixer to beat it at high speed until light and fluffy, about 2 minutes. Dollop the ganache onto the top of the cooled cake and spread and swoop it evenly over the top. If desired, decorate the cake with edible flowers, chocolate-covered espresso beans, and/or candied orange peel.

10. Any leftovers can be stored in an airtight container at room temperature for up to 3 days or in the refrigerator for up to 1 week.

CHOCOLATE LAYER CAKE WITH ADVIEH BUTTERCREAM

Makes one 8-inch (20 cm) round layer cake

There is nothing traditionally Jewish about this cake recipe, but it is deeply personal—the cake my mom made for every birthday celebration when I was growing up, and the one I now make for, and often with, my kids. It's a fabulously old-fashioned recipe that can be made in one bowl, and it amplifies the chocolate flavor with brewed coffee. (Yes, decaf works fine.) The cake has a moist and delicate crumb that is at once fluffy and rich. You can ice the cake with any frosting you prefer—my mom used a standard buttercream, but I like to mix things up with rose water, cinnamon, and cardamom, which give the frosting a Persian Jewish flavor profile. (Advieh is a Persian spice blend that combines this beguiling trio of spices.) Serve the cake as is, or, for a celebration, decorate it with natural sprinkles, dried rosebuds, and birthday candles.

FOR THE CAKE

2 cups (280 g) all-purpose flour or gluten-free all-purpose flour, sifted

1½ cups (300 g) granulated sugar

¾ cup (60 g) unsweetened cocoa powder, sifted

1½ teaspoons baking soda

1 teaspoon baking powder

¾ teaspoon kosher salt

1 cup (240 ml) neutral vegetable oil

1 cup (240 ml) milk or nondairy milk

1 cup (240 ml) brewed coffee (decaf or regular), slightly cooled

2 large eggs, lightly beaten

FOR THE ADVIEH BUTTERCREAM

20 tablespoons (2½ sticks / 284 g) unsalted butter or vegan butter, softened

5½ cups (660 g) confectioners' sugar, sifted, plus more if needed

3 tablespoons milk or nondairy milk, plus more if needed

1 teaspoon vanilla extract

½ teaspoon rose water

1¼ teaspoons ground cinnamon

½ teaspoon ground cardamom

A few drops of natural red or pink food coloring

1. Make the cake: Preheat the oven to 350°F (180°C). Line the bottoms of two 8-inch (20 cm) round cake pans with circles of parchment.

2. Whisk together the flour, sugar, cocoa powder, baking soda, baking powder, and salt in a large bowl. Add the oil, milk, coffee, and eggs and mix with a sturdy spoon to combine. The batter will be quite thin and loose.

3. Divide the batter evenly between the two cake pans. Bake until the tops of the cakes feel springy when gently pressed and a cake tester comes out clean, 30 to 35 minutes. Set the pans on a wire rack to cool completely.

4. Make the buttercream: In the bowl of a stand mixer fitted with the paddle attachment (or using a handheld mixer and a large bowl), beat the butter at medium speed until creamy, 1 to 2 minutes. Add the confectioners' sugar, milk, vanilla, rose water, cinnamon, cardamom, and food coloring and beat, starting on low speed and working up to medium, until fluffy. If the buttercream is too thick to spread, beat in additional milk, about 1 teaspoon at a time, until the desired consistency is reached. If it is too loose, beat in more confectioners' sugar, 1 tablespoon at a time.

recipe continues

NOTE: The cake layers are easiest to frost when they are cold from the fridge. I like to bake the cake the night before serving. I let the layers fully cool, then wrap them well and refrigerate until the next day.

5. Carefully remove the cooled cakes from the cake pans, remove and discard the parchment paper, and set the cakes on a cutting board. Using a serrated knife, slice off the domed top of each layer to create a flat surface. Place one layer on a serving plate and dollop with a generous scoop of the buttercream. Use an offset spatula or butter knife to spread the buttercream evenly across the top. (If necessary, dip the spatula or knife in hot water and wipe dry to help facilitate spreading.)

6. Place the second layer on top of the first one and dollop the remaining buttercream on top. Use the spatula or knife to spread the buttercream across the top and down the sides of the cake.

7. Serve slightly chilled or at room temperature. Store any leftovers, covered, in the fridge for up to 5 days or, well wrapped, in the freezer for up to 6 months.

BABKA, DOUGHNUTS & PASTRIES

HOW BABKA EVOLVED FROM HUMBLE PASTRY TO JEWISH FOOD ICON

Babka was not a big part of my childhood. But when the Ashkenazi cake-bread hybrid did show up on a holiday table or in the synagogue social hall after Shabbat morning services, it was invariably the same: a bit dry, parve (made with oil, not butter), densely swirled with chocolate or cinnamon paste, and coated with a thick layer of streusel. That iteration of babka still exists today, particularly in old-school kosher bakeries. But over the past fifteen years, a new babka has emerged that is almost unrecognizable as the same pastry.

Today's babka has had nothing short of a glow-up. The yeasted dough is more likely to be enriched with butter, rather than oil, giving it a tender, brioche-like crumb. Instead of streusel, the babka comes painted with a sugar syrup. And bakers have gotten wildly creative with fillings, rolling up everything from spiced pumpkin puree to dulce de leche (see the Chocolate Turtle Babka recipe on page 174) inside.

So what happened? The story begins in Poland in the nineteenth century, when Jewish home cooks would roll a mixture of jam, cinnamon, and chopped nuts or raisins into leftover challah dough, and bake it alongside the braided Sabbath loaves. (The word *babka* translates as "little grandmother," which is fitting, since it was often the family matriarch doing the baking.) When Polish Jewish immigrants settled in America, they continued to bake babka as a Shabbat morning treat in their new home. The addition of chocolate to the filling was a later, though probably inevitable, innovation.

By the mid-twentieth century, babka had spread beyond America's Polish Jewish community as it evolved from an almost exclusively home-baked pastry to one that could be readily found in American Jewish bakery cases. A 1994 episode of Seinfeld called "The Dinner Party," where Jerry and Elaine tussle with other customers over their local bakery's last chocolate babka, further expanded babka's profile from niche to national. But it wasn't until the 2010s that babka was transformed from a humble loaf into the Jewish pastry icon that it is today.

I credit three major influences for today's babka renaissance. The first is Yotam Ottolenghi, the Le Cordon Bleu–trained Israeli-born chef who, along with Palestinian chef Sami Tamimi, published the hugely influential *Jerusalem: A Cookbook* in 2012. The book included a recipe for Chocolate Krantz Cake (another name for babka in Israel), and it became an immediate sensation—both in the food media and in home kitchens.

Ottolenghi and Tamimi's babka seemed and tasted at once familiar and entirely new to American bakers. It was unapologetically buttery, for starters. And the surface was burnished and glossy, thanks to the coat of sugar syrup—an unmistakably Middle Eastern touch added to the Eastern European original. (Middle Eastern and Balkan pastries typically get their sweetness not from sugar in the dough, but from a sugar syrup, called *atar* or *shira*, that is brushed or poured over the top after baking.)

The recipe also introduced a different method for rolling and shaping the babka. The dough for old-school babka is filled and rolled up like a jelly roll, and then the filled log is twisted like a wrung-out dish towel to create a fat spiral. Slicing into a loaf sometimes reveals large sections of bready dough without filling.

Jerusalem's babka, however, is rolled up and cut vertically down the middle to expose the ripples of filling inside. Then the two strands are twisted around each other, ensuring that the filling is evenly distributed. It is a subtle tweak, but it makes all the difference.

A year after *Jerusalem* was published, Israeli chef and baker Uri Scheft opened Breads Bakery in New York City's bustling Union Square. Within a year, customers were flocking to the bakery from all over the world to try their chocolate babka. His babka followed the same split-log roll and syrup-brushing techniques, but Scheft took things a step further, rolling the decadent Nutella and chocolate chip filling up in a laminated dough, which gave the babka a flaky croissant-like texture.

If Ottolenghi, Tamimi, and Scheft opened the door to an American babka renaissance, the internet—particularly social media platforms like Instagram—solidified it. Even the humblest loaf of old-school babka is beautiful. But the new-school babkas, with their gooey strata of filling and glistening tops, have a particular star appeal. Other bakeries took a hint from Breads Bakery and began turning out their own modern babkas. And food magazines, bloggers, and recipe developers—both Jewish and not—began creating and sharing a myriad of gorgeous, creatively filled babka loaves with their hungry customers and followers. All of a sudden, there was carrot cake babka, halva babka, pesto and cheese babka, everything bagel babka, babka buns, and a million other varieties. Babka, in other words, had gone viral. And like its fellow Polish Jewish pastry, the bagel, it was on its way to entering the mainstream American baked goods lexicon.

CARAMELIZED WHITE CHOCOLATE–LIME BABKA

Makes two 9 × 5-inch (23 × 12 cm) loaves

Anyone who cooked their way through the 1990s might remember the combination of Key lime and white chocolate. Along with kiwi-strawberry, this duo could be found everywhere from cookies to yogurt cups. In this riff on Ashkenazi babka, the lime zest–scented filling is generously sprinkled with white chocolate chips. The chips melt into the dough as it bakes, leaving behind a sultry, caramel sweetness. And the lime syrup that is painted over the baked loaves doubles their citrusy flavor. Among all the dessert recipes my crew of volunteer testers tried, this babka got some of the most enthusiastic praise. As one tester put it, "The white chocolate chips got all caramelized together with the cashews and lime, and it was amazing." Another one simply said, "Utterly delicious." Like many babka recipes, this yields two loaves. Babka is relatively labor- and time-intensive to prepare, so it makes sense to make two—one to enjoy right away and one to share or freeze for another time.

FOR THE SYRUP

½ cup (120 ml) water

½ cup (100 g) granulated sugar

1 tablespoon fresh lime juice

FOR THE DOUGH

2¼ teaspoons (1 packet) active dry yeast

½ cup (100 g) plus 1 teaspoon granulated sugar

1 cup (240 ml) warm water (about 110°F / 45°C)

4 to 5 cups (560 to 630 g) all-purpose flour, plus more for rolling

1 teaspoon kosher salt

2 large eggs, lightly beaten

8 tablespoons (1 stick / 113 g) unsalted butter or vegan butter, cut into pieces and softened

Neutral vegetable oil for oiling the bowl

NOTE: To make a dairy-free version of this babka, use vegan or parve white chocolate chips.

1. Make the syrup: Combine the water and sugar in a small saucepan and bring to a boil over medium heat, stirring occasionally to dissolve the sugar, then turn the heat down to medium-low and cook until the syrup thickens slightly, 3 to 5 minutes. Remove from the heat, stir in the lime juice, and let cool completely. (*The syrup can be stored, covered, in the fridge for up to 2 weeks.*)

2. Make the dough: Stir together the yeast, 1 teaspoon of the sugar, and the warm water in a large bowl and let sit until bubbling and frothy, 5 to 10 minutes. Meanwhile, whisk together 4 cups (560 g) of the flour, the remaining ½ cup (100 g) sugar, and the salt in another bowl.

3. Stir the eggs into the yeast mixture, then add the flour mixture and stir until a shaggy dough comes together. Turn the dough out onto a work surface (set the bowl aside) and knead well, adding the softened butter pieces a few at a time, and up to 1 cup (140 g) of additional flour as needed, until the dough is supple and slightly sticky, about 10 minutes. The dough may feel greasy or too buttery at times, but just keep kneading and sprinkling additional flour over the top a little at a time until the desired consistency is reached. (The kneading step can also be done in a stand mixer fitted with a dough hook; knead the dough for 5 to 7 minutes.)

4. Rub about 1 teaspoon of vegetable oil over the inside of the large bowl; place the dough in the bowl and turn to coat. Cover the bowl and let sit in a warm place until the dough has nearly doubled in size, 1½ to 2 hours.

recipe continues

FOR THE FILLING

1 cup (140 g) raw or roasted unsalted cashews

8 tablespoons (1 stick / 113 g) unsalted butter or vegan butter, cut into pieces and softened

¾ cup (150 g) granulated sugar

2 packed teaspoons grated lime zest

1 teaspoon ground cinnamon

1 cup (180 g) white chocolate chips

5. Meanwhile, make the filling: Place the cashews, butter, sugar, lime zest, and cinnamon in the bowl of a food processor and pulse, scraping down the sides as necessary, until a smooth paste forms.

6. Line two 9 × 5-inch (23 × 12 cm) loaf pans with parchment paper, allowing the parchment to hang over the two long sides. Gently punch down the dough and turn it out onto a lightly floured surface. Divide it into 2 equal pieces, and keep one piece covered in the bowl while you work with the other.

7. Using a rolling pin, on a lightly floured surface, roll out the dough into a large rectangle that is ¼ inch (6 mm) thick. Spread about half of the filling evenly over the dough, leaving a ¼-inch- (6 mm) wide border around the edges, then sprinkle evenly with about half of the white chocolate chips. Starting at one of the short ends, roll up the dough tightly like a jelly roll. Cut off and discard about ½ inch (12 mm) of dough from each end, then cut the roll lengthwise in half. You will now have 2 long strands of dough, with layers of filling exposed. Twist the strands together, pinch them together at both ends, and carefully place in one of the prepared baking pans. Repeat the process with the remaining dough and filling.

8. Loosely cover the pans with a kitchen towel and let rise until lightly puffed, about 30 minutes. Meanwhile, preheat the oven to 350°F (180°C).

9. Bake the babkas until golden brown and cooked through, 45 to 50 minutes. If the tops are browning too quickly toward the end of baking, loosely tent the pans with aluminum foil.

10. Remove from the oven and immediately brush the top of each babka with three generous layers of the syrup. (You may not use all of the syrup; save the remainder for cocktails or another use.) Let the babkas cool in their pans on a wire rack for 20 minutes, then use the overhanging parchment to gently lift them out of the pans and onto a wire rack to cool slightly. (Or leave them in the loaf pans if you prefer to serve them that way.) Serve warm or at room temperature.

11. Store leftovers, covered, in the fridge for up to 3 days or, well wrapped, in the freezer for up to 6 months. Reheat in the oven or toaster oven before serving.

THE JEWISH HISTORY BEHIND COMMERCIAL YEAST

When home bakers in America want to make babka, doughnuts, or any number of pastries and breads today, they often reach for a packet of active dry yeast. And when they do, they have Jewish immigrants to thank.

In the mid-1860s, a Jewish Hungarian man named Charles Louis Fleischmann moved from Vienna, where he ran a distillery, to Cincinnati, Ohio. "Fleischmann was distressed by the poor quality of American bread," writes Gil Marks in his *Encyclopedia of Jewish Food*. He had ample reason to be concerned. At the time, there was virtually no regulation of the food industry. Commercial bakers sometimes used nonfood ingredients like plaster and sawdust in order to stretch their loaf yields, without regard to taste or human health. And, Marks writes, "many American bakers used fermented potato peelings for leavening their breads."

Determined to improve the quality of the bread in their new home, Fleischmann and his brother Maximilian developed a compressed, easy-to-distribute yeast cake made from a strain of yeast brought over from Austria. "They took it to the Philadelphia Exposition of 1876, setting up the 'Model Vienna Bakery,' as their display," writes Polly Campbell in *Cincinnati Food: A History of Queen City Cuisine*. "Vienna bread, a light, sweet-fermented white bread, became a huge favorite."

Building on its success, Fleischmann's introduced many other products in the ensuing decades, including vinegar, margarine, and, most notably, a dried granular yeast that did not require refrigeration and could be activated with warm water. Today Fleischmann's yeast, in its bright yellow packets, remains one of the leading brands of commercial yeast.

CHOCOLATE TURTLE BABKA

Makes two 9 x 5-inch (23 x 12 cm) loaves

I was obsessed with chocolate turtles when I was young—the heavenly confection that enrobes pecans and caramel in a thick layer of chocolate. This classic American candy, which dates back to the early 1900s, was named for its round, bumpy shape that resembles a turtle shell and feet. But as a kid, all I cared about was how many of them my mom would let me eat after a trip to the department store. Over the years, I have developed many nontraditional babka recipes, but one day it occurred to me that I had never made a chocolate turtle babka, and I immediately felt the urge to rectify that oversight. The sticky-sweet, nutty, chocolatey loaves that emerged from the oven were as every bit as decadent as the candy itself.

FOR THE DOUGH

- 2¼ teaspoons (1 packet) active dry yeast
- ½ cup (100 g) plus 1 teaspoon granulated sugar
- 1 cup (240 ml) warm water (about 110°F / 45°C)
- 4 to 5 cups (560 to 630 g) all-purpose flour, plus more for rolling
- 1 teaspoon kosher salt
- 2 large eggs, lightly beaten
- 8 tablespoons (1 stick / 113 g) unsalted butter or vegan butter, cut into pieces and softened
- Neutral vegetable oil for oiling the bowl

FOR THE FILLING

- 1½ cups (150 g) pecan halves
- 1½ cups (435 g) jarred dulce de leche
- 1½ cups (270 g) semisweet chocolate chips

NOTE: To make the babka dairy-free, use vegan dulce de leche and dairy-free chocolate chips.

1. Make the dough: Stir together the yeast, 1 teaspoon of the sugar, and the warm water in a large bowl and let sit until bubbling and frothy, 5 to 10 minutes. Meanwhile, whisk together 4 cups (560 g) of the flour, the remaining ½ cup (100 g) sugar, and the salt in another bowl.

2. Stir the eggs into the yeast mixture, then add the flour mixture and stir until a shaggy dough comes together. Turn the dough out onto a work surface (set the bowl aside) and knead well, adding the softened butter pieces, a few at a time, and up to 1 cup (140 g) additional flour as needed, until the dough is supple and slightly sticky, about 10 minutes. The dough may feel greasy or too buttery at times, but just keep kneading and sprinkling additional flour over the top a little at a time until the desired consistency is reached. (The kneading step can also be done in a stand mixer fitted with a dough hook; knead the dough for 5 to 7 minutes.)

3. Rub about 1 teaspoon of vegetable oil over the inside of the large bowl; place the dough in the bowl and turn to coat. Cover the bowl and let sit in a warm place until the dough has nearly doubled in size, 1½ to 2 hours.

4. Meanwhile, toast the pecans for the filling: Place the pecans in a dry frying pan set over medium heat and cook, stirring often, until toasted and fragrant, 3 to 5 minutes. Transfer the pecans to a cutting board and let cool, then roughly chop. Set aside.

FOR FINISHING

1 large egg, beaten

Granulated sugar for sprinkling (optional)

5. Assemble the babkas: Line two 9 x 5-inch (23 x 12 cm) loaf pans with parchment paper, allowing the parchment to hang over the two long sides. Gently punch down the dough and turn it out onto a lightly floured surface. Divide the dough into 2 equal pieces, and keep one piece covered in the bowl while you work with the other.

6. Using a rolling pin, on a lightly floured surface, roll out the dough into a large rectangle that is ¼ inch (6 mm) thick. Spread about half of the dulce de leche evenly over the dough, leaving a ¼-inch- (6 mm) wide border around the edges, then sprinkle evenly with about half of the toasted pecans and chocolate chips. Starting at one of the short ends, roll up the dough tightly like a jelly roll. Cut off and discard about 1 inch (2.5 cm) of dough from each end, then cut the roll lengthwise in half. You will now have 2 long strands of dough, with layers of filling exposed. Twist the strands together, pinch together at the top and bottom, and carefully place in one of the prepared baking pans. Repeat the process with the remaining dough and filling.

7. Loosely cover the pans with a kitchen towel and let rise until lightly puffed, about 30 minutes. Meanwhile, preheat the oven to 350°F (180°C).

8. Lightly brush the tops of each babka with some of the beaten egg (you will not use all of it) and sprinkle the tops with sugar, if desired. Bake the babkas until deeply golden brown and cooked through, 45 to 50 minutes. If the tops are browning too quickly toward the end of baking, loosely tent the pans with aluminum foil.

9. Remove from the oven and set the babkas, in their pans, on a wire rack to cool for about 30 minutes, then use the overhanging parchment to gently lift them out of the pans and onto the rack to cool slightly. (Or leave them in the loaf pans if you prefer to serve them that way.) Serve warm or at room temperature.

10. Store leftovers, covered, in the fridge for up to 3 days or, well wrapped, in the freezer for up to 6 months. Reheat in the oven or toaster oven before serving.

CINNAMON-PECAN DANISH RING

Serves 8 to 10

Some Jewish families bake, others outsource the sweets to Entenmann's. The iconic bakery, which was founded by a German immigrant named William Entenmann in Brooklyn in 1898, made a name for itself across the city—and later, the country—with its array of tempting cookies, crumb cakes, doughnuts, and Danishes. William Entenmann wasn't Jewish, but thanks to his company's many kosher-certified products (and wide availability at supermarkets), their desserts became standard fare at Jewish gatherings—everything from a synagogue kiddush to an afternoon mahjong game. One of my favorite Entenmann's treats, the wreath-shaped Pecan Danish Ring, was, unfortunately, discontinued years ago. My riff on the original, with its babka-like crumb, swirls of cinnamon and toasted pecans, and thick vanilla-scented icing, helps keep those sweet memories alive.

FOR THE DOUGH

2¼ teaspoons (1 packet) active dry yeast

⅓ cup (65 g) plus 1 teaspoon granulated sugar

½ cup (120 ml) warm water (about 110°F / 43°C)

3 to 3¼ cups (420 to 455 g) all-purpose flour

½ teaspoon kosher salt

1 teaspoon ground cinnamon

4 tablespoons (½ stick / 57 g) unsalted butter or vegan butter, melted and slightly cooled

¼ cup (60 g) plus 2 tablespoons sour cream or nondairy sour cream

1 large egg

Neutral vegetable oil for oiling the bowl

1. Make the dough: Stir together the yeast, 1 teaspoon of the sugar, and the warm water in a large bowl and let sit until bubbling and frothy, 5 to 10 minutes. Meanwhile, whisk together 3 cups (420 g) of the flour, the remaining ⅓ cup (65 g) sugar, the salt, and cinnamon in another bowl.

2. Stir the melted butter, sour cream, and egg into the yeast mixture, then add the flour mixture and stir until the dough comes together. Turn the dough out onto a work surface (set the bowl aside) and knead well, adding up to ¼ cup (35 g) additional flour if needed, until the dough is supple and slightly sticky, about 10 minutes. (The kneading step can also be done in a stand mixer fitted with the dough hook; knead for 5 to 7 minutes.)

3. Rub about 1 teaspoon of vegetable oil over the inside of the large bowl; place the dough in the bowl and turn to coat. Cover the bowl and let sit in a warm place until the dough has nearly doubled in size, 1½ to 2 hours.

4. Meanwhile, toast the pecans for the filling: Place the pecans in a dry frying pan set over medium heat and cook, stirring often, until toasted and fragrant, 3 to 5 minutes. Transfer the pecans to a cutting board and let cool, then chop. Set aside.

5. Make the filling: Combine the softened butter, sugar, cinnamon, almond extract, and salt in a bowl and stir to fully mix. Set aside.

FOR THE FILLING

1 cup (100 g) pecan halves

5 tablespoons (70 g) unsalted butter or vegan butter, softened

⅓ cup (65 g) granulated sugar

2½ teaspoons ground cinnamon

¾ teaspoon almond extract

⅛ teaspoon kosher salt

FOR THE GLAZE

1 cup (120 g) confectioners' sugar, sifted

1 to 2 tablespoons milk or nondairy milk

1 teaspoon vanilla extract or vanilla bean paste

6. Assemble the Danish ring: Line a large baking sheet with parchment paper and set nearby. Gently deflate the dough and turn it out onto a lightly floured surface. Roll it into a large ⅛-inch- (3 mm) thick rectangle and trim off any ragged edges. Spoon the filling onto the dough and use a butter knife or offset spatula to spread it into a thin, even layer. Sprinkle the top evenly with the toasted pecans.

7. Starting at one of the long ends, roll up the dough tightly like a jelly roll, then gently roll and stretch it into a 24-inch- (60 cm) long log. Transfer the log to the baking sheet, and bring the ends together to form a ring. Gently pinch the ends together to seal.

8. Using a pair of sharp scissors, make cuts all around the outer edge of the ring, leaving about 1 inch (2.5 cm) between the cuts and cutting about halfway into the ring. Cover the ring with a clean kitchen towel and let rise for 1 hour.

9. Meanwhile, preheat the oven to 375°F (190°C).

10. Bake the ring until it is golden brown and cooked through, 22 to 25 minutes. Remove from the oven and set the baking sheet on a wire rack to cool.

11. Make the glaze: Stir together the confectioners' sugar, 1 tablespoon milk, and the vanilla in a medium bowl to form a thick but pourable glaze. If the glaze is too thick, slowly add up to another tablespoon of milk, a little at a time, stirring until the desired consistency is reached.

12. Use a fork to generously drizzle the top of the Danish ring with the glaze (you might not use all of it). Serve slightly warm or at room temperature. Store any leftovers, covered, in the fridge for up to 3 days. Rewarm briefly in the microwave or toaster oven before serving.

CHOCOLATE PULL-APART CAKE

Makes one 9-inch (23 cm) round cake

Hungarian Jews are known for their memorable baked goods, including aranygaluska—a pull-apart cake that rolls small nuggets of yeasted dough (essentially the same as babka dough) in butter, sugar, and finely chopped walnuts before layering them into the baking pan. In Joan Nathan's *Jewish Holiday Cookbook*, she writes about an "outrageously delicious" variation of the cake that replaces the traditional ground walnuts with cocoa powder. Called *kuchem-buchem* ("one of those marvelous made-up Yiddish rhyming names," writes Nathan), the cake bakes up fluffy and fragrant with chocolate. Some versions of the recipe also fill the balls with the cocoa mixture, but I find that to be a lot of extra work without a noticeably different outcome. Serve this pull-apart cake for dessert, as a sweet centerpiece at brunch, or as an afternoon treat.

FOR THE DOUGH

2¼ teaspoons (1 packet) active dry yeast

½ cup (100 g) plus 1 teaspoon granulated sugar

1 cup (240 ml) warm water (about 110°F / 43°C)

4 to 4½ cups (560 to 630 g) all-purpose flour

1 teaspoon kosher salt

2 large eggs, lightly beaten

1 teaspoon vanilla extract

8 tablespoons (1 stick / 113 g) unsalted butter or vegan butter, cut into pieces and softened

1. Make the dough: Stir together the yeast, 1 teaspoon of the sugar, and the warm water in a large bowl. Let sit until bubbly, about 5 minutes.
2. Whisk together 4 cups (560 g) of the flour, the remaining ½ cup (100 g) sugar, and the salt in another large bowl.
3. Stir the eggs and vanilla into the yeast mixture. Add the flour mixture and gently stir until a shaggy dough forms. Turn the dough out onto a work surface (set the bowl aside) and knead well, adding the softened butter a few pieces at a time and up to ½ cup (70 g) additional flour as needed, until the dough is supple and elastic, about 10 minutes. (You might not need all of the flour.) The dough may seem dry or overly buttery at points, but stick with it until the desired texture is reached. The kneading step can also be done in a stand mixer fitted with a dough hook; knead for 5 to 7 minutes.
4. Place the dough back in the large bowl, cover, and let rise until nearly doubled in size, 1½ to 2 hours.
5. Make the topping: Melt the butter in the microwave or in a small saucepan over medium-low heat, then transfer to a bowl. Whisk together the sugar, cocoa powder, and salt in another bowl. Set aside.
6. Generously grease a 9-inch (23 cm) round springform pan.

FOR THE TOPPING

8 tablespoons (1 stick / 113 g) unsalted butter or vegan butter

⅔ cup (130 g) granulated sugar

⅓ cup (25 g) unsweetened cocoa powder, sifted

⅛ teaspoon kosher salt

½ cup (90 g) semisweet chocolate chips

7. Gently deflate the dough. Working in batches, pinch off walnut-sized pieces of dough and roll into balls, then dip the balls in the melted butter and the cocoa-sugar mixture, making sure all sides are coated, and place them in the prepared pan, sprinkling the chocolate chips into the pan as you go. (To avoid "cross-contamination" between the wet and dry toppings, use one hand for the butter bowl and one hand for the cocoa-sugar bowl.) Continue this process until all of the dough is used up. Drizzle any remaining melted butter over the top of the balls and sprinkle with any remaining cocoa-sugar.

8. Cover the pan and let the dough rise for 30 minutes. Meanwhile, preheat the oven to 350°F (180°C).

9. Bake the cake (if desired, set a parchment paper–lined baking sheet on the rack below to catch potential leaks) until it is puffed and cooked through, 40 to 45 minutes.

10. Remove from the oven and let the cake cool in the pan on a wire rack for at least 30 minutes, then carefully unmold the cake and transfer to a serving plate. Serve warm or at room temperature.

11. Store leftovers, covered, in the fridge for up to 3 days. Reheat in a toaster oven or the microwave before serving.

PUMPKIN CAKE DOUGHNUTS

Makes about 12 doughnuts

Eve Jochnowitz is a New York City–based Yiddish scholar, culinary ethnographer, and translator/editor of *The Vilna Vegetarian Cookbook*—a book originally published in 1938 by a Lithuanian-Jewish restaurateur, Fania Lewando. Jochnowitz is also a passionate home cook, and she chronicles her creative culinary projects on her dual-language blog, *In Mol Araan*. Jochnowitz has been making these pumpkin cake doughnuts (*banye pontshkes* in Yiddish) for Hanukkah for nearly twenty-five years. As an heirloom vegetable enthusiast, she prefers to make them with cooked and mashed zucca tonda padana—a dramatically beautiful pumpkin variety she describes as the "Elizabeth Taylor of squash." She sweetens the doughnuts with brown sugar and adds cinnamon, nutmeg, and vanilla for comforting warmth. "I love the doughnuts' contrast of a shatteringly crusty surface and the melt-in-your-mouth texture inside," she says. Fortunately, in case you don't have access to heirloom squash, the doughnuts are equally wonderful made with canned pumpkin puree.

2¾ to 3 cups (385 to 420 g) all-purpose flour, plus more for rolling

1½ teaspoons baking powder

½ teaspoon baking soda

½ teaspoon kosher salt

¼ cup (60 ml) buttermilk

2 large eggs

½ cup (115 g) pure pumpkin puree (not pumpkin pie filling)

4 tablespoons (½ stick / 57 g) unsalted butter or vegan butter, melted

½ packed cup (100 g) light brown sugar

1 teaspoon vanilla extract

1 teaspoon ground cinnamon

⅛ teaspoon ground nutmeg

1 packed teaspoon grated lemon zest

Neutral vegetable oil for frying

Confectioners' sugar for dusting (optional)

1. Whisk together 2¾ cups (385 g) flour, the baking powder, baking soda, and salt in a large bowl.
2. Whisk together the buttermilk, eggs, pumpkin puree, melted butter, brown sugar, vanilla, cinnamon, nutmeg, and lemon zest in a medium bowl. Make a well in the center of the dry ingredients and pour in the wet, then stir until a soft dough forms. If it is too sticky to roll out, stir in up to ¼ cup (35 g) additional flour as needed.
3. Line a large baking sheet with paper towels and set nearby. Heat about 2 inches (5 cm) of vegetable oil in a large saucepan over medium heat until it reaches 350°F (180°C) on a digital thermometer.
4. Meanwhile, transfer the dough to a well-floured surface and use a lightly floured rolling pin to roll it out to a ½-inch (12 mm) thickness. Using a 3-inch (7.5 cm) round cookie cutter, stamp out as many circles as possible. Then use a 1-inch (2.5 cm) round cookie cutter to stamp out a hole in the center of each doughnut. (If desired, reserve the holes to fry along with the doughnuts.)
5. Working in batches of 3 or 4, using floured hands to help prevent sticking, carefully drop the doughnuts into the hot oil and fry, flipping once, until puffed up and cooked through, 2 to 4 minutes. Use a slotted spoon or spider to transfer the doughnuts to the paper towel–lined baking sheet to drain.

VARIATION: To make these dairy-free, substitute the buttermilk with ¼ cup (60 ml) nondairy milk mixed with 1 teaspoon fresh lemon juice and allowed to stand for 5 minutes.

6. Transfer the doughnuts, while still warm, to a serving platter and use a fine-mesh sieve to dust generously with confectioners' sugar, if desired. Serve immediately.

HOW POLISH JELLY DOUGHNUTS BECAME AN AMERICAN HANUKKAH SENSATION

In the weeks leading up to Hanukkah, Jewish bakeries across America begin turning out jelly doughnuts by the dozen. It is quite the experience to walk into one of these bakeries and be greeted by heaping piles of glistening doughnuts, not to mention the heady aroma of fried dough. Stuffed with jam or other tempting fillings and sprinkled with confectioners' sugar or coated with a glaze, these doughnuts—called *sufganiyot*—offer a sweet way to fulfill the Hanukkah custom of eating fried foods in commemoration of the holiday's miracle of oil (see page 19).

Before there were sufganiyot, there were ponchiks. In Poland, jelly doughnuts—traditionally filled with apricot or prune jam—go by the name *paczki*, which translates rather lyrically as "flower bud." Before World War II, Polish Jews enjoyed these doughnuts just as much as their neighbors did. But while most of the country served them to celebrate the end of Lent, many Polish Jewish families ate them on Hanukkah. Instead of frying them in lard (which is not kosher), they used oil. And instead of paczki, they called them by their Yiddish name, *ponchiks*.

In the years after World War II, when many Polish Jews emigrated to the newly formed State of Israel, they introduced ponchik recipes to their new home. Other Jewish communities settling in Israel had variations of doughnuts too—like the rustic Moroccan ring doughnuts called *sfenj* and Greek *loukoumades* (page 191). But it was ponchiks that caught on like wildfire. Within a generation or two, jelly doughnuts had been officially adopted in Israel as a Hanukkah food for everyone—not just Polish Jews. They also received a new Hebrew name, *sufganiyah* (*sufganiyot* is plural), which translates roughly as "spongy dough" and refers to the soft, pillowy texture of the yeasted doughnuts.

Starting in the 1970s, Jewish American travelers who had tried sufganiyot in Israel began to introduce them back home. I can track the rise in sufganiyot's popularity across my personal timeline. When I was a child growing up in suburban Chicago in the 1980s and '90s, sufganiyot were not a regular part of my Hanukkah experience. There was plenty of chocolate gelt and an endless supply of potato latkes, but I do not remember jelly doughnuts at my family's or synagogue's holiday celebrations. (And I'm certain I would remember if there were doughnuts.)

But in more recent decades, they have become more and more common—both in New York City, where I now live (and delight my own kids by making or buying Hanukkah doughnuts), and across the country. While still not quite as widely known or eaten in America as latkes or gelt, sufganiyot have become one of the most beloved Hanukkah treats.

APPLE CIDER SUFGANIYOT WITH SALTED CARAMEL

Makes about 16 doughnuts

I first developed this recipe fifteen years ago for the now-defunct food website *Chow*. It was part of a larger "creative sufganiyot" package that resulted in my frying approximately ten dozen doughnuts (no joke) and ending up with many quarts of used frying oil to dispose of. Fortunately, my roots as a professional Jewish environmentalist meant I knew a guy who ran his car on biodiesel and was thrilled to take the oil off my hands. All that oill was worth it, because these doughnuts are incredible. They take the best parts of the apple cider doughnuts I love buying at the farmers' market (autumn spices! Apple cider! A crunchy sugar cap!) and fills them with rich homemade salted caramel. They are a great starter doughnut recipe, since you do not need a piping bag to fill them.

FOR THE SALTED CARAMEL

2 cups (475 ml) whole milk

1 cup (200 g) granulated sugar

½ teaspoon baking soda

2 teaspoons vanilla extract

¾ teaspoon kosher salt

FOR THE DOUGHNUTS

2¼ teaspoons (1 packet) active dry yeast

¾ cup (180 ml) apple cider, heated to 110°F (45°C) (see Note)

2½ to 2¾ cups (350 to 385 g) all-purpose flour

½ cup (100 g) granulated sugar, divided

1½ teaspoons ground cinnamon

¼ teaspoon ground nutmeg

¼ teaspoon ground cloves

¾ teaspoon kosher salt

1 tablespoon apple butter

2 large egg yolks (reserve one of the whites for the egg wash)

1 teaspoon vanilla extract

1 tablespoon unsalted butter, cut into small pieces

Neutral vegetable oil for greasing the bowl and frying

1. Make the caramel: Pour the milk into a large saucepan and bring to a boil over medium-high heat, stirring occasionally, then whisk in the sugar, baking soda, vanilla, and salt. Keep whisking until the sugar is completely dissolved, 3 to 5 minutes.

2. Reduce the heat to low and cook (do not stir, but occasionally skim off and discard any foam that accumulates at the sides of the saucepan) until the mixture turns deep brown and is the consistency of a loose caramel, 30 to 40 minutes.

3. Remove the pan from the heat and pour the caramel through a fine-mesh strainer into a heatproof bowl. Let cool for 30 minutes, then cover and refrigerate until set, about 2 hours. (*The caramel can be made up to 3 days in advance and stored in the fridge.*)

4. Make the doughnuts: Stir together the yeast and warm apple cider in a large bowl and let sit until bubbling and frothy, about 5 minutes.

5. Meanwhile, whisk together 2½ cups (350 g) flour, ¼ cup (50 g) of the sugar, the cinnamon, nutmeg, cloves, and salt in a medium bowl.

recipe continues

NOTE: To warm the apple cider, heat it in a small pot on the stove or in the microwave until just steaming (not boiling). This should take a few minutes on the stove and about 1 minute in the microwave.

NOTE: I don't recommend making these with nondairy milk because the caramel will not reliably set in the fridge.

6. Stir the apple butter, egg yolks, and vanilla into the yeast and cider mixture. Add the flour mixture and stir until a dough begins to form. Transfer the dough to a work surface (set the bowl aside). Add the butter pieces and knead, slowly adding up to ¼ cup (35 g) additional flour as needed, until the dough is smooth and supple, about 10 minutes. (The kneading can also be done in a stand mixer fitted with the dough hook; knead for 5 to 7 minutes.)

7. Rub about 1 teaspoon of oil over the inside of the large bowl. Add the dough and turn to coat. Cover the bowl and let the dough rise until doubled in size, 1½ to 2 hours.

8. Form and fry the doughnuts: Line a large baking sheet with parchment paper. Deflate the dough, transfer it to a lightly floured surface, and use a lightly floured rolling pin to roll it out to a ¼-inch (6 mm) thickness. Using a 2½-inch (6 cm) round cookie cutter, stamp out as many circles of dough as possible. Arrange the rounds on a baking sheet and spoon a rounded ½ teaspoon of the salted caramel onto the center of half of them. Beat the reserved egg white and use a pastry brush to lightly brush the outer edges of the filled rounds with the egg wash. (You will not use all of it.) Gently stretch the reserved rounds and fit them over the filled rounds, pinching the edges firmly to seal.

9. Gather up the dough scraps and repeat the process to make additional doughnuts. Cover the filled doughnuts with a clean dish towel and let rise until puffed, about 30 minutes.

10. Meanwhile, line a large baking sheet with paper towels and set nearby. Heat 2 inches (5 cm) of oil in a large heavy-bottomed saucepan over medium heat until it reaches 350°F (180°C) on a digital thermometer.

11. If any of the filling is peeking out of the doughnuts, pinch the edges together again with floured fingers. Working in batches of 2 or 3, gently drop the doughnuts into the hot oil and fry, turning once, until golden brown and cooked through, 1 to 2 minutes. Remove the doughnuts with a slotted spoon and drain on the paper towel–lined baking sheet.

12. While the doughnuts are still warm, spread the remaining ¼ cup (50 g) sugar on a plate and roll the doughnuts in the sugar to coat. Serve immediately.

FLUFFY APRICOT JAM DOUGHNUTS

Makes about 16 doughnuts

Most jelly doughnuts are filled with jam or jelly. But these saucer-shaped Hungarian fritters, called *fánk*, are instead piled with scoops of thick apricot preserves (also known as *lekvar*; see page 190), like some kind of magical bialy-doughnut hybrid. It is much simpler to dollop doughnuts with jam than to inject it into their doughy centers: jelly doughnuts, quicker?—that's a win-win scenario. In Hungary, these fluffy deep-fried delights are traditionally served during the carnival season preceding Ash Wednesday, but they also make excellent Hanukkah doughnuts. My recipe was inspired by the top-notch fánk served at Agi's Counter, a Hungarian-and-Jewish-inspired restaurant and bakery in Brooklyn, New York.

- 1½ teaspoons active dry yeast
- ¼ cup (60 ml) warm water (about 110°F / 43°C)
- 3½ to 4 cups (490 to 560 g) all-purpose flour, plus more for kneading and shaping
- ¾ cup (90 g) confectioners' sugar, sifted, plus more for dusting
- ¾ teaspoon kosher salt
- ¾ cup (180 ml) milk or nondairy milk
- 1 large egg plus 1 large egg yolk
- 1 packed teaspoon grated lemon zest
- 4 tablespoons (½ stick / 57 g) unsalted butter or vegan butter, cut into small pieces and softened
- Neutral vegetable oil for frying
- Apricot jam for filling

1. Stir together the yeast and warm water in a large bowl. Let the mixture sit until bubbling and foamy, about 5 minutes.
2. Meanwhile, whisk together 3½ cups (490 g) flour, the confectioners' sugar, and salt in a medium bowl.
3. Stir the milk, egg, egg yolk, and lemon zest into the yeast mixture. Add the flour mixture and stir until the dough begins to come together. (The dough might feel quite wet at this point.) Turn the dough out onto a floured surface and knead well, adding the softened butter pieces a few at a time and up to ½ cup (70 g) additional flour as needed, until you have a supple, slightly sticky dough, about 10 minutes. (The kneading step can also be done in a stand mixer fitted with the dough hook; knead for 5 to 7 minutes.)
4. Return the dough to the large bowl. Cover the bowl and let the dough rise until it has nearly doubled in size, 1½ to 2 hours.
5. Line one large baking sheet with a clean dish towel, and line a second large baking sheet with a layer of paper towels.
6. Gently deflate the dough and transfer it to a floured work surface. Roll it out with a rolling pin to a ¼-inch (6 mm) thickness. Using a 3-inch (7.5 cm) round cookie cutter, stamp out as many rounds as possible and place them on the baking sheet lined with a dish towel. Gather the scraps, reroll, and cut out more rounds; add them to the baking sheet.

recipe continues

7. Using the tip of your finger, press an indentation into the center of each doughnut. (Do not make a hole; the indentation should not go through the dough.) Cover the dough rounds loosely with a second dish towel and let rise until puffed, about 30 minutes.

8. Meanwhile, heat 2 inches (5 cm) of oil in a large heavy-bottomed pot over medium heat until it reaches 350°F (180°C) on a digital thermometer.

9. Working in batches of 4, gently add the dough rounds to the oil, indentation side down, and fry, flipping once, until puffed and golden on both sides, about 2 minutes. Transfer the doughnuts to the baking sheet lined with paper towels to drain. Let cool slightly.

10. Spoon about 1 tablespoon of apricot jam into each doughnut's indentation. Using a fine-mesh sieve, dust the tops of the doughnuts with confectioners' sugar. Serve warm.

LEKVAR: THE QUINTESSENTIAL JEWISH JAM

Many years ago, my husband, Yoshie, and I were enjoying a bowl of hot borscht at B&H Dairy, a beloved restaurant that has been serving Eastern European staples in New York City's East Village since 1938. We started chatting with a sweet and seemingly lonely older man who was eating a plate of kasha and gravy next to us at the counter. As we got up to leave, he said, "My name is Simon Fischer. You know, like the prune butter." I smiled politely and nodded but had no clue what he was talking about.

A few months later, while browsing the jam aisle at a supermarket, I noticed a glass jar with a blue-and-yellow label that read "Simon Fischer Prune Butter." It felt like bumping into an old friend! I brought the jar of prune butter home and was delighted to discover that it tasted exactly like the prune-filled hamantaschen I remembered from childhood.

Prune butter, I would learn, is a thick, concentrated fruit preserve made from cooked-down plums or prunes. Called *povidl* in Yiddish and *lekvar* in Hungarian, it serves as the filling for a wide variety of Ashkenazi pastries, cakes, and cookies, including Danishes, doughnuts, sweet dumplings, fluden, and hamantaschen. The word *lekvar* originally referred just to plums and prunes, but its meaning eventually expanded to encompass jams made from other fruits, particularly apricots and peaches.

In Europe, the jams were made in summer when the fruit was ripe and sweet, then stored in large crocks to be used throughout the cold winter. In New York City, which became the home of many Jewish immigrants from Hungary, some stores sold prune and apricot lekvar by the pound to bakers hungry for a taste of the Old Country. Lekvar fell out of fashion in America as other jams and fillings (most notably chocolate) became widely available. But its complex, concentrated sweetness is worthy of a revival.

GREEK DOUGHNUTS WITH HONEY AND WALNUTS

Makes about 24 doughnuts

Greek Jews celebrate Hanukkah with loukoumades—small balls of fried dough that are drizzled with honey and sprinkled with cinnamon and chopped walnuts. According to Nicholas Stavroulakis' *Cookbook of the Jews of Greece*, the deep-fried treat is related to the Sephardi doughnut holes called bimuelos. The batter for loukoumades is quite wet and sticky, which results in ethereally light doughnuts but can be difficult to work with. Greek home cooks typically pick up a handful of the loose batter and gently squeeze out balls of dough between their thumbs and index fingers, using an oiled spoon to then scrape the dough into the hot oil. Keep practicing, and you will get the hang of it.

- 2¼ teaspoons (1 packet) active dry yeast
- 3 tablespoons plus 1 teaspoon granulated sugar, divided
- ¼ cup (60 ml) warm water (about 110°F / 43°C)
- 2 cups (280 g) all-purpose flour
- ½ teaspoon kosher salt
- ¾ cup (180 ml) milk or nondairy milk
- 1 large egg
- Neutral vegetable oil for frying
- Honey, ground cinnamon, and finely chopped walnuts for finishing

1. Stir together the yeast, 1 teaspoon of the sugar, and the warm water in a large bowl. Let the mixture sit until bubbling and foamy, about 5 minutes.
2. Meanwhile, whisk together the flour, the remaining 3 tablespoons sugar, and the salt in a medium bowl.
3. Stir the milk and egg into the yeast mixture, then stir in the flour mixture to form a loose, sticky dough. Cover the bowl and let rise until the dough has doubled in size, 1 to 2 hours.
4. Heat about 2 inches (5 cm) of oil in a large heavy-bottomed saucepan over medium heat until it reaches 350°F (180°C) on a digital thermometer. Line a large baking sheet with paper towels and set nearby.
5. Working in batches of 5 or 6, using a lightly oiled hand, pick up a handful of the dough (it will feel very wet and sticky), close your hand into a fist over the pot, squeezing a small ball of dough through your thumb and index finger, and use an oiled spoon to scrape the ball into the hot oil. Fry, flipping the doughnuts once, until golden and cooked through, 3 to 4 minutes. Nudge the heat up or down as necessary to keep the temperature consistent.
6. Transfer the doughnuts to the lined baking sheet to drain briefly, then arrange on a serving platter. Drizzle the doughnuts with honey and sprinkle with cinnamon and chopped walnuts. Serve immediately.

HUNGARIAN APPLE SQUARES

Makes one 9 × 13-inch (23 × 33 cm) pastry

Whenever life gives me an abundance of sweet-tart baking apples, I start dreaming about making this Hungarian slab pie. Its Hungarian name, *almás pite*, translates literally as "apple pie," but it is quite distinct from American apple pie. It sandwiches sweetened grated apples between two sheets of sour cream–enriched dough. As the pastry bakes and turns golden in the oven, the apples cook down and compact into an almost apple butter consistency. There is nothing fancy about these apple squares. Instead, they are wonderfully rustic—homey, gently sweet, and uncomplicated. I like to serve them as a simple dessert on Rosh Hashanah, as an afternoon sweet with coffee on Sukkot, or as a treat after an afternoon of apple picking.

FOR THE DOUGH

2½ cups (350 g) all-purpose flour, plus more for rolling

½ cup (60 g) confectioners' sugar, sifted

½ teaspoon baking powder

½ teaspoon kosher salt

12 tablespoons (1½ sticks / 170 g) unsalted butter or vegan butter, cut into pieces and softened

2 large egg yolks (reserve one of the whites for the egg wash)

½ cup (120 g) sour cream or plain nondairy yogurt

1 packed teaspoon grated lemon zest

1. Make the dough: Combine the flour, confectioners' sugar, baking powder, and salt in the bowl of a stand mixer fitted with the paddle attachment (or use a handheld electric mixer and a large bowl), and beat briefly at low speed to combine. Add the softened butter, egg yolks, sour cream, and lemon zest and beat until a soft dough comes together. (It is okay, even preferable, if the dough is still a little crumbly.)

2. Divide the dough into 2 equal pieces, form each into a disk, and wrap well with parchment paper. Refrigerate while you make the filling.

3. Prepare the apples for the filling: Peel the apples and grate on the large holes of a box grater, discarding the cores and seeds. Or cut the peeled apples into quarters, core them, and grate in a food processor fitted with the grating disk. Gently squeeze out some of the juice from the grated apples (don't squeeze them completely dry) and transfer to a large bowl. (Reserve the juice for drinking or another use.) Add the confectioners' sugar, cinnamon, and lemon juice to the apples and mix well to combine.

4. Preheat the oven to 350°F (180°C).

5. Remove one of the dough disks from the refrigerator and place it on a floured work surface. Using a lightly floured rolling pin, roll the dough into a large rectangle approximately ¼ inch (6 mm) thick. Transfer the dough to a 9 × 13-inch (23 × 33 cm) baking dish, fitting it over the bottom and up the sides (do not trim the excess dough yet).

FOR THE FILLING AND ASSEMBLY

6 large baking apples (about 2 pounds / 1 kg)

1¼ cups (150 g) confectioners' sugar, sifted

1 tablespoon ground cinnamon

1 teaspoon fresh lemon juice

½ cup (30 g) plain panko breadcrumbs, for assembly

Confectioners' sugar for dusting

6. Sprinkle the dough evenly with the breadcrumbs, then pile the apple filling on top, spreading it out into an even layer.

7. Roll out the second dough disk to a ¼-inch (6 mm) thickness and drape it over the filling. Trim the excess dough on all sides so that it is flush with the filling. (You do not need to crimp or seal the dough.) Use a sharp knife to cut a few small slits in the top crust to allow steam to escape.

8. Beat the reserved egg white in a small bowl then brush the top crust evenly with the egg wash. (You will not use all of it.) Bake the pastry until the top is golden brown, 45 to 50 minutes. Remove from the oven and set the baking dish on a wire rack to cool.

9. Just before serving, dust the top of the pastry with confectioners' sugar and then cut into squares. Serve slightly warm or at room temperature. Store any leftovers, covered, in the fridge for up to 5 days.

RASPBERRY AND SWEET CHEESE STRUDEL

Serves 4 to 6

Many years ago on a trip to Hungary, I spent the better part of a morning watching bakers make strudel, called *rétes* in Hungarian, at Strudel House in Budapest. The bakers skillfully pulled and stretched the dough until it was paper-thin, sprinkled it with breadcrumbs to keep the dough crisp as it baked, and filled it with any of a dozen sweet or savory fillings. For me, the standout favorite was the raspberry curd strudel, which rolled a filling of sweetened farmer's cheese and ruby-colored raspberry jam up in the dough and baked it until the outside was golden and crunchy and the inside was creamy and bright.

Jewish home cooks traditionally used a kitchen table to stretch strudel dough, gently coaxing it until it was as large as the tabletop and thin enough to read the newspaper through. This recipe mimics the raspberry and sweet cheese filling from Strudel House but substitutes store-bought phyllo dough for homemade strudel dough. While I love a good baking project, I worried that the time and steep learning curve that goes into homemade dough would deter people from making and enjoying this exceptional strudel. Fortunately, when it comes to the thin, crispy crunch I love in homemade strudel, phyllo delivers.

FOR THE RASPBERRY FILLING

1 cup (120 g) fresh raspberries

2½ tablespoons granulated sugar

½ teaspoon grated orange zest

1 tablespoon fresh orange juice

FOR THE SWEET CHEESE FILLING

¾ cup (150 g) unsalted farmer's cheese or ricotta

2 tablespoons sour cream

1 large egg yolk

3 tablespoons granulated sugar

1 tablespoon all-purpose flour

½ teaspoon vanilla extract or vanilla bean paste

¼ teaspoon kosher salt

NOTE: To save time, you can substitute about ½ cup (140 g) of good-quality store-bought raspberry jam for the jam filling.

1. Make the raspberry filling: Combine the raspberries, sugar, orange zest, and orange juice in a small saucepan and bring to a boil over medium heat, stirring often, then reduce the heat to medium-low and cook, stirring occasionally, until the mixture thickens enough to coat the back of a spoon, 10 to 15 minutes. Remove from the heat and let cool. (*The filling can be made up to 5 days ahead and stored, covered, in the fridge.*)

2. Make the sweet cheese filling: Combine the farmer's cheese, sour cream, egg yolk, sugar, flour, vanilla, and salt in a medium bowl and stir to fully combine. Set aside.

3. Assemble and bake the strudel: Preheat the oven to 375°F (190°C). Line a large baking sheet with parchment paper.

4. Melt the butter in a small saucepan over low heat, or in a bowl in the microwave in 20-second intervals, stirring after each. Remove from the heat.

recipe continues

FOR THE STRUDEL

- 8 tablespoons (1 stick / 113 g) unsalted butter
- 7 sheets frozen phyllo dough (9 × 14 inches; 23 × 35 cm), thawed
- 2 tablespoons unseasoned panko breadcrumbs
- Sliced almonds for topping (optional)
- Confectioners' sugar for dusting (optional)

5. Lay a piece of parchment on a work surface and place 1 sheet of phyllo on top. (Keep the remaining phyllo sheets covered with a damp cloth so they don't dry out.) Brush and dot the sheet evenly with the melted butter. (It is okay if it tears a little bit.) Place a second piece of phyllo on top of the first and brush with melted butter. Repeat the process 5 more times, brushing each layer of phyllo with butter, to make a stack of 7 sheets.
6. Sprinkle the breadcrumbs evenly over the top of the phyllo stack, then spoon the sweet cheese filling in a thick line across one of the short ends of the dough, leaving about ¾ inch (2 cm) space along the bottom edge and both sides. Spread the raspberry filling in a second line just above the cheese filling.
7. Use the parchment paper to help roll the dough up around the filling, tucking it inside as necessary and ending up with a long stuffed cylinder. Pat down the ends of the phyllo to seal in the filling. (It is okay if some of the filling squishes out.) Use a sharp serrated knife to score the unbaked strudel into pieces, slicing about halfway through the pastry.
8. Brush the top of the phyllo with a little more melted butter. If desired, sprinkle the top of the strudel with sliced almonds.
9. Carefully transfer the strudel to the prepared baking sheet, seam side down, and bake, rotating the baking sheet back to front halfway through, until the phyllo is crisp and golden brown, 25 to 30 minutes. (Some of the butter might leak out onto the baking sheet during baking; that is okay.)
10. Remove the strudel from the oven, carefully transfer it to a cutting board, and let cool for at least 30 minutes.
11. If desired, just before serving, use a fine-mesh sieve to dust the top of the strudel with confectioners' sugar, then use a serrated knife to slice it into pieces along the scoring lines. Serve warm or at room temperature.
12. Store any leftovers, well wrapped, in the fridge for up to 3 days. Rewarm briefly at 350°F (180°C) in the oven or a toaster oven to recrisp the phyllo.

SWEET WALNUT AND ALMOND TURNOVERS

Makes about 24 pastries

Pastries, both savory and sweet, are the heart of Turkish and Greek Jewish cuisine, including these nut-filled turnovers called *travados*. According to Jewish food historian Gil Marks, *travado* means "joined" in Ladino and refers to how the pastries are pressed closed to hold the filling inside. However, in her book *Jewish Cookery from Boston to Baghdad*, Malvina Liebman suggests that the name may have come from the old Spanish word *trova*, meaning "love song"; travados were often included as part of a larger exchange of food gifts between bride and groom in the weeks leading up to a wedding. Turkish recipes for travados usually call for walnuts, while Greek recipes call for almonds—I like a mixture of the two. And while most recipes are made with a flour-and-oil-based dough, they are simpler and delicious made using store-bought puff pastry.

FOR THE FILLING

½ cup (50 g) walnut halves

½ cup (70 g) whole, unsalted almonds

½ cup (100 g) granulated sugar

1 teaspoon almond extract

1 teaspoon ground cinnamon

⅛ teaspoon kosher salt

1 teaspoon water, plus more if needed

FOR ASSEMBLY AND BAKING

All-purpose flour for dusting

One 17-ounce (482 g) package frozen puff pastry (2 sheets), thawed

1 large egg

Confectioners' sugar for dusting (optional)

NOTE: Sprinkle any leftover walnut-almond filling on yogurt, granola, or berries.

VARIATION: For vegan turnovers, omit the egg wash. They will not get quite as golden in the oven, but they will still taste delicious.

1. Make the filling: Combine the walnuts, almonds, sugar, almond extract, cinnamon, salt, and 1 teaspoon water in a food processor and pulse, scraping down the sides of the bowl as necessary, until the nuts are very finely ground and the mixture has the texture of slightly damp sand. If the mixture is too dry, add a little more water, 1 teaspoon at a time, until the desired consistency is reached.
2. Assemble and bake the turnovers: Preheat the oven to 350°F (180°C). Line two large baking sheets with parchment paper.
3. On a lightly floured surface, gently roll out 1 sheet of puff pastry until it is ⅛ inch (3 mm) thick. Using a 3-inch (7.5 cm) round cookie cutter, stamp out as many circles of pastry as you can and transfer them to one of the baking sheets.
4. Scoop out rounded teaspoons of the filling, gently squeeze each one to form a football shape, and place in the center of a pastry circle. Fold the circles in half to form a half-moon shape, and use the tines of a fork to gently press the edges together to seal. Repeat with the remaining pastry and filling.
5. Beat the egg in a small bowl and brush the tops of the turnovers with this egg wash. (You will not use all of it.) Bake the turnovers, rotating the baking sheets back to front and top to bottom once halfway through baking, until they are puffed and golden brown, 20 to 25 minutes. Set the baking sheets on wire racks to cool.
6. Just before serving, use a fine-mesh sieve to lightly dust the tops of the turnovers with confectioners' sugar, if desired.

CHOCOLATE AND CINNAMON PALMIERS

Makes about 32 pastries

Many Jewish communities celebrate Purim by baking up treats meant to symbolize the Purim story's villain, Haman. The most widely known example is hamantaschen (see page 66), triangular-shaped cookies that Ashkenazi Jews say look like Haman's hat or pockets. In France, some Jewish families serve the sweet coiled puff pastry treats called palmiers. The pastries are rolled and sliced to resemble Haman's misshapen ears, rather than a hat (or pocket). My take on the classic French pastry adds cocoa powder and cinnamon to the traditional sugar coating, along with chocolate chips for a double dose of chocolate. Serve these crisp, gently sweet pastries with a cup of tea or coffee.

¾ cup (150 g) granulated sugar

2 tablespoons unsweetened cocoa powder

1½ teaspoons ground cinnamon

⅛ teaspoon kosher salt

One 17-ounce (482 g) package frozen puff pastry (2 sheets), thawed

½ cup (90 g) mini chocolate chips for sprinkling

NOTE: Start with thawed but still-cold-from-the-fridge puff pastry.

1. Preheat the oven to 400°F (200°C). Line two large baking sheets with parchment paper.
2. Stir together the sugar, cocoa powder, cinnamon, and salt in a medium bowl. Sprinkle a large clean work surface with 2 tablespoons of this mixture. Unfold one of the puff pastry sheets on the sugared surface and use a rolling pin to roll it into a 9 × 12-inch (23 × 30 cm) rectangle.
3. Sprinkle the top of the dough evenly with ¼ cup (50 g) of the remaining sugar mixture, followed by half of the mini chocolate chips. Gently run the rolling pin over the pastry a few times to press the sugar mixture and chips into it.
4. Roll the short sides of the dough over toward the center so they meet in the middle. Flip the rolled pastry over and gently press together. Using a sharp serrated knife, cut the pastry into ½-inch- (12 mm) wide slices and place the slices on their sides on one of the baking sheets, leaving about 1 inch (2.5 cm) between them.
5. Repeat the process with the remaining pastry, cinnamon-sugar mixture, and mini chocolate chips.
6. Bake, carefully flipping the palmiers over halfway through with a thin metal spatula, until puffed and golden, 14 to 16 minutes. Remove from the oven and let the palmiers cool on the baking sheets for a few minutes, then transfer to wire racks to cool completely.
7. Store any leftovers, covered, at room temperature for up to 3 days or in the fridge for up to 1 week. Rewarm briefly in the oven or toaster oven before serving.

CLASSIC WALNUT BAKLAVA

Makes one 9 × 13-inch (23 × 33 cm) pastry

This *is* your grandma's baklava—or rather, it's Alex Artinian's grandma's baklava. As a chef at Lehrhaus—an innovative Jewish restaurant in Somerville, Massachusetts—Artinian is accustomed to giving creative spins to familiar Jewish sweets. But when it comes to baklava, she swears by her Armenian grandmother's Old World approach. So while many contemporary baklava recipes switch up the type of nuts used, stir in spices like cardamom or ginger, or add splashes of orange blossom water and lemon juice to the sticky syrup that is poured over top, she keeps things simple. "My grandmother is adamant that no other nuts besides walnuts belong in baklava," she said. With all due respect to culinary experimentation, sometimes you just can't beat a classic. As one of my volunteer testers commented after making the baklava, "I initially wondered if it would taste flat without the little flourishes I've added to other recipes, but it was great—buttery, nutty, and balanced."

FOR THE SYRUP

1 cup (200 g) granulated sugar

1 cup (240 ml) water

FOR THE BAKLAVA

3½ cups (350 g) walnut halves

½ cup (100 g) granulated sugar

1 tablespoon ground cinnamon

½ teaspoon kosher salt

16 tablespoons (2 sticks / 227 g) unsalted butter or vegan butter, cut into pieces

1 box frozen phyllo dough sheets (9 × 14 inches; 23 × 35 cm), thawed

1. Make the syrup: Combine the sugar and water in a medium saucepan and bring to a boil over high heat, stirring to dissolve the sugar, then reduce the heat to medium-low and cook, stirring occasionally, until the syrup is slightly thickened, about 5 minutes. Remove from the heat and set aside to cool completely.

2. Make the baklava: Combine the walnuts, sugar, cinnamon, and salt in a food processor and pulse, scraping down the sides of the bowl as necessary, until the mixture resembles crumbs. Set aside.

3. Arrange a large cutting board and a 9 × 13-inch (23 × 33 cm) baking dish side by side.

4. Melt the butter in a small saucepan over medium heat or in the microwave in 20-second bursts, stirring after each. Remove from the heat.

5. Unwrap the phyllo sheets and use a pair of sharp scissors to trim them to fit the baking dish—you should be able to cut the entire stack at once. Place the trimmed stack on the cutting board and cover it with a damp dish towel to prevent it from drying out as you work.

6. Fit one sheet of phyllo into the bottom of the baking dish and use a large pastry brush to brush it evenly with melted butter. Repeat this process 9 more times, brushing each sheet with butter and ending up with a stack of 10 phyllo sheets.

7. Scoop the ground walnut mixture on top of the buttered phyllo and spread into an even layer. Repeat the stacking process with the remaining 10 phyllo sheets, brushing each layer with butter. Transfer the baking dish to the refrigerator and chill for 20 to 30 minutes.
8. Preheat the oven to 350°F (180°C).
9. Use a sharp knife to cut a square or diamond pattern into the chilled baklava (making sure to cut all the way through to the bottom). Bake until the top is deep golden brown and crisp, 35 to 40 minutes.
10. Remove the pan from the oven and set the baking sheet on a wire rack. Carefully and evenly pour the cooled syrup over the hot baklava (it should sizzle on contact), and let it fully cool. Just before serving, cut the pastry along the original scored lines.
11. Store leftovers, covered, at room temperature for up to 3 days or in the refrigerator for up to 1 week. If desired, briefly rewarm the baklava in the oven or toaster oven before serving.

SWEET CHEESE BOUGATSA

Makes one 9 × 13-inch (23 × 33 cm) pastry

I find it hard to think of a dessert more bewitching than bougatsa—a Greek pie that fills phyllo with a thick layer of sweet custard and bakes it until crunchy and golden. Try as I might, it is nearly impossible to limit myself to one slice. In Nicholas Stavroulakis's *Cookbook of the Jews of Greece* (published in 1986), he writes that in the Greek town of Ioannina, "bougatsa was traditionally prepared from what is known in Greek as *staka*, a rich, heavy cream obtained from water buffalo or sheep milk." Stavroulakis's 1980s spin on the Old World recipe calls for cream cheese or another "very soft, very creamy, white unsalted cheese." Other versions of bougatsa I have come across fill the pie with a milky semolina custard instead of sweetened cheese. I decided to take a "best of all worlds" approach, mixing softened cream cheese, Italian mascarpone, and a bit of semolina for a simple-to-prepare but undeniably sumptuous pastry. Serve bougatsa on Shavuot along-side cheesecake, at a Yom Kippur break fast meal, or as a centerpiece for brunch.

8 ounces (226 g) cream cheese, softened

8 ounces (226 g) mascarpone, at room temperature

1 cup (200 g) granulated sugar

4 large eggs

2 tablespoons fine semolina

1 teaspoon vanilla extract or vanilla bean paste

Grated zest of 1 large orange

10 tablespoons (1¼ sticks / 142 g) unsalted butter

10 frozen phyllo dough sheets (9 × 14 inches / 23 × 35 cm), thawed

Confectioners' sugar for dusting

1. In the bowl of a stand mixer fitted with a paddle attachment (or using a handheld electric mixer and a large bowl), beat the cream cheese, mascarpone, and granulated sugar together until creamy, about 1 minute. Add the eggs, semolina, vanilla, and orange zest and beat, scraping down the sides of the bowl as necessary, until fully combined.

2. Arrange a large cutting board and a 9 × 13-inch (23 × 33 cm) baking dish side by side on a work surface.

3. Melt the butter in a small saucepan over medium heat or in the micro-wave in 20-second bursts, stirring after each. Remove from the heat.

4. Unwrap the phyllo sheets and use a pair of sharp scissors to trim them to fit the baking dish (you should be able to cut the entire stack at once). Place the trimmed phyllo stack on the cutting board and cover it with a damp dish towel to prevent it from drying out as you work.

5. Fit one sheet of phyllo into the bottom of the baking dish and use a large pastry brush to brush it evenly with melted butter. Repeat this process 4 more times, brushing each sheet with butter and ending up with a stack of 5 phyllo sheets.

6. Pour the sweet cheese filling over the top of the buttered phyllo and smooth the top. Repeat the stacking process with the remaining 5 phyllo sheets and remaining melted butter. Cover the baking dish and refrigerate for 30 minutes to allow the butter to firm up.

7. Preheat the oven to 375°F (190°C).

8. Using a sharp knife, score the pastry into 15 squares. Bake until the top is flaky and deep golden brown, about 40 minutes. Remove from the oven and transfer the baking dish to a wire rack. Cut through the pastry again along the original scoring lines (making sure to reach the bottom of the pan), then let cool until slightly warm or room temperature.

9. Just before serving, use a fine-mesh sieve to dust the top of the pastry with confectioners' sugar. Store any leftovers, covered, in the fridge for up to 5 days.

PUDDINGS & FRUIT DESSERTS

PERSIAN RICE PUDDING

Serves 6 to 8

This rice pudding, called *shir berenj* ("milk rice"), is beloved by Jewish and non-Jewish Iranians alike. Muslims serve it to break the fast after Ramadan, while Jews enjoy it for Passover and Shavuot. (It is also a nourishing anytime favorite among children.) The rice is cooked for an extended time, which breaks down the grains' starches and results in a sweet, comforting porridge that is then flavored with cardamom and rose water. This sweet is typically served chilled, but I also like it warm from the pot.

- ¾ cup (135 g) jasmine rice, rinsed and drained
- 4 cardamom pods, cracked
- 1 cinnamon stick
- ¼ teaspoon kosher salt
- 4 cups (945 ml) water
- 4 cups (945 ml) milk or nondairy milk, warmed
- ½ cup (100 g) granulated sugar
- ¾ teaspoon rose water, plus more if desired
- Finely chopped pistachios for serving

1. Combine the rice, cardamom pods, cinnamon stick, salt, and water in a large wide pot and bring to a boil over medium-high heat, then turn the heat down to medium and cook, stirring occasionally, until almost all of the liquid is absorbed and the rice is very tender and beginning to fall apart, about 20 minutes.
2. Stir in the warmed milk, turn the heat back up to medium-high, and bring to a boil. Turn the heat down to medium-low and continue cooking the mixture at a slow bubble, stirring often, until it thickens into a soupy porridge, about 20 minutes. (It will still be loose at this stage, but it will continue to thicken as it cools.)
3. Remove the pot from the heat and immediately stir in the sugar and rose water. Let the pudding cool for 30 minutes, stirring occasionally, then taste and add more rose water, if desired.
4. Remove and discard the cardamom pods and cinnamon stick, then transfer the rice pudding to a container with a lid and chill for at least 4 hours, and up to overnight.
5. Serve the pudding chilled, sprinkled with chopped pistachios. Store any leftovers, covered, in the fridge for up to 3 days.

NOTE: Warm the milk on the stovetop, or in the microwave for 20 to 30 seconds, until steaming but not boiling.

VARIATION: Many recipes for shir berenj are additionally flavored with saffron. If desired, mix a pinch of crumbled saffron threads with 1 tablespoon of boiling water and let steep for at least 5 minutes. Stir the mixture into the rice pudding along with the sugar and rose water.

RICE-FLOUR PUDDING

Serves 4 to 6

The first time I tried sutlach—a milky pudding thickened with rice flour—was at a Turkish café deep in South Brooklyn. As a longtime New Yorker, I have enjoyed countless bowls of the thick raisin-studded rice pudding served in the city's many Greek diners. But sutlach's silky texture, as smooth as the surface of a lake, was something entirely different (and wonderful). Sephardi Jews serve sutlach for Shabbat breakfast, as a treat on Purim, and to break the Yom Kippur fast. The top of the pudding is typically sprinkled with cinnamon—sometimes in the shape of Hebrew letters, a Star of David, or, especially when served to children, with the child's initials. Simple, sweet, and soothing, a bowl of rice-flour pudding makes the perfect end to any light meal.

½ cup (85 g) white rice flour

⅔ cup (130 g) granulated sugar

¼ teaspoon kosher salt

4 cups (945 ml) milk or nondairy milk

2 teaspoons vanilla extract or vanilla bean paste

½ packed teaspoon grated lemon zest

Ground cinnamon for dusting

1. Whisk together the rice flour, sugar, and salt in a medium saucepan (off the heat). Whisk in about ⅓ cup (80 ml) of the milk until the mixture forms a smooth paste.

2. Set the saucepan over medium heat and whisk in the remaining milk. Switch to a spoon or silicone spatula and stir constantly as the mixture heats up and thickens, about 10 minutes. (Do not let it come to a full boil; nudge the heat down a bit if necessary.)

3. Once the mixture has thickened into a soupy pudding, remove it from the heat and stir in the vanilla and lemon zest. Transfer the pudding to a container or divide among individual bowls or ramekins and let cool to room temperature. The pudding will continue to thicken a bit as it cools.

4. Cover the pudding and refrigerate for at least 4 hours, and up to overnight. Serve chilled, lightly dusted with cinnamon.

JEWS AND THE SUGAR TRADE

As a diasporic people spread throughout the world, Jews have played a central role in many global industries, including the sugar trade. In the fifteenth and sixteenth centuries, Portuguese Jews and Crypto-Jews (people who were coerced into converting to Christianity during the Spanish Inquisition) were central in helping Dutch companies establish a cane sugar industry in Brazil and, later, in countries like Jamaica, Barbados, and Suriname.

These Sephardi immigrants and refugees worked as merchants and shippers, operated sugar mills and refineries, and became distillers who transformed cane sugar into rum. They established some of the oldest Jewish communities and synagogues in the Americas. Some also owned sugarcane plantations, which, regrettably, meant that Jews were involved in the slave trade and owned enslaved people—all the while facing discrimination themselves. (In the 1630s, for example, the Dutch expelled all Jews from Brazil.)

In Eastern Europe, where sugarcane could not be grown reliably, honey was originally the primary sweetener. That changed in the eighteenth and nineteenth centuries with the introduction of the sugar beet—a variety of the root vegetable with a high concentration of sucrose that could be refined into table sugar. Before long, Jewish sugar beet farmers throughout the Russian Empire began producing beet sugar to supply both local and European markets.

Sugar beets grew readily in the region's soils, and before long, Ukraine became a center of the sugar trade. As professor Jenna Weissman Joselit writes in an article for *Tablet Magazine*, "Jewish entrepreneurs, among them Yisra'el Brodsky and his sons, Lev and Lazar (who was known as the 'Sugar King'), developed their own network of sugar refineries, which, by the late nineteenth century, reportedly supplied nearly 25 percent of all the sugar consumed throughout Tsarist Russia." The connection between Jews and the sugar industry has faded in more recent decades, but the community's impact on sugar production reverberates through to today.

BAKED PUMPKIN PIE CUSTARD

Serves 6

In *The Book of Jewish Food*, Claudia Roden includes a recipe for a Venetian Jewish pumpkin custard called Budino di Zucca Gialla. "This creamy specialty of Veneto is my favorite Italian pumpkin dish," she writes. "Everyone marvels at how good it is." Similar to many Ashkenazi kugels, Roden's budino, which contains only a couple of teaspoons of sugar, straddles the line between sweet and savory and is typically served as a side dish. My version adds just enough brown sugar, cinnamon, and ginger to nudge the baked custard more decisively toward dessert. (If you use potato starch instead of flour, it also makes a welcome addition to the Passover dessert table.) As one of my volunteer recipe testers described it, "It tastes like pumpkin pie without the crust." Serve the custard as is or topped with crushed graham crackers, whipped cream, and chocolate shavings.

One 15-ounce (425 g) can pure pumpkin puree (not pumpkin pie filling)

3 large eggs

¾ packed cup (150 g) light brown sugar

2 tablespoons all-purpose flour or potato starch

1 teaspoon vanilla extract or vanilla bean paste

2 teaspoons ground cinnamon, plus more for serving

½ teaspoon ground ginger

¼ teaspoon allspice

¼ teaspoon kosher salt

½ cup (120 ml) milk or nondairy milk, warmed

1. Preheat the oven to 350°F (180°C). Lightly grease six 6-ounce (170 g) ramekins.
2. Whisk together the pumpkin puree, eggs, brown sugar, flour, vanilla, cinnamon, ginger, allspice, and salt in a large bowl until well combined. Slowly pour in the warmed milk, whisking constantly until fully incorporated.
3. Divide the pumpkin mixture evenly among the ramekins and place the ramekins in a 9 × 13-inch (23 x 33 cm) baking dish. Carefully pour enough boiling water into the baking dish to come about halfway up the sides of the ramekins.
4. Bake until the custard is just set (it should still feel soft at the center), 35 to 40 minutes. Immediately remove the ramekins from the water bath and set on a wire rack to cool.
5. Serve the custard slightly warm, dusted with a little cinnamon. Or let cool, cover, and refrigerate until chilled, about 4 hours. Store any left-overs, covered, in the fridge for up to 3 days.

NOTE: Warm the milk on the stovetop, or in the microwave for 20 to 30 seconds, until steaming but not boiling.

STRAWBERRY RHUBARB MALABI

Serves 6

Variations of this silky custard are popular throughout the Middle East, including Israel, where it is a common street food and ubiquitous on restaurant dessert menus. The cornstarch-thickened custard is most often served with a bright-pink, rose-raspberry syrup. It is beautiful to look at but too aggressively sweet for my taste. I prefer this seasonally inspired version, which is topped with springtime's dynamic duo of strawberries and rhubarb cooked into a slumpy compote. The bright-red compote spooned on top of the snowy-white pudding maintains the dramatic visual contrast of the original, while the rhubarb lends a welcome tartness.

When rhubarb is out of season, top the malabi with date syrup (silan), raspberry jam, sour cherry jam, or another topping of your choice.

FOR THE MALABI

4 cups (945 ml) milk or nondairy milk), divided

½ cup (70 g) cornstarch or potato starch

½ cup (100 g) granulated sugar

2 teaspoons vanilla extract or vanilla bean paste

FOR THE STRAWBERRY-RHUBARB COMPOTE

1 pound (454 g) fresh strawberries, stems removed and quartered

8 ounces (227 g) rhubarb (about 3 medium stalks), ends trimmed and sliced into ½-inch- (12 mm) wide pieces

½ cup (100 g) granulated sugar

2 thick strips lemon or orange peel

NOTE: Use a vegetable peeler to peel off wide, thick strips of the citrus peel.

NOTE: This recipe makes more compote than you need for the malabi—spoon leftovers over yogurt, pancakes, or granola.

1. Make the malabi: Whisk together 1 cup (240 ml) of the milk and the cornstarch in a small bowl until the cornstarch dissolves. Set aside.
2. Whisk together the remaining 3 cups (705 ml) milk and the sugar in a medium saucepan. Set the pan over medium heat and bring to a simmer, whisking often.
3. Pour in the cornstarch-milk slurry and cook, whisking constantly, until the mixture thickens into the consistency of a loose pudding, 2 to 3 minutes. Remove from the heat and immediately whisk in the vanilla.
4. Divide the mixture evenly among six small serving bowls or ramekins and let cool to room temperature, then cover and refrigerate until chilled, about 4 hours. (*The malabi can be made up to 2 days in advance and kept refrigerated.*)
5. Make the compote: Stir together the strawberries, rhubarb, sugar, and citrus peel in a medium saucepan and bring the mixture to a simmer over medium heat, then turn the heat down to low and cook, stirring occasionally, until the fruit is very soft and falling apart and the liquid has thickened into a syrup, 15 to 20 minutes.
6. Remove from the heat and transfer the compote to a heatproof bowl. Let cool, then remove and discard the citrus peel, cover, and refrigerate until chilled, 2 to 3 hours. (*The compote can be made ahead and stored in the fridge for up to 5 days.*)
7. To serve, spoon some of of the compote over each bowl of malabi and serve the remainder alongside at the table.

SILKY VEGAN CHOCOLATE PUDDING

Serves 4 to 6

I am a sucker for a great chocolate pudding—the deeper the chocolate flavor, the better. But it is a challenge to create a thick, silky-smooth, dairy-free chocolate pudding that can be served after kosher meat meals. This recipe takes a lesson from the vegan playbook, using silken tofu (the soft, wobbly kind) in place of cream and eggs. Combined with melted chocolate, cocoa powder, vanilla, and just a hint of coffee to amplify the chocolate (don't skip it!), it makes a rich, creamy pudding that leaves absolutely nothing to be desired. Serve it in small ramekins or bowls, topped with fresh berries, shaved chocolate, or sprinkles.

⅓ cup (65 g) granulated sugar

⅓ cup (80 ml) almond milk or other nondairy milk

4 ounces (113 g) semisweet baking chocolate, chopped

½ teaspoon instant coffee granules (regular or decaf)

16 ounces (454 g) silken tofu, drained and roughly chopped

3 tablespoons unsweetened cocoa powder, sifted

2 teaspoons vanilla extract

¼ teaspoon kosher salt

1. Combine the sugar and almond milk in a small saucepan set over medium heat, and slowly bring to just shy of a boil, stirring often to dissolve the sugar. Remove from the heat and immediately whisk in the chopped chocolate and coffee granules until the chocolate is fully melted. Set aside to cool slightly.
2. Place the tofu in the bowl of a food processor, followed by the cocoa powder, vanilla, and salt. Pour in the warm chocolate mixture and pulse, scraping down the sides of the processor bowl as necessary, until the mixture is completely smooth.
3. Transfer the pudding to a container, cover, and refrigerate until chilled, about 3 hours.
4. Serve the pudding cold. Store any leftovers, covered, in the fridge for up to 3 days.

TEA BISCUIT TIRAMISU

Serves 6 to 8

Many celebrations in Israel (particularly during the hottest months, when turning on the oven to bake feels cruel) feature ugat bisquvitim, or "biscuit cake." The no-bake icebox cake is made from petit beurre–style biscuits layered with a combination of vanilla pudding mix, whipped heavy cream, and, sometimes, a soft white cheese called gvina levana. As the cake chills in the fridge, the biscuits are softened by all that luscious dairy, forming a soft, scoopable, entirely decadent dessert. In this variation, I nixed the instant pudding in favor of tangy sour cream and leaned into the cake's obvious tiramisu parallels. Each biscuit is briefly dipped in espresso (spiked with Cognac, if you'd like), dolloped with the sour cream and whipped cream mixture, and generously sprinkled with cocoa powder. Serve it for Shavuot, when eating dairy foods is de rigueur, or as a special birthday dessert.

2 cups (475 ml) heavy cream

½ cup (100 g) granulated sugar

1 cup (240 g) sour cream

2 teaspoons vanilla extract or vanilla bean paste

½ teaspoon kosher salt

1½ cups (355 ml) espresso or strong brewed coffee, cooled

1 to 2 tablespoons dark rum or Cognac (optional)

About 45 petit beurre biscuits (tea biscuits; about 2½ × 1½ inches / 6 × 8 cm)

Cocoa powder for dusting

1. In the bowl of a stand mixer fitted with the whisk attachment (or using a handheld electric mixer and a large bowl), whisk the heavy cream on medium-high speed, adding the sugar a couple of tablespoons at a time, until the cream holds stiff peaks. Whisk in the sour cream, vanilla extract, and salt.
2. Pour the espresso into a medium bowl and whisk in the rum, if using.
3. Assemble the dish: Spread about one-quarter of the whipped cream mixture over the bottom of a 9-inch (23-cm) square baking dish. Working with a few at a time, briefly dip the biscuits on both sides in the espresso mixture (not too long, or they will fall apart) and arrange in the baking dish in a single, even layer.
4. Dollop another quarter of the whipped cream mixture onto the biscuits and spread it evenly over them. Use a fine-mesh sieve to dust the whipped cream with about 1 tablespoon cocoa powder. Repeat the layering process twice with two more layers of biscuits, and end with the last quarter of the whipped cream and a final dusting of cocoa powder.
5. Cover the baking dish and refrigerate until chilled, at least 4 hours, and up to overnight, before serving.

FLAN NAPOLITANO

Makes one 8-inch (20 cm) flan

From her Mexican sweets company, La Newyorkina, to her popular Brooklyn doughnut shop, Fan Fan Donuts, chef Fany Gerson is one of the most innovative pastry chefs in New York City. She credits much of her creative spirit to growing up in a Mexican Jewish family in Mexico City. "I love finding ways for my two cultures to come together," she says. And yet sometimes tradition takes center stage—as with her family's Flan Napolitano recipe.

Flan's origins date back to ancient Rome. In pre-Inquisition Spain, cooks began adding caramelized sugar to the egg-based custard, and Sephardi Jews developed dairy-free versions. Spanish settlers introduced flan to Latin America, where it quickly took root. In Mexico, the dessert evolved again and a new variation with cream cheese, called *flan Napolitano*, emerged. Gerson shared her family's favorite recipe for flan, which they serve on Passover. "With no crust, flan is naturally Passover-friendly, and so delicious," she said.

FOR THE CARAMEL

1¼ cups (250 g) granulated sugar

¼ cup (60 ml) water

½ teaspoon fresh lemon juice

FOR THE CUSTARD

One 14-ounce (395 g) can sweetened condensed milk

One 12-ounce (355 ml) can evaporated milk

4 large eggs

4 ounces (113 g) cream cheese, softened

2 teaspoons vanilla extract or vanilla bean paste

½ teaspoon kosher salt

1. Preheat the oven to 350°F (180°C). Make the caramel: Stir together the sugar, water, and lemon juice in a medium saucepan. Set the saucepan over medium heat and bring the mixture to a simmer (do not stir), then reduce the heat to medium-low and cook, swirling the saucepan occasionally, until a rich amber caramel forms, 10 to 20 minutes.

2. Pour the caramel evenly over the bottom of an 8-inch (20 cm) round cake pan and let cool a bit while you make the custard.

3. Make the custard: Combine the sweetened condensed milk, evaporated milk, eggs, cream cheese, vanilla paste, and salt in a high-powered blender and blend until completely smooth. Pour the custard mixture over the caramel in the cake pan. Cover the pan tightly with foil and set it in a 9 × 13-inch (23 × 33 cm) baking dish.

4. Place the baking dish in the oven and carefully pour enough boiling water into the dish to come about halfway up the sides of the cake pan. Bake until the flan has set but is still a bit jiggly at the center, 50 to 65 minutes. Remove from the oven.

5. Carefully take the cake pan out of the baking dish, remove the foil, and set the pan on a wire rack to cool for 1 hour, then cover and refrigerate until the flan is chilled, at least 4 hours, and up to overnight.

6. When ready to serve, run a wet knife around the sides of the cake pan to loosen the caramel, then carefully invert the pan onto a serving plate and lift it off. Store any leftovers, covered, in the fridge for up to 5 days.

MILK TART

Makes one 9-inch (23 cm) round tart

For nearly a decade, Philadelphia's Essen Bakery was a beloved local hub of Jewish breads and pastries. (The shop closed in late 2025.) Owner Tova du Plessis's menu offered everything from chocolate halva babka and apple cake to fresh loaves of challah and rye bread. She drew inspiration from her upbringing in Johannesburg, South Africa, where her mother baked babka and chiffon cakes for Shabbat and holidays. But she was also exposed to South African desserts like malva pudding and this milk tart. Called *melktert* in South Africa, the dessert bakes a wobbly, vanilla-flecked custard inside a buttery crust. "Growing up, if it was Shavuot, or if someone was making a dairy meal or had an event with a dessert spread, milk tart would be there," du Plessis says. Milk Tart was not on the menu at Essen Bakery, but du Plessis shared her recipe with me, so unadulterated dairy goodness is only a mixing bowl away.

FOR THE CRUST

1½ cups (210 g) all-purpose flour
1 tablespoon granulated sugar
¼ teaspoon baking powder
¼ teaspoon kosher salt
8 tablespoons (1 stick / 113 g) cold unsalted butter, cut into pieces
¼ cup (60 ml) cold water, plus more if needed

NOTE: You can make decorations for the top of the tart using any excess pie dough. After rolling out the crust, gather up and reroll the trimmings to a ⅛-inch (3 mm) thickness. Stamp out shapes with cookie cutters and bake on a parchment-lined baking sheet at 350°F (180°C) until golden, 10 to 15 minutes. Let cool, then arrange the shapes on top of the cooled tart.

1. Make the crust: Combine the flour, sugar, baking powder, and salt in the bowl of a food processor and pulse briefly to combine. Add the butter pieces and pulse until the mixture resembles coarse crumbs, with some larger, pea-sized clumps of butter.

2. Drizzle in the cold water and pulse until a crumbly dough forms. If the mixture is too dry to hold together when pinched, add more cold water, about 1 teaspoon at a time, until the desired consistency is reached.

3. Transfer the dough to a work surface, knead briefly to bring it together, and form into a disk. Wrap the disk well in parchment paper and refrigerate for at least 1 hour, and up to overnight.

4. On a lightly floured surface, using a lightly floured rolling pin, roll the dough into a 13-inch (33 cm) circle. Carefully transfer the dough to a 9-inch (23 cm) pie pan and fit it over the bottom and up the sides of the pan.

5. Trim off the excess dough, leaving about ½ inch (12 mm) of overhang, and flute the edges. Poke the bottom of the crust in several places with a fork and freeze the crust while you preheat the oven to 350°F (180°C).

6. Bake the crust until it is set and golden, 25 to 30 minutes. Remove from the oven and set on a wire rack to cool completely.

FOR THE FILLING AND TOPPING

3 cups (710 ml) whole milk

½ cup (100 g) granulated sugar, divided

1 tablespoon unsalted butter

2 teaspoons vanilla bean paste (or 1 vanilla bean pod, seeds scraped out and reserved)

2 tablespoons cornstarch

2 tablespoons all-purpose flour

¼ teaspoon kosher salt

1 large egg

Ground cinnamon for dusting

7. Make the filling: Whisk together the milk, ¼ cup (50 g) of the sugar, the butter, and vanilla bean paste in a medium saucepan, set it over medium heat, and let the mixture heat up until it is just shy of boiling, regularly stirring and scraping the bottom of the saucepan with a silicone spatula.

8. Meanwhile, whisk together the cornstarch, flour, salt, the remaining ¼ cup (50 g) sugar, and the egg in a medium bowl until smooth. When the milk is steaming, but not boiling, pour about ⅓ cup (80 ml) of the hot milk into the flour and cornstarch mixture, whisking to form a slurry.

9. Turn the heat under the milk down to medium-low and pour the slurry into the saucepan. Whisk constantly until the mixture thickens, about 2 minutes. Remove from the heat and let cool for a few minutes, then pour the hot custard through a fine-mesh sieve into the cooled crust, using a silicone spatula to push it through if needed.

10. Let the custard cool to room temperature, then cover and chill in the fridge until fully set, about 4 hours, or up to overnight.

11. Just before serving, use a fine-mesh sieve to lightly dust the top of the tart with cinnamon. Store any leftovers, covered, in the fridge for up to 5 days.

SWEET SEMOLINA PUDDING WITH TOASTED NUTS

Serves 4 to 6

The majority of India's historic Jewish communities now live in Israel, where they continue to prepare many traditional dishes, including this sweet semolina pudding. Called *sheera* by the Cochin Jews who originally hailed from southwestern India, the dish gets its complexity from the ghee (clarified butter) used to toast the semolina grains, and from the addition of cardamom and saffron. Sweet, fragrant, and nourishing, it is served for both breakfast and dessert.

- 4 tablespoons clarified butter (ghee), divided
- ¼ cup (35 g) raw cashews
- ¼ cup (35 g) raw almonds
- ½ cup (80 g) fine semolina
- 2 cups (475 ml) boiling water
- ½ cup (100 g) granulated sugar
- ¼ teaspoon ground cardamom, plus more for sprinkling
- Small pinch of saffron threads, crumbled
- ⅛ teaspoon kosher salt
- ¼ cup (35 g) dark raisins

1. Heat 2 tablespoons of the butter in a medium saucepan over medium-low heat. Add the cashews and almonds and cook, stirring often, until fragrant and golden, 2 to 3 minutes. (Watch carefully so they do not burn.) Remove from the heat and transfer the nuts to a cutting board to cool briefly, then chop them. (Do not start step 2 until the nuts have cooled and been chopped.)
2. Add the remaining 2 tablespoons ghee to the same saucepan and set it over medium heat. Add the semolina and cook, stirring often, until it begins to take on a golden color, 1 to 2 minutes.
3. Meanwhile, stir together the boiling water, sugar, cardamom, saffron, and salt in a medium bowl.
4. Stirring constantly, slowly pour the hot water-sugar mixture into the semolina. Bring the mixture to a low boil and cook, stirring frequently, until the semolina thickens into a soupy porridge, 2 to 5 minutes.
5. Remove the saucepan from heat and stir in the raisins and about half of the nuts. Divide the semolina pudding among small bowls or ramekins and serve hot or warm, sprinkled with the remaining nuts and a pinch of additional cardamom.

SERVING VARIATION: Spoon the hot semolina mixture into small bowls or ramekins, gently smoothing the tops with the back of a spoon. Refrigerate for 30 minutes, or until the semolina has set. Run a butter knife around the edges of each bowl, then invert the bowls to release the dome-shaped semolina puddings onto serving plates.

ANCIENT-GRAINS APPLE CRISP

Serves 8 to 10

The Torah mentions seven agricultural products that were cultivated in the land of Israel during biblical times: barley, wheat, figs, dates, olives, grapes, and pomegranate. In homage to Jewish tradition's ancient agricultural roots, I swapped sweet and nutty barley flour for the usual all-purpose flour in this crumble. Paired with oats for texture and ground ginger and cinnamon for warmth and complexity, the crumble topping serves as a majestic cap for the sweet, bubbly fruit below. My family's annual apple picking trip usually lands somewhere right around Sukkot, which means this crisp—made with local apples—is often on our holiday dessert table.

FOR THE CRUMBLE TOPPING

- 1 cup (100 g) old-fashioned rolled oats
- ¾ cup (110 g) barley flour
- ¾ packed cup (150 g) light brown sugar
- 1½ teaspoons ground cinnamon
- 1 teaspoon ground ginger
- ¾ teaspoon baking powder
- ½ teaspoon kosher salt
- 8 tablespoons (1 stick / 113 g) unsalted butter or vegan butter, cut into pieces and softened

FOR THE FILLING

- 8 medium baking apples (about 3 pounds / 1.4 kg), peeled, quartered, cored, and thinly sliced lengthwise
- 3 tablespoons cornstarch
- ¼ cup (60 ml) apple juice or apple cider
- ⅔ cup (130 g) granulated sugar
- ½ packed teaspoon grated lemon zest (optional)
- 1 tablespoon fresh lemon juice

1. Preheat the oven to 350°F (180°C).
2. Make the topping: Stir together the oats, barley flour, brown sugar, cinnamon, ginger, baking powder, and salt in a medium bowl. Add the butter pieces and press the mixture together with your fingers to combine. You should end up with small clumps. Set aside.
3. Make the filling: Combine the sliced apples, cornstarch, apple juice, sugar, lemon zest, if using, and lemon juice in a large bowl and stir to mix. Transfer the fruit to a 9 × 13-inch (23 × 33 cm) baking dish and gently smooth it into an even layer. Scatter the topping evenly over the fruit.
4. Bake the crisp until the top is golden and the fruit is tender and bubbling, 45 to 55 minutes. Remove from the oven and let cool for at least 30 minutes before serving, to allow the juices to thicken.
5. Store any leftovers, covered, in the fridge for up to 4 days.

SYRUP-POACHED APRICOTS WITH CLOTTED CREAM

Makes 18 stuffed apricots

Turkey is the world's largest apricot producer, so it is no wonder that Turkish cuisine (both within the Jewish community and beyond) includes many ways to serve the juicy stone fruit. In this dessert, called *kaymakli kayisi tatlisi*, dried apricots are poached in syrup until they plump up, then are split and stuffed with a thick clotted cream called *kaymak*. Mascarpone, the soft fresh Italian cheese, makes a worthy substitute if you cannot find kaymak. The combination of sweet, succulent fruit; rich cream; and a sprinkle of chopped pistachios makes a simple but beguiling dessert. For the best results, use the largest, most succulent dried apricots you can find.

- 1½ cups (355 ml) water
- 1 cup (200 g) granulated sugar
- 18 large dried apricots (about 8 ounces / 225 g)
- 1 tablespoon fresh lemon juice
- About 1 cup (240 g) kaymak (or substitute clotted cream or mascarpone)
- Finely chopped roasted salted pistachios for dipping

1. Combine the water and sugar in a medium saucepan and bring to a boil over medium-high heat. Add the apricots and lemon juice, lower the heat to medium, and simmer, stirring occasionally, until the apricots are tender, 10 to 15 minutes. Remove from the heat and let the apricots cool completely in the poaching liquid.
2. Using a small, sharp knife, make a slit down one side of an apricot and fill with about 1 tablespoon of kaymak. Spread a layer of chopped pistachios on a plate. Dip the stuffed side of the apricot into the pistachios and transfer to a serving platter. Repeat with the remaining apricots, kaymak, and chopped nuts.
3. Serve the apricots drizzled with some of the poaching liquid. Store any leftovers in an airtight container in the fridge for up to 3 days.

NOTE: Any leftover syrup can be combined with seltzer for a refreshing spritzer.

STREUSEL-TOPPED PLUM GALETTE

Serves 6

At the end of summer, right on the cusp of early fall, German Jews bake plum cake (*pflaumenkuchen* in Yiddish) to celebrate the peak of the stone fruit's season. There are many iterations of plum cake, but my favorite ones come topped with a layer of cinnamon-perfumed streusel. In this riff on German plum cake, I traded cake batter for piecrust—specifically, for a free-form galette. I love how the buttery crust drapes over just the edges of the filling, letting the spiral of jammy, streusel-topped plums take center stage. You can use any kind of ripe in-season plum you like, but red-fleshed plums are particularly beautiful here.

FOR THE DOUGH

1½ cups (210 g) all-purpose flour

12 tablespoons (1½ sticks / 170 g) cold unsalted butter or vegan butter, cut into small pieces

½ teaspoon kosher salt

3 to 5 tablespoons ice water

FOR THE FILLING

1 pound (454 g) plums (5 to 7 medium), pitted and cut lengthwise into ¼-inch (6 mm) slices

⅓ cup (65 g) granulated sugar

½ teaspoon grated lemon zest

1 tablespoon fresh lemon juice

1 tablespoon all-purpose flour

NOTE: To give the crust a slightly nuttier flavor profile, substitute up to half of the all-purpose flour with whole wheat flour.

1. Make the dough: Combine the flour, butter, and salt in a food processor and pulse several times until the mixture resembles coarse crumbs. Drizzle in 3 tablespoons ice water and continue pulsing until the dough begins to clump together. (It should hold together when squeezed.) If it is still too dry and crumbly, drizzle in up to 2 additional tablespoons of water, a little at a time, as needed.
2. Turn out the dough, gather it together, and form it into a disk. Wrap in parchment paper and refrigerate for at least 3 hours, and up to overnight.
3. When ready to bake, preheat the oven to 375°F (190°C). Line a large baking sheet with parchment paper.
4. Make the filling: Combine the sliced plums, sugar, lemon zest, lemon juice, and flour in a medium bowl, stirring to coat the plums with sugar. Set aside.
5. Make the streusel: Combine the flour, brown sugar, cinnamon, salt, and butter in a medium bowl and rub the ingredients together until the mixture resembles coarse crumbs. (Do not overmix.) Set aside.
6. On a floured work surface, using a floured rolling pin, roll the dough out into an approximately 12-inch (30 cm) circle; trim off and discard any jagged edges. Carefully transfer the dough circle to the baking sheet.
7. Arrange the plums in an overlapping circular pattern on top of the dough, leaving about a 1½ inch- (4 cm) border all around. (Discard any

FOR THE STREUSEL AND FINISHING

¼ cup (35 g) all-purpose flour

¼ packed cup (50 g) light brown sugar

¾ teaspoon ground cinnamon

⅛ teaspoon kosher salt

2 tablespoons cold unsalted butter or vegan butter, cut into small pieces

1 large egg, beaten, for egg wash

juices in the bottom of the bowl.) Sprinkle the streusel evenly over the plums. Fold the border of dough up over the filling at overlapping intervals, leaving most of the plums visible.

8. Use a pastry brush to brush the crust (not the plums or streusel) with a layer of egg wash. (You will not use all of it.)

9. Bake the galette until the fruit is bubbling and the crust is dark golden brown, 50 to 55 minutes. Remove from the oven and set the baking sheet on a wire rack. Let the galette cool before slicing. Serve warm or at room temperature.

10. Leftovers can be stored, covered, in the fridge for up to 3 days.

WHITE WINE–POACHED PEARS WITH CHOCOLATE SAUCE

Serves 6

Poached pears are simple to make and punch well above their weight to yield an impressively elegant dessert. The dish originated in France's wine-growing Beaujolais region, but its naturally dairy-free status has made it a favorite on American Jewish tables. My version poaches snappy Bosc pears in white wine steeped with cinnamon sticks and orange zest until they are spoon-tender, then enrobes the pears in a luscious chocolate sauce. The wine-drunk pears are particularly nice on Purim, when, according to Talmudic wisdom, Jewish people are obligated to drink until they cannot tell the difference between the phrases "cursed be Haman" (the Purim story's villain) and "blessed be Mordechai" (one of the story's heroes). Of course, the intoxicating alcohol gets cooked away as the pears simmer, but the sentiment remains. If you have any leftover pears after serving the dessert, they make a decadent breakfast alongside a scoop of yogurt. Any extra chocolate sauce can, and arguably should, be drizzled over ice cream.

FOR THE PEARS

- 2 cups (475 ml) dry white wine
- ¾ cup (180 ml) water
- ¾ cup (150 g) granulated sugar
- 2 cinnamon sticks
- 1 large orange
- 6 firm Bosc pears, peeled, with stems intact

FOR THE CHOCOLATE SAUCE

- 8 ounces (225 g) semisweet or bittersweet baking chocolate, chopped (or ¾ cup chocolate chips)
- ⅓ cup (80 ml) heavy cream, milk, or nondairy milk
- 3 to 5 tablespoons of the pear poaching liquid

1. Make the pears: Combine the wine, water, sugar, and cinnamon sticks in a large heavy-bottomed saucepan. Use a vegetable peeler to remove two long, wide strips of peel from the orange, then halve and juice the orange. Add the orange peel and juice to the saucepan and stir to combine.
2. Bring the mixture to a simmer over medium heat, stirring occasionally to dissolve the sugar. Add the pears to the liquid (they will not be fully submerged), turn the heat down to medium-low, and cover the pan. Cook, turning the pears occasionally to ensure all sides soak up the liquid, until tender all the way through when pierced with a knife but not falling apart, 30 to 45 minutes. Remove the saucepan from the heat and let the pears cool completely in the liquid, turning them occasionally, then remove and discard the orange peel and cinnamon sticks.
3. Refrigerate the pears in their liquid, covered, for at least 4 hours, and up to 3 days. The longer they sit, the more flavor they will develop.

recipe continues

4. When ready to serve, make the chocolate sauce: Combine the chopped chocolate, heavy cream, and 3 tablespoons poaching liquid in a microwave-safe bowl and microwave for 20-second intervals, stirring after each, until the chocolate is melted and the sauce is smooth and glossy. (The sauce can also be made in a double boiler.) If the sauce is too thick to drizzle, stir in up to 2 more tablespoons poaching liquid, 1 tablespoon at a time, until the desired consistency is reached.

5. The pears can served be chilled, at room temperature, or slightly warmed. Lay them on serving plates, or stand them up, if preferred. Spoon a heaping tablespoon of the chocolate sauce over one side of each pear, letting any excess pool at the bottom of the plate, and serve immediately, with any remaining chocolate sauce in a bowl alongside.

GRAPE SPOON SWEET

Serves 6

Many Sephardi families across Turkey, Greece, and the Balkans followed the custom of greeting visitors to their homes with "spoon sweets"—a variety of preserves made from quince, apple, oranges, apricots, cherries, figs, or grapes, among other fruits. The jams and preserves were meant to delight and revive guests who may have traveled long distances, and were elegantly served in small crystal bowls on a silver tray with dainty teaspoons alongside, and glasses of chilled water for sipping. Spoon sweets were also served on Jewish holidays, particularly Rosh Hashanah, when they symbolized hopes for a sweet year ahead. While not traditionally served on the holiday of Tu Bishvat, they would make a fitting sweet for the Tu Bishvat seder (see page 19).

Many traditional spoon sweet recipes call for extended cooking times and massive quantities of sugar. My modified version, which comes together quickly, tastes like a cross between a fruit compote and a quick jam. Serve the syrupy grapes in small glasses or bowls for a light dessert, or spoon them over yogurt at breakfast.

3 cups (525 g) seedless red grapes
½ cup (100 g) granulated sugar
2 cinnamon sticks
2 tablespoons fresh lemon juice
⅛ teaspoon kosher salt

1. Combine the grapes, sugar, cinnamon sticks, lemon juice, and salt in a medium saucepan and bring to a boil over medium-high heat, stirring to dissolve the sugar.
2. Reduce the heat to medium and cook, stirring occasionally, until the grapes soften and burst, but still hold their shape, and the liquid turns syrupy, 15 to 20 minutes.
3. Remove from the heat, discard the cinnamon sticks, and let cool to room temperature. The grapes will continue to shrivel (and may slip loose from their skins) and sweeten as they cool, and the flavors will continue to develop. Then cover and refrigerate until chilled, at least 4 hours.
4. Serve the syrupy grapes chilled. Store any leftovers, covered, in the fridge for up to 1 week.

BERRIES WITH HONEY AND SOUR CREAM

Serves 4 to 6

In his cookbook *Jewish Home Cooking: Yiddish Recipes Revisited*, Arthur Schwartz writes about the summertime Ashkenazi tradition of eating sour cream with just about any fresh fruit or vegetable. "A favorite dairy meal of my mother was a bowl of sour cream with whatever," he writes. "My father and I preferred it with boiled potatoes, butter, salt, and pepper. My sister went for sour cream with sliced bananas and a sprinkling of sugar. When in season, my mother usually liked strawberries, blueberries, or cantaloupe." My dessert-friendly riff on the "sour cream plus whatever" tradition briefly macerates fresh berries with sugar and lemon zest to bring out their juicy sweetness. Then I amp up the sour cream with a little honey and cinnamon, and fold in whipped cream to add lightness. When serving company, I spoon the berries and cream into small teacups or coupe glasses for an elegant and fun presentation.

4 cups (600 g) mixed berries (blueberries, quartered strawberries, raspberries, and/or blackberries)

2 tablespoons granulated sugar

1 packed teaspoon grated lemon zest

1 cup (240 g) sour cream, ideally full-fat

3 tablespoons runny honey or maple syrup

¾ teaspoon ground cinnamon, plus more for sprinkling

½ cup (120 ml) heavy cream

Finely chopped roasted almonds, pistachios, or pecans for sprinkling (optional)

1. Combine the berries, sugar, and lemon zest in a large bowl and gently toss. Let the berries sit, tossing occasionally, until juicy, 15 to 20 minutes.

2. Whisk together the sour cream, honey, and cinnamon in a medium bowl. In the bowl of a stand mixer fitted with the whisk attachment (or using a handheld electric mixer and a medium bowl), beat the heavy cream until it holds soft peaks. Spoon the whipped cream into the sour cream mixture and gently swirl together. (Do not fully combine.)

3. Divide the macerated berries among small serving bowls or cups. Dollop generously with the sour cream mixture and use a fine-mesh sieve to dust with a little cinnamon. Sprinkle with chopped nuts, if using, and serve immediately.

CHOCOLATE & CONFECTIONS

CHOCOLATE TAHINI-STUFFED DATES

Makes 12 stuffed dates

These stuffed dates are one of my favorite “no-recipe recipes”—a dessert you can throw together in minutes that will immediately soothe an unexpected craving for sweets and also tastes special enough to serve to company. Recipes for stuffed dates, usually filled with nuts or marzipan, abound in Middle Eastern and North African Jewish cuisines. This combination of bittersweet chocolate, fudgy Medjool dates, and a drizzle of earthy tahini is untraditional but especially magical. Use the fattest, squishiest, best-quality Medjool dates you can find, and don’t be tempted to substitute another drier variety.

12 Medjool dates

4 ounces (113 g) bittersweet baking chocolate

About 2 tablespoons well-stirred tahini

Flaky sea salt for sprinkling (optional)

1. Use a sharp paring knife to slice each date open lengthwise, taking care not to go completely through it. Remove and discard the pits.
2. Chop the chocolate into 12 pieces. (It is okay if they are not all the same shape or size.) Tuck a piece of chocolate into the center of each date and arrange the dates on a small serving platter.
3. Drizzle each stuffed date with about ½ teaspoon tahini and sprinkle with a small pinch of sea salt, if using. Serve immediately, or store, covered, in the fridge for up to 2 days. Bring to room temperature before serving.

CHOCOLATE SALAMI

Makes one 9-inch- (23 cm) long log

This "salami" has nothing to do with garlicky cured meat. Instead, it is made from melted chocolate combined with crushed tea biscuits, dried fruits, and nuts. The mixture gets shaped into a log and rolled in parchment paper, then chilled until set. When unwrapped and sliced, it closely resembles its meaty namesake and delivers a fun surprise when served at dessert. According to a *Tablet Magazine* article by Joan Nathan, chocolate salami was "probably invented [in Europe] before or during WWI . . . and became popular with Ashkenazi Jews and non-Jews alike before WWII." It is still enjoyed today in several Jewish communities, going by the names *schokoladenwurst* in Germany, *shokoladnaya kielbasa* in Russia, *salame di cioccolato* in Italy, and *naknik shokolad* in Israel. (Each one essentially translates as "chocolate sausage.") Chocolate salami is a no-bake confection that is as easy to make as it is to enjoy. It keeps for several months in the freezer, making it a lovely at-the-ready treat to serve unexpected guests.

4 ounces (85 g) bittersweet baking chocolate, roughly chopped

5 tablespoons (70 g) unsalted butter or vegan butter, cut into pieces

¼ cup (50 g) granulated sugar

2 tablespoons unsweetened cocoa powder

1 teaspoon vanilla extract

¼ teaspoon kosher salt

1 cup (55 g) crumbled petit beurre biscuits (tea biscuits) or plain graham crackers

½ cup (70 g) mixed dried fruit (e.g., cherries, raisins, apricots, and/or crystallized ginger), chopped

⅓ cup (35 g) mixed nuts (e.g., slivered almonds, pecans, cashews, and/or walnuts), chopped (optional)

Confectioners' sugar for dusting

NOTE: Crumble your biscuits into small pieces, about ⅛ to ¼ inch (3 to 6 mm). It is okay for the pieces to be irregularly shaped and sized, but be careful not to grind them too fine. You want a little texture in your chocolate salami.

1. Combine the chocolate, butter, granulated sugar, cocoa powder, vanilla, and salt in a small saucepan and cook over medium-low heat, stirring often to help dissolve the sugar, until the chocolate and butter are fully melted and combined, 2 to 3 minutes.

2. Remove from the heat and immediately fold in the crumbled tea biscuits, dried fruit, and nuts, if using. Stir well to make sure the biscuits and mix-ins are coated with chocolate.

3. Scoop the mixture onto the center of a large piece of parchment paper and form into a rough log shape using a silicone spatula. Fold the bottom edge of the parchment paper up around the log, then continue rolling and pressing the mixture in the parchment until you have a 9-inch- (23 cm) long log. (It is okay if the log isn't perfectly cylindrical.) Twist the ends of the parchment firmly together, and refrigerate the log until firm enough to slice, about 3 hours.

4. When ready to serve, use a fine-mesh sieve to dust the entire outside of the log with confectioners' sugar. Then, using a sharp serrated knife and starting from the middle of the log, carefully slice it into thin rounds. If it is difficult to slice straight from the fridge, let it sit at room temperature for 5 minutes. Store leftovers, well wrapped, in the fridge for up to 2 weeks or in the freezer for up to 3 months.

JEWISH AMERICAN CANDY COMPANIES

When I was young, I harbored a minor obsession with Peeps—the bunny- or bird-shaped marshmallows that would show up in the grocery store in the weeks leading up to Easter. Although they were just candy, I always felt a little strange pining for a confection so closely tied to a Christian holiday. As it turns out, I can thank a Russian Jewish immigrant named Sam Born for my beloved marshmallow confections.

Born founded Just Born, Inc., in Brooklyn in 1923 and went on to launch many popular candies, including Mike & Ike and Hot Tamales. In 1953, Just Born acquired the Rodda Candy Company, which made jellybeans and marshmallow candies, including Peeps. The animal-shaped marshmallows were handmade and quite labor-intensive until Born's son, Bob Born, created a machine that could produce them quickly and efficiently. Thanks to his innovation, the treats were able to take off nationally. Never mind that Peeps include gelatin and are therefore not kosher. And never mind that my grown-up palate does not particularly like them. To me, they are an American classic with a Jewish pedigree.

Just Born is only one of many revolutionary American candy companies founded by Jewish immigrants. Here are a few more:

✻ **Barton's Candy Corporation.** Founded in New York City by a Viennese Jewish immigrant named Stephen Klein in 1940, Barton's made a name for itself with its high-end chocolate bonbons and confections. Klein had been a candy-making apprentice in Austria, and he brought his expertise and elevated tastes to America. "With their magenta-and-chartreuse-striped awnings and handsome, streamlined interiors, Barton's shops were a cut above the neighborhood candy store," writes Professor Jenna Weissman Joselit in *Tablet Magazine*. One of their most beloved products, Barton's Almond Kisses, were for many decades a standard on American Jewish Passover tables. (See my Almond Kiss–inspired blondies on page 54.)

✻ **Bazooka Bubble Gum.** Russian Jewish brothers Abram, Ira, Joseph, and Philip Shorin founded the Topps Company in 1938 in Brooklyn, New York. Nine years later, they introduced Bazooka Bubble Gum, a chewy pink gum packaged in a red, white, and blue wrapper to capitalize on post–World War II patriotism. In 1953, the company began including a comic strip featuring Bazooka Joe in each package, and the gum's popularity skyrocketed. The comic was discontinued in 2012, but the gum remains.

✻ **Chunky.** My favorite candy bar always "felt Jewish" to me. Now I know why. The trapezoid-shaped chocolate was created by Polish-Jewish immigrant, Phil Silvershein, in 1943. It was originally packed with raisins and almonds, in homage to the iconic Yiddish song "Rozhinkes mit Mandlen." Later, the almonds were replaced with less-expensive peanuts, but Chunky's sweet appeal remained.

✻ **Goldenberg Peanut Chews.** In 1880, David Seltzer emigrated from Romania to Philadelphia, Pennsylvania, changing his last name to Goldenberg upon arrival. A decade later, he founded Goldenberg Candy Company, which would go on to create Peanut Chews—roasted peanuts and chewy molasses coated in dark chocolate. (The candy was originally made with walnuts.) Today Peanut Chews are manufactured by Just Born, Inc. (see above).

✻ Leaf Brands Candy. In 1907, Russian Jewish immigrants Louis and Clara Lifschitz arrived in New York City and established a candy-making business. (The family later changed their surname to the more American-sounding Leaf.) In the 1920s, their sons Sol and Harry founded several gum and penny candy companies in Chicago that eventually merged to create Leaf Confectionery Company. Leaf would go on to become the fourth-largest candy producer in North America, manufacturing many beloved candies, including Whoppers, Jolly Ranchers, Heath Bar, Payday, and Milk Duds. In 1996, the U.S. division was sold to The Hershey Company.

✻ Joyva. If you have ever enjoyed a chunk of sweet sesame-based halva, chocolate-covered Jell Rings, or Marshmallow Twists, you likely know and love Joyva. The Brooklyn-based company was founded in 1907 by Nathan Radutzky, a Jewish immigrant from Kiev, Ukraine. Today Joyva is run by third- and fourth-generation members of the Radutzky family, still turning out their iconic confections and halva in a variety of flavors.

✻ Tootsie Rolls. These candies were the brainchild of Leo Hirshfield, a Jewish immigrant from Austria who opened a candy shop in New York City in 1896. In 1908, he debuted his individually-wrapped chewy chocolate confections, named "Tootsie Rolls," after his daughter Clara's nickname. The cylindrical candies became a sensation and continue to be one of the most popular candies sold in America—and around the world—today.

Bazooka
BAZOOKA JOE
FORTUNE
Goldenberg's
Peanut Chews
Original Dark
NET WT 2 OZ (56 g)
6 PIECES

Tootsie Roll

CHOCOLATE TAHINI TRUFFLES

Serves 8

These four-ingredient truffles are decadent and intensely chocolatey, while being completely free of dairy, gluten, and eggs. The recipe is inspired by Rachel Simons, founder of the New York City–based artisanal tahini and halva company, Seed + Mill. Simons demonstrated how to make chocolate tahini truffles on YouTube several years ago, and that was all it took to convince me to make them a regular part of my sweet treat rotation. A generous pour of tahini gives the truffles their fudgy, melt-in-your-mouth texture while adding a welcome hint of complexity. Although any good-quality sesame paste will work in this recipe, if you can get your hands on Seed + Mill's ultrasmooth tahini, I highly recommend using it. The truffles store well in the freezer, and can be served chilled, making them a wonderful treat to keep on hand for company.

8 ounces (227 g) bittersweet baking chocolate, finely chopped

½ cup (120 g) runny, well-stirred tahini

1 tablespoon unsweetened cocoa powder, plus more for coating

⅛ teaspoon kosher salt

1. Line an 8 × 4-inch (20 × 10 cm) metal loaf pan with parchment paper and set it nearby.
2. Melt the chopped chocolate in a bowl in the microwave in 20-second intervals, stirring after each, until it is completely melted and smooth. (You can also use a double boiler.)
3. Add the tahini, cocoa powder, and salt to the melted chocolate and stir to fully combine. Pour the mixture into the loaf pan, cover, and freeze until the chocolate is completely set, at least 2 hours, and up to overnight.
4. Spread a few tablespoons of cocoa powder on a small plate and set it nearby. Turn the loaf pan upside down to release the chocolate onto a cutting board. Use a sharp knife to cut the chocolate into small squares, rectangles, or diamond shapes, then add each piece to the plate of cocoa powder and turn to coat on all sides. Transfer the truffles to a serving plate.
5. Serve immediately, or store, covered, in the freezer until ready to serve.

CHAROSET TRUFFLE BALLS

Makes about 15 truffles

On Passover, Moroccan Jews make a special charoset, the fruit-and-nut paste eaten during the seder as a symbol of the mortar the ancient Israelites used while enslaved in ancient Egypt. Instead of serving charoset in a bowl, they roll the thick date-based mixture into individual balls. These Charoset Truffle Balls take that tradition to its next logical conclusion, adding cocoa powder to the mix for a hint of rich chocolate flavor. I like to roll the truffles in more cocoa powder—the bitter, unsweetened cocoa perfectly complements the sweet dates. You can also roll them in dried coconut, cacao nibs, finely chopped nuts, or whatever you fancy. Serve these as a treat at the seder, or as a sweet snack or dessert all Passover (and all year) long.

Half of a small sweet apple (like Gala), peeled, cored, and roughly chopped

1 cup (125 g) pitted Medjool dates, roughly chopped

¼ cup (35 g) dark raisins

½ cup (70 g) roasted unsalted almonds

½ cup (70 g) roasted unsalted cashews

2 tablespoons unsweetened cocoa powder, plus more for rolling

½ teaspoon ground cinnamon

⅛ teaspoon kosher salt

1. Combine the apple, dates, raisins, almonds, cashews, cocoa powder, cinnamon, and salt in the bowl of a food processor and pulse, scraping down the sides of the bowl as necessary, until a thick paste forms.
2. Spread a few tablespoons of cocoa powder on a plate and set nearby. Using lightly moistened hands to prevent sticking, scoop out a tablespoon of the charoset and roll into a ball. Roll the ball in the cocoa powder, then transfer to a serving plate. Repeat with the remaining charoset, adding more cocoa powder to the plate as needed.
3. Cover and chill for at least 4 hours before serving. The charoset balls will firm up a bit as they chill.

CHOCOLATE-COVERED PRETZELS

Serves 8 to 10

It is hard to imagine a Shabbat dinner at my in-laws' home that doesn't end with chocolate-covered pretzels (among myriad other dessert options, of course!). There is nothing traditionally Jewish about chocolate-covered pretzels, but over the last few decades, they have become an increasingly popular offering from American kosher candy companies and a favorite hostess (or host) gift in many Jewish communities. Chocolate-covered pretzels are also incredibly simple to make at home, and a fun cooking project to collaborate on with kids. You can leave them simply coated in chocolate, or dip them into sprinkles, chopped nuts, mini candies, or another topping. Either way, they are festive, joyous, and sweet—the perfect ending to any celebratory meal.

Mini candy-coated chocolates, natural sprinkles, natural colored sugar, finely chopped nuts, and/or toffee bits for decorating (optional)

12 ounces (340 g) semisweet or bittersweet baking chocolate, chopped

1 teaspoon neutral vegetable oil

4 cups (160 g) mini pretzel twists

1. Line a large baking sheet with parchment paper. If decorating the pretzels, spread your desired toppings out on a few small plates and set nearby.
2. Combine the chopped chocolate and oil in a microwave-safe bowl and microwave for 20-second intervals, stirring after each, until the chocolate is completely melted and smooth. (You can also use a double boiler.)
3. Working with a few pretzels at a time, dip them into the melted chocolate, using a fork to make sure they are fully submerged. Then use the fork to remove the pretzels from the chocolate one at a time, gently shaking the pretzel and tapping it against the side of the bowl to remove any excess chocolate. If you are not decorating the pretzels, set them on the baking sheet as you go.
4. If decorating, dip or lightly press each chocolate-coated pretzel into the toppings on one or both sides and set on the baking sheet.
5. When all the pretzels are coated, refrigerate them on the baking sheet until the chocolate has set, 10 to 15 minutes, before serving.
6. Serve the pretzels slightly chilled or at room temperature. Store leftovers in an airtight container in the fridge for up to 1 week.

VARIATION: Swap in pretzel rods for the mini pretzel twists.

ROSY MARZIPAN

Makes about 30 pieces

Persian Jews end Shabbat dinner and other festive meals with fresh fruit, nuts, and tut—small marzipan confections perfumed with rose water. The word *tut* means "mulberry" in Farsi, and the sweets are often formed into petite ovals to resemble the berry, which is considered one of the national fruits of Iran. (Marzipan tut are also served as part of the spread for Nowruz, the Iranian New Year.) Some Persian marzipan recipes call for food coloring, which lends festive hue to the sweet almond paste. The naturally off-white treats are already beautiful, but I've included instructions for coloring the almond paste if you would like to do so.

1½ cups (150 g) almond flour
¾ cup (90 g) confectioners' sugar, sifted
⅛ teaspoon kosher salt
1 teaspoon rose water
2 tablespoons water, plus more if needed
2 or 3 different colors of natural food coloring (optional)
Granulated sugar, for rolling
Slivered almonds for decorating

1. Combine the almond flour, confectioners' sugar, salt, rose water, and water in the bowl of a food processor and pulse to combine, scraping down the sides of the bowl as necessary, until the mixture begins to come together in a large clump. If it is too dry, add more water, 1 teaspoon at a time, until the desired consistency is reached.
2. Transfer the almond mixture to a bowl; or, if using food coloring, divide the mixture among two or three bowls. Add a few drops of a food color to each bowl and stir to combine. Adjust the color with more food coloring if desired.
3. Spread a little granulated sugar on a plate and set nearby. Pinch off rounded teaspoons of the almond mixture and roll into small ovals. (Moisten your hands lightly with water if the mixture is sticking.) Stick a slivered almond into one end of each oval (like a stem), then gently roll the oval in the sugar to lightly coat and arrange the ovals on a serving platter.
4. The marzipan confections can be stored, covered, in the fridge for up to 2 weeks.

NOTE: Rose water brands vary in strength, so adjust the amount you use up or down as needed.

CHEATER'S TEIGLACH

Makes 24 teiglach

Teiglach translates from Yiddish as "little dough pieces," and the Eastern European Jewish dessert is exactly that—petite nuggets of a chewy dough simmered in a ginger-scented honey syrup, and sometimes mixed with nuts or candied cherries. Teiglach are typically served in small, sticky mounds or piled high on serving platters, like a French croquembouche. For generations, teiglach could reliably be found on Jewish holiday tables (particularly during Rosh Hashanah), at weddings and bar mitzvahs, and in kosher bakeries.

Over time, though, the beloved treat began to fall by the wayside—in large part because rolling out all those tiny individual pieces of dough is time-consuming. My "cheater's" version maintains a lot of the original's characteristics but substitutes store-bought puffed wheat cereal for the dough nuggets. And in place of the honey syrup, which requires an extended cooking time, I combine brown sugar, corn syrup, and a little butter (or vegan butter) for a syrup that comes together in minutes and coats the puffed wheat in caramel sweetness.

- 6 cups (110 g) unsweetened puffed wheat cereal
- 1 cup (100 g) walnut halves or pecan halves, coarsely chopped (optional)
- 5 tablespoons (70 g) unsalted butter or vegan butter
- ¾ packed cup (150 g) light brown sugar
- ⅓ cup (80 ml) light corn syrup
- ¾ teaspoon ground ginger
- 1 teaspoon vanilla extract
- ¼ teaspoon kosher salt

1. Line two 12-cup muffin tins with paper liners. Combine the cereal and nuts, if using, in a large bowl and set nearby.
2. Combine the butter, brown sugar, and corn syrup in a medium saucepan and cook over medium heat, stirring occasionally, until the mixture begins to bubble vigorously. Let bubble for 1 minute, then remove from the heat and immediately whisk in the ginger, vanilla, and salt.
3. Pour the mixture over the cereal and stir to completely coat the cereal. Divide the mixture evenly among the muffin cups, gently pressing it down into the cups. Let set for at least 15 minutes before serving.
4. Leftovers can be stored, covered, in the fridge for up to 3 days.

VARIATIONS: You can substitute puffed rice for the puffed wheat to make these gluten free. If you like, you can also add a handful of chopped crystallized ginger in the place of or along with the nuts, use ground cinnamon instead of ginger, stir a few tablespoons of peanut butter into the brown sugar mixture, or top the teiglach with sprinkles or mini chocolate chips.

GERMAN-CHOCOLATE MATZO TOFFEE

Serves 6

If you look up the term "instant classic" in the dictionary, you might just see a photo of matzo toffee. First developed in the 1980s by Canadian baker and author Marcy Goldman, it has become a beloved fixture of my family's (and countless other families') Passover celebrations. Goldman's original recipe enrobes squares of matzo in a combination of homemade caramel and melted chocolate. The toffee tastes absolutely bewitching as is, but is also an ideal canvas for creativity and experimentation. I like to dress it up with a German chocolate cake–inspired duo of chopped pecans and coconut. The floral coconut and buttery pecans bring just the right amount of "something extra" to the mix. You might as well make a double batch, because this treat is going to go quickly.

4 to 6 sheets regular matzo or gluten-free matzo

16 tablespoons (2 sticks / 227 g) unsalted butter or vegan butter

1 packed cup (200 g) light brown sugar

½ cup (50 g) pecan halves, chopped, plus chopped pecans for topping

⅓ cup (25 g) unsweetened dried shredded coconut

1 teaspoon vanilla extract

½ teaspoon kosher salt

1½ cups (270 g) semisweet chocolate chips

Toasted coconut flakes, gently crushed if in large pieces, for topping

NOTE: If you cannot find toasted coconut flakes, simply sprinkle the toffee with more shredded coconut. Or toast the coconut yourself by spreading the coconut flakes on a baking sheet and baking in a 350°F (180°C) oven until golden, 4 to 5 minutes.

1. Preheat the oven to 350°F (180°C). Line a large baking sheet with foil, then cover with a sheet of parchment paper.
2. Arrange as many matzo sheets as needed to make a single layer on the baking sheet, breaking pieces in half to fit if necessary.
3. Combine the butter and brown sugar in a medium saucepan and bring to a bubble over medium heat, then cook, stirring often, until the sugar dissolves and the mixture begins to thicken, 2 to 3 minutes. Stir in the pecans and shredded coconut and cook for 1 more minute. Remove the pan from the heat, stir in the vanilla and salt, and immediately pour the caramel mixture over the matzo, spreading it into an even layer.
4. Transfer the baking sheet to the oven and bake until the toffee is bubbling and deep brown, 10 to 15 minutes. (Watch carefully near the end of baking time so it doesn't burn.)
5. Remove from the oven and immediately scatter the chocolate chips evenly over the top of the matzo. Let stand until the chocolate melts, about 5 minutes, then use an offset spatula or a butter knife to spread the chocolate evenly over top. Sprinkle with more chopped pecans and the flaked coconut and transfer the baking sheet to the refrigerator to allow the chocolate to set, about 30 minutes.
6. Break the toffee into pieces and serve chilled or at room temperature. Leftovers can be stored, covered, in the fridge for up to 1 week.

ICE CREAM & DESSERT DRINKS

FL. OZ.
BROS.

A BROOKLYN ORIG
SINCE 1900
Fox'
HOCOLA
FLAVORED SYR
NET WT 22 OZ (624

NO-CHURN COFFEE HAWAIJ ICE CREAM

Serves 6 to 8

The word *hawaij* refers to two distinct Yemenite spice blends—a savory one used to flavor soups and stews, and a sweet one that gets stirred into coffee. Sweet hawaij's mix of ground ginger, cinnamon, cloves, and cardamom brings warmth and depth to your morning coffee routine. And here it lends those same spicy, cozy vibes to dessert. The no-churn base of sweetened condensed milk and billowy whipped cream freezes into an ice cream with the texture of soft-serve, no ice cream maker required. And the spiced coffee flavor is next-level—it both wows dinner guests and makes the perfect late-night sweet treat.

2 teaspoons vanilla extract or vanilla bean paste

2 teaspoons instant coffee granules (regular or decaf)

One 14-ounce (395 g) can sweetened condensed milk

1½ teaspoons ground cinnamon

½ teaspoon ground cardamom

½ teaspoon ground ginger

¼ teaspoon ground cloves

⅛ teaspoon kosher salt

2 cups (475 ml) heavy cream, well chilled

1. Whisk together the vanilla and instant coffee in a small bowl until the coffee granules mostly dissolve. Transfer to a medium bowl, add the sweetened condensed milk, cinnamon, cardamom, ginger, cloves, and salt, and whisk together.

2. In the bowl of a stand mixer fitted with the whisk attachment (or using a handheld electric mixer and a large bowl), whip the heavy cream until stiff peaks form, 1 to 3 minutes. Using a silicone spatula, fold about one-third of the whipped cream into the condensed milk mixture, then fold in the remainder of the whipped cream until fully blended.

3. Pour the mixture into a 9 × 5-inch (23 × 12.5 cm) metal loaf pan, cover, and freeze until scoopable, at least 5 hours, and ideally overnight. Store any leftovers, covered, in the freezer for up to 3 months.

DATE AND PISTACHIO ICE CREAM

Serves 6 to 8

It doesn't get much dreamier than homemade ice cream—especially when that ice cream is inspired by ma'amoul, the Middle Eastern butter cookies beloved by both Muslims and Jews from Syria, Lebanon, Egypt, and beyond. They are traditionally filled with either a thick date paste or sweetened chopped nuts. This creamy ice cream base, which is spiced with cinnamon and cardamom, brims with bites of sweet and chewy dates and roasted pistachios. Serve scoops drizzled with date syrup (silan) and a little tahini for one heck of a sundae. (Pictured on page 280.)

- ⅔ cup (135 g) granulated sugar
- 1 teaspoon ground cinnamon
- ½ teaspoon ground cardamom
- ¼ teaspoon kosher salt
- 1 cup (240 ml) whole milk
- 2 cups (475 ml) heavy cream
- 1½ teaspoons vanilla extract or vanilla bean paste
- ½ cup (65 g) pitted Medjool dates, chopped
- ⅓ cup (35 g) roasted salted or unsalted pistachios, roughly chopped

1. Whisk together the sugar, cinnamon, cardamom, and salt in a medium bowl, then add the milk and whisk until most of the sugar has dissolved, about 1 minute. Stir in the heavy cream and vanilla.
2. Transfer the mixture to an ice cream maker and churn according to the manufacturer's directions until thickened. Add the chopped dates and pistachios to the ice cream and churn to incorporate them.
3. Transfer the ice cream to a freezer-safe container and smooth the top. Cover and freeze until firm enough to scoop, about 4 hours. Let the ice cream sit at room temperature for 5 to 10 minutes before scooping. Store any leftovers, covered, in the freezer for up to 3 months.

NOTE: You can use either salted or unsalted roasted pistachiols, depending on whether or not you prefer a sweet-salty contrast in your ice cream.

EGG CREAM FLOAT

Makes 1 drink

There are several competing stories about how the first egg cream—a frothy, slurpable combination of chocolate syrup, cold milk, and bubbly seltzer water—came to be. One of the more popular tales is that the drink was invented in the 1890s by a Jewish immigrant and candy store operator named Louis Aster. And meanwhile, in Brooklyn, Herman and Ida Fox were busy developing their recipe for Fox's U-Bet, the chocolate syrup that would become forever linked to making a "proper" egg cream.

In the early twentieth century, when soda fountains and Jewish candy shops were king, you could find an egg cream just about anywhere in New York City. For generations, egg creams quenched New Yorkers' thirst and became a fixture of childhood memories. But over time, the drink has largely vanished—a relic of another time. While I love the idea of an egg cream, as someone who grew up drinking thick chocolate milk shakes, I have always found them to be lacking the creaminess and decadence that only ice cream can bring. So in this spin on a classic egg cream, I add an untraditional (but decadent!) scoop of chocolate ice cream to the mix. I also suggest swapping in orange-flavored seltzer for plain—a subtle change that adds another dimension to the classic.

1 tablespoon Fox's U-Bet chocolate syrup

3 tablespoons very cold milk

Orange-flavored seltzer or plain seltzer to top off the drink, chilled

1 generous scoop chocolate ice cream

1. Combine the chocolate syrup and milk in a 12-ounce (355 ml) glass. Add enough seltzer to almost fill the glass, then use a long-handled spoon to quickly stir the syrup and milk together.
2. Add the ice cream and drink immediately.

NOTE: Fox's U-Bet is the classic chocolate syrup for making egg creams, but if you cannot find it, another good-quality chocolate syrup will work fine.

POPPY SEED ICE CREAM

Serves 6 to 8

This ice cream was inspired by a photo my friend and fellow food writer Devra Ferst shared of an ice cream cone she ate in Belgrade, Serbia. The cone was arrestingly beautiful–a craggy mountain peak of black and white poppy seed gelato. I knew that a trip to Serbia wasn't in the cards for me anytime soon, so I decided to re-create it at home. The recipe for my first iteration, a no-churn poppy seed ice cream, originally ran in my newsletter, "The Jewish Table." It was very good, but I had a hunch that I could improve upon the flavor and texture if I used an ice cream maker. This updated version is a knockout–a rich vanilla custard densely speckled with nutty poppy seeds that have been toasted and finely ground for maximum flavor. Scoop it into a cone or serve it in a bowl with sour cherry jam spooned over the top for an unbeatable sundae.

⅓ cup (50 g) poppy seeds
¾ cup (150 g) granulated sugar
1 cup (240 ml) whole milk
¼ teaspoon kosher salt
2 cups (475 ml) heavy cream
2 teaspoons vanilla extract or vanilla bean paste

1. Pour the poppy seeds into a medium frying pan and cook over medium heat, stirring often, until fragrant and toasty, 2 to 3 minutes. Watch carefully so the seeds do not burn. Remove from the heat and let cool slightly, then transfer the poppy seeds to a spice grinder or coffee grinder and pulse until finely ground. The poppy seeds should be fluffy and have the texture of slightly damp soil. Set aside.
2. Combine the sugar, milk, and salt in a medium bowl and whisk until most of the sugar is dissolved, about 1 minute. Whisk in the heavy cream and vanilla.
3. Transfer the mixture to an ice cream maker and churn according to the manufacturer's directions until thickened. Add the ground poppy seeds to the ice cream and churn to incorporate them.
4. Transfer the ice cream to a freezer container and smooth the top. Cover and freeze until firm enough to scoop, about 4 hours. Let the ice cream sit at room temperature for 5 to 10 minutes before scooping. Store any leftovers, covered, in the freezer for up to 3 months.

SHTETL FRUIT SORBET

Serves 6

Asheknazi cuisine is most often defined by its heaviest and heartiest dishes (think brisket, matzo balls, and potato kugel). But Eastern European summers provided a colorful bounty of fresh berries and stone fruits to the Jews living in the *shtetl* (the Yiddish word for a small, predominantly Jewish town). These fruits made their way into baked goods and jams and were also devoured by the abundant handful. In homage to those fruitful shtetl summers, this simple, four-ingredient sorbet pairs blueberries, raspberries, floral honey, and apricot jam for a sweet-tart, intensely fruit-forward frozen treat. For the best texture, start with frozen (not fresh) berries that are thawed but still cold from the fridge.

2½ cups (340 g) thawed frozen blueberries

2½ cups (340 g) thawed frozen raspberries

½ cup (140 g) apricot jam

2 tablespoons honey (ideally orange blossom or clover), plus more if desired (see Note)

1. Add the blueberries, raspberries, jam, and honey to the bowl of a food processor and pulse, scraping down the sides of the bowl as necessary, until fully combined and smooth, about 1 minute. Taste and blend in another tablespoon or two of honey if you want a sweeter sorbet.

2. Set a fine-mesh sieve over a large deep bowl. Scoop about half of the fruit mixture into the sieve and, using the back of a spoon or a silicone spatula, press the mixture through the sieve; use the spatula or a butter knife to periodically scrape any puree clinging to the underside of the sieve into the bowl. Discard the seeds and repeat with the remaining fruit mixture. The process of pressing the mixture through the sieve takes a bit of patience and time (5 to 10 minutes), but it will result in a smooth, luscious-textured sorbet.

3. Transfer the fruit puree to an ice cream maker and churn according to the manufacturer's directions until thickened. The sorbet can be served right away, with a soft-serve consistency, or transferred to a freezer-safe container and frozen until firm, about 4 hours. Let the ice cream sit at room temperature for 5 to 10 minutes before scooping. Store any leftovers, covered, in the freezer for up to 3 months.

NOTE: To make this sorbet completely vegan, substitute agave for the honey.

COFFEE SODA

Makes 1 drink

A few years back, my husband, Yoshie, and I ordered (and immediately fell in love with) the coffee soda at Russ & Daughters Cafe—the sister restaurant of the Lower East Side's century-old smoked fish shop. The blend of chilled coffee, simple syrup, and bubbly seltzer was the perfect mix of bitter, sweet, and effervescent. It tasted both deeply nostalgic—like something you might have ordered at a Jewish soda fountain in the 1930s—and excitingly new. My spin on Russ & Daughters' drink sweetens cold brew and seltzer with maple syrup and adds a twist of orange that makes the other flavors sing. The recipe scales up easily, so serve these coffee sodas as a mocktail at brunch, for the Yom Kippur break fast meal, or as a refreshing afternoon pick-me-up.

⅓ cup (80 ml) strong cold-brew coffee

2 teaspoons maple syrup, plus more to taste if desired

Ice cubes

⅓ to ½ cup (80 to 120 ml) chilled seltzer

Dash of orange bitters (optional)

Twist of orange peel

1. Stir together the coffee and maple syrup in a tall glass. Taste and add a little more syrup, if desired. Fill the glass with ice, then top off with desired amount of seltzer and stir gently to combine.
2. Add the orange bitters, if using, and garnish with the orange peel twist. Serve immediately.

ALMOND MILK AND ROSE WATER DRINK

Makes about 8 drinks

This light, almondy frappe (called *schrab el'loz* in Arabic) is traditionally served in glasses set on silver trays at engagement parties among Syria's Aleppian Jewish community—a symbol of sweetness and fertility for the betrothed couple's life together. It also makes a refreshing drink on steamy summer nights. You start by making a thick and creamy almond paste accented with rose water, then blend the paste with ice and water to taste into a frothy, snowy-white drink that is reminiscent of horchata. Serve it in your most elegant glasses, and for a sensational (if untraditional) variation, spike it with a little cold brew or a shot of cooled espresso.

FOR THE ALMOND PASTE

1½ cups (205 g) blanched whole almonds

1¼ cups (250 g) granulated sugar

1 cup (240 ml) water

1 teaspoon rose water, or more to taste

FOR ASSEMBLY

Water

Ice cubes

Ground cinnamon for sprinkling (optional)

1. Make the almond paste: Combine the almonds, sugar, water, and rose water in a high-powered blender and blend at high speed for a full minute. Taste and add a little more rose water if a stronger flavor is desired.

2. Pour the mixture through a fine-mesh sieve into a bowl, then transfer it to a glass jar or pitcher. Cover and refrigerate until needed. (*The mixture can be stored in the fridge for up to 1 week.*)

3. To make one drink: Combine ¼ to ⅓ cup (60 to 80 ml) of the almond paste, depending on desired sweetness, with 1 cup (240 ml) water and 5 to 6 ice cubes (depending on the size of your ice cubes and how frothy you want the drink to be) in the blender and blend at high speed until frothy. Pour into a tall glass and serve immediately, sprinkled with a little cinnamon, if desired.

NOTE: A high-powered blender is important to the success of this recipe because it can pulverize the almonds effectively; I do not recommend trying it with a standard blender.

NOTE: If you cannot find blanched whole almonds, substitute skin-on raw almonds. The drink won't be quite as light in color, but the taste will be the same.

CONCORD GRAPE SODA

Makes about 10 sodas

Concord grapes are arguably the "grapiest" of grapes–floral and perfume-sweet with thick purple-blue skins and translucent, juicy flesh. They are also the primary ingredient in Manischewitz wine, which might as well be the official wine of the American Passover seder. This refreshing spritzer capitalizes on the grapes' unique flavor, adding cardamom pods and a squeeze of lemon to complement the sweetness. I save this recipe for early autumn, when fat clusters of grapes start to show up at the farmers' market.

FOR THE GRAPE SYRUP

1½ cups (355 ml) water

1 cup (200 g) granulated sugar

2 cups (320 g) Concord grapes removed from their stems

3 cardamom pods, cracked

1 tablespoon fresh lemon juice

FOR ASSEMBLY

Ice cubes

Seltzer

1. Make the grape syrup: Combine the water and sugar in a medium saucepan and bring to a boil over medium-high heat. Add the grapes, cardamom pods, and lemon juice, lower the heat to medium, and simmer, stirring occasionally and lightly smashing the grapes with a potato masher or sturdy fork, until the liquid is slightly thickened, 5 to 10 minutes. Remove from the heat and let cool completely.
2. Pour the syrup through a fine-mesh sieve into a jar or other container, pressing down on the grapes with the back of a spoon to extract as much syrup as possible; discard the solids. Cover and refrigerate until chilled. (*The syrup can be refrigerated for up to 2 weeks.*)
3. To assemble one drink: Pour a few tablespoons of the syrup into the bottom of a tall glass. Add ice and seltzer to taste, gently stirring to combine the seltzer and syrup. Serve immediately.

NOTE: You can substitute an equal amount of blackberries if Concord grapes are not in season.

TURKISH COFFEE IN A FRENCH PRESS

Serves 6

Across the Middle East, Turkish coffee is king. I have vivid memories of sipping bracingly dark coffee out of tiny porcelain cups at hole-in-the-wall cafés in Tel Aviv and Jerusalem—invariably with a bite of something sweet alongside. Turkish coffee is traditionally prepared in a small long-handled pot called a *cezve* (or *ibrik*), in which finely ground coffee and water are boiled together to create the thick, aromatic brew.

As a longtime devotee of my French press coffee maker, I wondered if I might mimic the richness of Turkish coffee without the thick layer of coffee grounds that invariably settles at the bottom of the cup. Turns out the answer is a resounding yes! I added a few spices—cardamom, cinnamon, and ginger—to make a pot of smooth, full-bodied coffee that is wonderful to sip while enjoying Classic Walnut Baklava (page 202), Sweet Walnut and Almond Turnovers (page 199), or a slice of Yogurt Semolina Loaf Cake (page 135).

½ cup (40 g) coarsely ground coffee
2½ tablespoons granulated sugar (optional)
½ teaspoon ground cardamom
¼ teaspoon ground cinnamon
¼ teaspoon ground ginger
3½ cups (830 ml) boiling water

1. Combine the coffee, sugar, if using, cardamom, cinnamon, and ginger in a 32-ounce (946 ml) French press pot.
2. Slowly add the boiling water, then gently stir to dissolve the sugar. Let the mixture stand for 3 to 5 minutes and then use the plunger to filter the coffee from the grounds.
3. Pour into small cups and serve hot.

NOTE: For best results, use coarse-ground coffee rather than finely ground in the French press pot. Adjust the amount of sugar according to your taste—or leave it out entirely.

SIPPING CHOCOLATE

Serves 2 or 3

Today the island of Curaçao is home to only about 500 Jews, but up until the early nineteenth century, it had the largest Jewish community in the New World. (The community's circa-1732 synagogue is the oldest one in continuous use in the Americas.) I recently learned, while reading Rabbi Deborah Prinz's book *On the Chocolate Trail*, that Curaçao's Sephardi Jews traditionally enjoyed hot chocolate and crisp sponge cookies called *panlevi* (see page 111) to celebrate a b'rit milah (circumcision ceremony, also called a bris). What a sweet and comforting pairing to serve while welcoming a new baby into the community. Curaçaoan hot chocolate combines evaporated milk with cocoa powder, sugar, and an egg to help thicken the mixture. My version strays from that tradition, but it still makes a rich, decadent drink for sipping and cookie dipping. Serve it in small cups as is, or top with marshmallows or barely sweetened whipped cream and chocolate shavings. (Pictured on page 113.)

- 2 tablespoons unsweetened cocoa powder
- 1½ tablespoons granulated sugar
- 1¼ cups (300 ml) milk or nondairy milk
- 2 ounces (57 g) bittersweet baking chocolate, chopped

1. Whisk together the cocoa powder and sugar in a small saucepan (off the heat). Add ¼ cup (60 ml) of the milk and whisk until the cocoa and sugar have dissolved.
2. Set the saucepan over medium heat, add the remaining 1 cup (240 ml) milk and the chopped chocolate, and cook, whisking often, until steaming but just shy of boiling.
3. Pour the hot chocolate into mugs or teacups and serve.

NOTE: If you are serving a larger group, scale up the ingredients (and pot size) accordingly. Once the hot chocolate is ready, transfer it to a slow cooker set to "Keep Warm" to hold the temperature steady.

"I CAN'T BAKE" DESSERT RECIPES

Maybe you are the kind of home cook who manages to burn ice cream. Or maybe you like baking but need a dessert right now and don't have time to separate eggs or let cookie dough chill in the fridge. I see you! These dozen recipes are foolproof, simple, and quick, but deliver maximum dessert joy.

BAKE

NO-BAKE

VEGAN DESSERT RECIPES

The majority of recipes in this book—far too many to list here—are either naturally dairy-free or offer simple substitutions to make them dairy-free. But the recipes listed here are completely vegan (or can be made vegan with a slight adjustment), which means they are free from dairy, eggs, and any other animal products.

Right to left: Poppy Seed Ice Cream (page 268), Date and Pistachio Ice Cream (page 266)

GLUTEN-FREE DESSERT RECIPES

These desserts bring all the sweet joy with none of the gluten. Keep this list of treats handy if you are gluten-free yourself or baking for a loved one who avoids gluten.

ACKNOWLEDGMENTS

It is an incredible honor to write a cookbook. *The Dessert Table* is my eighth book, and watching it come out into the world is every bit as thrilling as it was with my first. I am so grateful for the opportunity to share the magic of the global Jewish dessert canon with readers, and I am endlessly thankful for the people who helped make it happen.

Thank you to my wonderful agent, Meg Thompson of Thompson Literary Agency, for her steadfast support and wise guidance.

Thank you to the talented team at W. W. Norton, especially my editor, Melanie Tortoroli, whose thoughtful questions and creative insights always make my writing stronger, and whose indefatigable love of good food makes her a pleasure to collaborate with. Thank you also to Norton's Allison Chi and Huneeya Siddiqui for bringing extra joy to the photo shoot and adding their brilliance to these pages.

Huge thanks to everyone who made *The Dessert Table* look so darn beautiful: photographer Nico Schinco, food stylist Kaitlin Wayne, food styling assistant James Tenenhouse, prop stylist Maeve Sheridan, and prop styling assistant Ashleigh Sarbone. It is rare for a cookbook photo shoot to be both wildly productive and genuinely fun—but they made it happen! I am thrilled by the photos, which perfectly capture the unique beauty of Jewish sweets. Thank you also to Mia Johnson for bringing the photos and recipes to life with her gorgeous and creative book design and illustrations.

I am grateful to the chefs, pastry chefs, bakers, and cookbook authors who shared their Jewish dessert recipes and stories with me for this book: Jodi Geren, Tal Mor, and Kristina Costa of Loquat Bakery in San Francisco; Tova Du Plessis of Essen Bakery in Philadelphia; Maaryasha Werdiger of Zelda Bakery in Ripponlea, Australia; Lori and Paul Kettelle of Oak Bakeshop in Providence, Rhode Island; Ron and Leetal Arazi of NY Shuk in Brooklyn; Katreena Kanney of K'far Philly and K'far Brooklyn; Jessica and Trina Quinn of Dacha 46 in Brooklyn; Fany Gerson of Fan Fan Doughnuts and La Newyorkina in New York City; Eli Sussman of Gertrude's in Brooklyn; Alex Artinian of Lehrhaus in Somerville, MA; Vered Guttman; and Eve Jochnowitz. They all make it look easy!

Thank you to the amazing crew of volunteer recipe testers—their feedback made this book infinitely more delicious: Alice Adams, Rebecca Alpert, Sally Alterman, Julie Alterman Stifel, Elizabeth Andrade, Tammy Aronson, Melissa Baker, Rachel Barrick, Jessica Beer, Cori Benson, Erica Benton, Toby Bloomberg, Felice Bogus, Jenn Book Haselswerdt, Helena Brodsky, Roi Brown, Shauna Burke, Sara Catterall, Julia Clancy,

Sophia Cohen, Graham Cooper, Emily Croft, Rebecca Davids, Alyssa Davidson, Aliza Donath, Dave Dreifus, Barb Engler, Sylvia Fallas, Scott Filkins, Debbie Fine, Liz Fisher, Nicole Fisher, Karen Folz, Pamela Freedman, Gabriella Gershenson, Rachel Glicksman, Rachel Gold, Ilene Goldman, Deborah Greene, Jessica Grosman, Jocelyn Gross, Myra Grunfeld, Rebecca Guber, Mara Hausler, Lori Heisler, Melissa Herling, Alexandra Holbrook, Jennifer Hutzel, Sarah Gordon, Jessica Iverson, Madison Jackson, Sarah Joselow Parris, Vicky Kaufman, Laura Kiger, Laura Kirby Pardo, Carol Koenig, Abbie Kozolchyk, Laura Kumin, Samantha Lande, Gail Lansky, Kate Leeder, Rosa Leon Lumagbas, Eliana Leader, Sara Beth Levavy, Emily Levin, Miriam Liebman, Sue Ann Lipsey, Yana Lvovich, Sasha Luks-Morgan, Tziporah Markowitz Santos, Elizabeth Michael, Avia Moore, Rebekah Moran, Jennifer Neiman, Marilyn Newman, Tamara Noble, John Odum, Nicola Orlov, Marci Ortega, Rebecca Park, Sarah Parris, Sukey Pett, Sophie Press, Emy Ray, Rebecca Richards, Amy Rogers, Nancy Rosenberg, Nathalie Ross, Johanna Rothenberg, Rose Sadler, Jamie Schenk, Lisa Schwartz, Alexis Segal, Rob Shostak, David Siegel, Jennifer Simon, Michelle Simon, Lorin Sklamberg, Jennifer Slothower, Ellen Ahern, Monica Spitzer, Daryl Stein, Amy Steiner, Ruth Stroud, Ava Vatsky, Kath Vincent, Gail Vladimir, Jamie Wei, Cora Weissbourd, Molly Weisman, Jenny Werbell, Zack Zaban, and Betsy Zalaznick.

Love and thanks to my besties Ellen Ahern, Hannah Giles, Kate Elias, Elizabeth Lambshead, and Anna Hanau for being sounding boards, cheering crews, and unshakably supportive friends.

Many thanks to my Koenig and Fruchter families for their continued enthusiasm and encouragement: Carol Koenig and Herb Golinkin, Seth Koenig, Dr. Chaim and Rena Fruchter, Temim Fruchter and Erin Anthony, Ora Fruchter, Bradford Jordan and Gideon Jordan, Rabbanit Dasi Fruchter, Daniel Krupka, and Ada Krupa.

Eternal love and gratitude to my husband, Yoshie Fruchter (team tahini-almond cookie), and our two wonderful children, Max (team black-and-white cookie) and Beatrice (team chocolate rugelach) for making life together so meaningful and sweet. (Additional thanks to Max for helping me spot typos in the manuscript. What a dream it is to get to collaborate with you!)

INDEX

Note: Page references in *italics* indicate photographs.

Patrick Donovan

ABOUT THE AUTHOR

Leah Koenig is the author of eight cookbooks, including *Portico: Cooking and Feasting in Rome's Jewish Kitchen*, which was the IACP 2024 International Cookbook winner and a finalist in the National Jewish Book Awards. Leah's writing and recipes can be found in *The New York Times*, *The Washington Post*, and *Food & Wine*, among other publications. She also writes a weekly newsletter, "The Jewish Table," which shares recipes and stories from the world of Jewish food. In addition to writing, Leah regularly leads cooking demonstrations and workshops. She lives in Brooklyn, New York, with her husband, Yoshie Fruchter, and two children, Max and Beatrice Fruchter.

Printed in China
First Edition

Manufacturing by Toppan Leefung
Book design by Mia A. Johnson
Production manager: Gwen Cullen

Library of Congress Cataloging-in-Publication Data

Names: Koenig, Leah author | Schinco, Nico photographer
Title: The dessert table : 100 joyful Jewish sweets / Leah Koenig ; photography by Nico Schinco.
Description: First edition. | New York, NY : W.W. Norton & Company, [2026] | Includes index.
Identifiers: LCCN 2026001671 | ISBN 9781324076599 hardcover
Subjects: LCSH: Desserts | Jewish cooking | LCGFT: Cookbooks
Classification: LCC TX773 .K5756 2026 | DDC 641.86–dc23/eng/20260126
LC record available at https://lccn.loc.gov/2026001671

W. W. Norton & Company, Inc.
500 Fifth Avenue, New York, NY 10110
www.wwnorton.com

W. W. Norton & Company Ltd.
15 Carlisle Street, London W1D 3BS

Authorized EU representative:
EAS, Mustamäe tee 50, 10621 Tallinn, Estonia

1 2 3 4 5 6 7 8 9 0